Fun Places to Go

with Children in

Northern California

30TH-ANNIVERSARY 9TH EDITION!

Over 350 Listings, Completely Revised & Updated

By Elizabeth Pomada

CHRONICLE BOOKS

SAN FRANCISCO

This book is dedicated to the thousands of volunteers who eagerly help bring history, science, and new worlds to life for children of all ages.
  Happy Trails!

Library of Congress Cataloging-in-Publication Data available.
ISBN: 0-8118-3815-3

Manufactured in the United States of America
Cover design by Aya Akazawa
Maps by Eureka Cartography
Illustrations by Willow Cook
Typesetting by Jack Lanning

Distributed in Canada by Raincoast Books
9050 Shaughnessy Street
Vancouver, British Columbia V6P 6E5

10 9 8 7 6 5 4 3 2 1

Chronicle Books LLC
85 Second Street
San Francisco, California 94105

www.chroniclebooks.com

CONTENTS

Needless to say, this book was not done by just one person. I must say thank you to Lauren and Jennifer, Elizabeth and Deborah, Diana and Marc, Eric and Chris, Cindy and Christopher, and Alan, Emma, and Elizabeth and Maxim, our "test" children. But most of all, thank you to my pal, editor, chauffeur, idea man, hero, husband, and the biggest child of them all—M.F.L.

—EP

After living in New York City for 30 years, Elizabeth Pomada moved to San Francisco. She learned about Northern California by traveling more than 4,000 miles of it to write *Places to Go with Children in Northern California*. Her other books include *California Publicity Outlets*, now *Metro California Media*. She and her partner, Michael Larsen, have created the Painted Ladies® series: *Painted Ladies: San Francisco's Resplendent Victorians; Daughters of Painted Ladies: America's Resplendent Victorians; How to Create Your Own Painted Lady; The Painted Ladies Guide to Victorian California;* and *America's Painted Ladies: The Ultimate Guide to Our Resplendent Victorians*. Elizabeth frequently writes about France. Michael and Elizabeth also run the oldest literary agency in Northern California.

A Word Before You Go

HERE, BIGGER AND I HOPE better than ever, is the ninth edition of *Fun Places to Go with Children in Northern California.* The countryside is as gorgeous and varied as ever, and it was a pleasure exploring again, both to check on places already in the book and to find new discoveries to share with you. Maybe it's just provincial pride, but Michael, my husband, and I think that the ocean, rivers, trees, sunshine, mountains—all of the breathtaking beauty and richness that Northern California has been blessed with—make it one of the most beautiful areas on earth. More remarkable still is that so much of it has been protected or left in its natural state for us to marvel at.

We found an increasing number of places geared to awakening young minds. There are dozens of new science and discovery museums, and most of the history and art museums have a "hands-on" section, as well as special children's activities. Again, we were pleased to find that the interest in preserving the state's colorful historical heritage continues. More museums and historic houses than ever dot the landscape. We believe that if you and your children can learn something and have fun at the same time, then the good time is worth twice as much. And of course, most of the places listed here are enjoyable no matter how old you are.

The big new thing this time is websites! You can travel the state (or the world) with your computer. We've tried to include a website for every *Fun Place* here; those *Fun Places* without a website at this writing are probably developing one as you read this. The websites will give you up-to-date hours of operation and costs and may include driving directions if needed.

You'll note that we've added a recommended age range for each attraction. This reflects my opinion of the optimal age range for each place; you'll find them in bold in the listings.

Practically all of the locations in *Fun Places* have wheelchair access—indicated with a W at the end of the entries—and almost all of the attractions with educational value present special tours for schools and other groups. Just call to arrange your tour. Infants and toddlers are usually free, unless noted.

Many nonprofit institutions have gift shops, the sales from which help to sustain museums and nature centers. If you are pleased with what you see, these shops are one way of showing your support. Often a nonprofit will not charge for entrance, but a small donation will be gratefully accepted. If you see a "Donation" listing instead of a fee for a particular site, please support the nonprofit with a contribution, if you can.

Most of the nonprofit attractions are staffed largely by volunteers. If you live in the area, another way of showing your support and making new friends is helping out. Some places even have volunteer programs for children, which will be learning experiences for the kids and might even lead to a career.

The goal of *Fun Places* is to include every attraction and special event in Northern California that youngsters and the young at heart will enjoy. Since the book concentrates on places to visit rather than things to do, playgrounds, arcades, and activities such as bowling, skateboarding, skiing, skating, shooting pool, and miniature golf aren't included. So if a water slide or balloon site is mentioned in one area, and that sounds like a good idea to you, check the local Yellow Pages to see if there's one nearby. One adventure may lead to another.

I hope that you will help to make the next edition even better. Please write to me at 1029 Jones Street, San Francisco 94109, or call me at (415) 673-0939 if you find an attraction that should be included, or if you think of a way to make *Fun Places* more helpful to parents and teachers. I'd like to create a dialogue around *Fun Places,* so it will continue to improve. This edition has benefited from the many people who have contacted us. I'll be happy to send an autographed copy of the next edition to the first person to suggest a new place or one we have overlooked for future publications.

If you have any unusual experiences, good or bad, at one of the places in this book, I'd like to know about them. Also, if your children or students write anything memorable about the places they visit, I would like to see it—and perhaps quote them in the next edition. We've included comments from youngsters when it seemed appropriate. After all, a book for children should have input from children!

This book is arranged with downtown San Francisco as a starting point, with you traveling out from there, first in nearby neighborhoods, then out around San Francisco by county and region.

Prices go up and schedules change, especially in winter and on holidays, so if you're going far, call for up-to-the-minute information and driving and lodging tips. Most places are closed on Thanksgiving, Christmas, and New Year's Day. Local chambers of commerce, tourist offices, and the American Automobile Association will also help you plan your trip.

Don't forget to buckle your seatbelts and stock the car with drinks and travel snacks, games, books and books on tape, tissues, wet wipes, and a lot of good humor. Giving each child a bag full of coloring or puzzle books and toys to be used only in the car can make each trip special. Gameboys and in-car DVDs and VCRs may keep kids quiet, but they won't help family interaction, which is the reason for the trip. Rand McNally's website (www.randmcnally.com) generates colorful maps that can be printed and laminated so the kids can "navigate" as you drive. One change of clothing per person might be a good idea, as well as an extra sweater. Extra plastic bags of all sizes pack small and can be extremely useful. Bring a cooler and a small first-aid kit. And remember that an unopened can of cold soda works on sprains, bumps, and mosquito bites. While driving, we also like to play alphabet, cow count, "name the clouds," and license plate state spotting.

I hope that you will enjoy *Fun Places* and the places it inspires you to visit. Bon voyage!

Northern California's Top 11 Places

1. Monterey Bay Aquarium
2. Exploratorium, San Francisco
3. Yosemite National Park
4. Tech Museum of Innovation, San Jose
5. Six Flags Marine World, Vallejo
6. Steinbeck Center, Salinas
7. Lawrence Hall of Science, Berkeley
8. San Francisco Zoo
9. California State Railroad Museum, Old Sacramento
10. Point Reyes National Seashore
11. Ardenwood Farm, Fremont

To which I add my personal favorites:
1. Santa Cruz Beach and Boardwalk
2. Columbia State Historic Park
3. San Juan Bautista State Historic Park
4. Oakland Museum of California
5. Jack London State Historic Park, Glen Ellen
6. Safari West, Santa Cruz
7. John Muir National Historic Site, Martinez

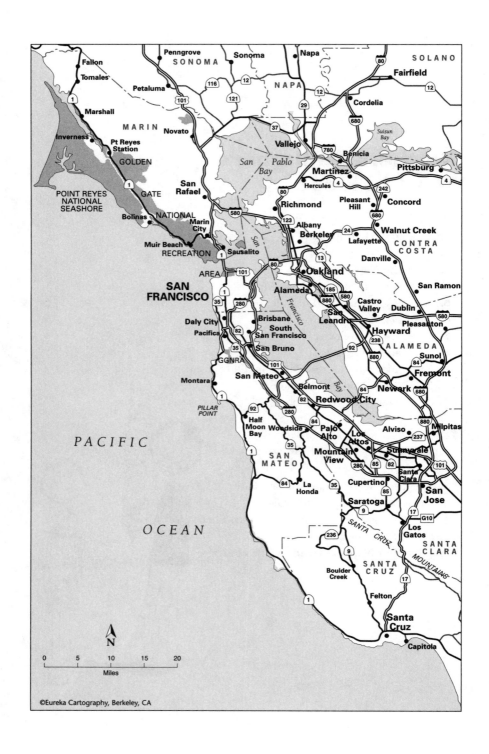

PACIFIC

OCEAN

SOLANO

SONOMA

NAPA

MARIN

Fallon
Tomales
Penngrove
Sonoma
Napa
Fairfield
Petaluma
Marshall
Cordelia
Inverness
Pt Reyes
Station
GOLDEN
Novato
Vallejo
Benicia
Pittsburg
San
Pablo
Bay
Suisun
Bay
Martinez
Hercules
POINT REYES
NATIONAL
SEASHORE
GATE
San
Rafael
Richmond
Pleasant
Hill
Concord
Bolinas
NATIONAL
Marin
City
Albany
Berkeley
Walnut Creek
CONTRA
COSTA
Muir Beach
RECREATION
Sausalito
Lafayette
Danville
San Ramon
SAN
FRANCISCO
AREA
Oakland
Alameda
San
Leandro
Castro
Valley
Dublin
Pleasanton
Daly City
Pacifica
Brisbane
South
San Francisco
San Bruno
Hayward
ALAMEDA
Sunol
Montara
San Mateo
Belmont
Redwood City
Newark
Fremont
PILLAR
POINT
Half
Moon
Bay
Woodside
Palo
Alto
Los
Altos
Alviso
Milpitas
SAN
MATEO
Mountain
View
Sunnyvale
Santa
Clara
San
Jose
La
Honda
Cupertino
Saratoga
Los
Gatos
SANTA
CLARA
Boulder
Creek
SANTA
CRUZ
SANTA CRUZ MOUNTAINS
Felton
Santa
Cruz
Capitola

San Francisco Bay
GGNR A
GG NRA

N

| 0 | 5 | 10 | 15 | 20 |

Miles

©Eureka Cartography, Berkeley, CA

San Francisco and the Bay Area

■ San Francisco

San Francisco has been called a peninsula bounded on three sides by water and on one side by reality. What makes the city special? It's both large and small. At about 750,000 people, it's small for a major city. Yet it has the amenities of any great city: opera, ballet, theater, a symphony, shopping galore, and restaurants that will please any palate.

San Francisco is a unique blend of elements:
- a beautiful natural setting
- cool, fair weather
- a history that makes up in color what it lacks in length
- a rich multicultural heritage that makes the city hospitable to new people, ideas, and lifestyles
- old and new architecture, with the greatest, most beautiful collection of redwood Victorians in the world (The famous "postcard row" of Painted Ladies standing in front of a view of downtown's skyscrapers is on Alamo Square, Steiner and Hayes Streets. Don't miss it!)
- a collection of distinct neighborhoods worthy of wandering and exploration
- a world-class mixture of education, business, culture, and religion that attracts visitors and immigrants from all over the world
- a size small enough to walk around in yet large enough to provide kids of all ages with plenty of things to see and do.

Consider transportation. You can see San Francisco by foot, bicycle, moped, car, taxi, bus (single- or double-decker), cable car (regular or motorized), trolley car, subway, helicopter, ferry, sailboat, and even by blimp!

Riding the cable car up and down hills can be more fun than Disneyland. Hungry? San Francisco provides an excellent opportunity to expand your children's enjoyment of the world's cuisines. The first ten blocks of Clement Street (starting at Arguello) in the Richmond District offer the most cosmopolitan concentration of delectable food we know of anywhere. Here, you can feast on Chinese (dim sum dumplings as well as Cantonese, Mandarin, Shanghai, Fukien, Taiwanese, Hakka, and Hunan cooking), Japanese, Italian, Indonesian, French, Russian, Persian, Vietnamese, Irish, Thai, and American food, plus health food and barbecue. The town's best secondhand bookstore, Green Apple, is there, too.

San Francisco suffers from the same problems as any other metropolis, but the city's size, human-scale architecture (outside our mini-Manhattan downtown), and sunny weather give urban blights a more benign quality.

The city has a remarkable capacity for self-renewal. Although still largely populated by the poor and the lost, the Tenderloin is being revitalized by

Vietnamese immigrants. Kids are playing in the streets, and new stores and restaurants have sprouted up, adding another neighborhood to the city's rich ethnic mix.

Much of the best of what the city has to offer costs nothing. More than one-third of the attractions in this chapter are free. San Francisco is a walker's paradise. Just strolling around Golden Gate Park or the city's neighborhoods—Chinatown, Japantown, the Mission, the Haight, Noe Valley, Clement Street, Union Street, or anywhere on the waterfront from Land's End to the Embarcadero—on a sunny, breezy day is delightful. The Marina is great for walking, kite flying, and boat watching.

Coit Tower, on the top of Telegraph Hill, has fabulous views. The observation platform at the top is 210 feet high (open daily, 10–6, $3.75). In the outer room, huge wall paintings portray the wonders of California. Take the #39 bus to the top of Telegraph Hill (415-673-6864 for MUNI information) to avoid parking problems.

Upon climbing the nearby Greenwich Street steps and discovering a flock of green parrots escaped from North Beach homes, 14-year-old Sam, honoring novelist Ray Bradbury, wrote:

And then I saw them, perching
on the telephone wires above my head.
Green they were, and red-faced.

Take the family on a "Hollywood Tour"—walking down Lombard Street, "The Crookedest Street in the World"; "flying" down Jones between Union and Filbert Streets, or Filbert between Hyde and Leavenworth Streets, pretending to be in the car chase in either *Bullitt* or *The Rock;* driving to the southeast corner of Broadway and Pierce Streets to see Mrs. Doubtfire's house; attend church service at St. Paul's Roman Catholic Church, Valley Street between 29th and Church Streets, to see if you can catch Whoopi Goldberg in *Sister Act* and ending at Land's End under the Golden Gate Bridge where Kim Novak jumped into the bay in *Vertigo.*

Unless you hit one of the city's few hot days, the temperature is usually in the low 60s. So the layered look, which enables you to peel off a jacket or sweater if it gets toasty, is always appropriate.

The entertainment section of the Sunday *Chronicle* will fill you in on special events that are taking place while you are in town. The Visitors Bureau offers free orientation information at www.sfvisitor.org. Download self-guided walking tours for free at www.destinationssf.com. Or call (415) 391-2000, the San Francisco Convention and Visitors Bureau.

Museum fans might want to invest in a CITYPASS, which offers admission to the six top S.F. attractions (the Museum of Modern Art) a Blue and Gold Fleet Bay Cruise, the Exploratorium, the Palace of the Legion of Honor, the California Academy of Sciences, and a seven-day passport to MUNI and Cable Cars) for one half-priced payment. You buy it at your first visit, then use it for the next week (888-299-6633/707-256-0490, www.citypass.com). MUNI Passports offer unlimited passes for one, three, or seven days and are available at cable car turnarounds and the Visitors Information Center at Hallidie Plaza, (415) 673-6864. The #45 bus will take you through Chinatown, North Beach, and onto the classy Union Street. Or catch the F Line at Fisherman's Wharf and ride the vintage streetcars along the Embarcadero and Market Street out to the Castro District. The #6, #7, or #71 will take you out to the Haight-Ashbury. Then transfer to the #37, which winds around Buena Vista Park, past an array of Victorians and up the side of Twin Peaks.

Whether you live in the city or are just visiting, whether you are young or just young at heart, whether you want cultural enrichment or just plain fun, San Francisco is one of the best places in the world to spend a week or a lifetime. Happy Trails!

● Ferries to Larkspur, Sausalito, Tiburon, and Vallejo

San Francisco Ferry Terminal, San Francisco 94111. Behind the Ferry Building at the foot of Market Street. (415) 923-2000. Telecommunication Device for the Deaf (TDD): (415) 257-4554. Ferries run daily to/from Larkspur and Sausalito in Marin County. Call for up-to-date fares and schedules. Bicycles okay. Assistance for the disabled available.

The Golden Gate Ferry leaves its slip at the foot of Market Street, passes Alcatraz Island, and docks across the bay. The snack bar serves coffee and snacks, and whether it's sunny or foggy, the views are wonderful. Take a camera. The Ferry Terminal itself will soon be a wonderful shopping and "museum" mall.

The Vallejo Baylink travels daily from Vallejo to the S.F. Ferry Building and Pier 41½. Call (877) 64-FERRY or visit www.baylinkferry.com for up-to-date schedules and fares. Although the Harbor Bay Express is a commuters special, it will still take you from Bay Farm Island in San Leandro to the Ferry Building. Call (510) 769-5500 or check out www.harborbayferry.com, or www.baycrossings.com, for fares and schedule.

● Yank Sing

Rincon Center, 101 Spear Street, between Mission and Howard Streets, (415) 781-1111. Open for lunch, daily. Reservations accepted. www.yanksing.com

The world's best dim sum is not in Chinatown! Yank Sing offers the freshest, most interesting dim sum, or "heart's delights," in town. The constantly expanding selection of little tastes makes it possible to have a completely vegetarian meal or dim sum that's just seafood. And it's fun to eat with your hands or with chopsticks. The individual portions of Peking duck or minced squab in lettuce cups, the flaky curry cakes, the chicken in avocado halves, and the steamed chicken *bao* are all special. Even desserts run from the ancient sweetened silky tofu to the modern mango ice cream cakes. Kids like the orange Jell-O quarters best. You choose from the wheeled carts going by. The server marks your billing slip, and then the headwaiter totes them up for your bill.

Forced to move when its home on Battery was torn down, Yank Sing is now in a modern building with an 85-foot-tall waterfall, or "Rain Column," in the center of the atrium. Rincon Center itself, built as a post office in 1939, stills boasts magnificent WPA murals by Anton Refregier that depict the history of Northern California. It remains the largest single commission by the Painting and Sculpture Division for the WPA and is now on the National Registry of Historic Places.

● Magnes Museum

121 Steuart Street, off Mission Street, San Francisco 94103. (415) 543-8880. Sun.–Wed., 12–5; Thurs., 2–7. Closed on Jewish holidays. Adults, $4; seniors and ages 12 and over, $3. Tours by appt. **Ages 8 & up.** *W. www.magnesmuseum.org*

In cultural partnership uniting the Judah L. Magnes Museum and the Jewish Museum of San Francisco, the Magnes Museum brings together preeminent collections, special exhibitions, and educational and public programs to explore the contemporary relevance of Jewish art, history, and culture. Changing exhibits vary from comic strip art by Ben Katchor to sacred paintings, photographs, and sculpture.

● Pacific Bell Park/Pac Bell Park

Home of the San Francisco Giants. 24 Willie Mays Plaza, 3rd and King Streets, San Francisco 94107. (415) 972-2000. Tours daily, 10–2 on nongame days, 10–1 on game days: adults, $10; seniors, $8; ages 12 and under, $5. Group tours and birthday parties by appt. (415) 972-2361 at group rates. Game tickets range from $12.00 for bleacher seats to $24.00 for arcade seats, and up to $35.00 for lower boxes. Restaurants and snack bars. Gift shops. **Ages 3 & up.** *W. www.sfgiants.com/www.pacbellpark.com*

Now you can take the whole family out to the ballpark! The Coca-Cola Fan Lot, just inside, is a family attraction, open year-round, that allows young fans to feel what it's like at a ball game. Inside, Little Giants Park is a mini-version of Pacific Bell Park for the youngest fans, with a base race, a giant baseball glove offering great views of the game, a Coca-Cola Superslide, and Giants-at-Their-Best themed interactives to enhance fan visits. It's free for ticket holders during the game; there's a small charge on nongame days.

The Coca-Cola Superslide is only 465 feet from home plate and offers four slides, two 56-foot-long curving slides, and two 20-foot-long twisting slides. The bottle lights up whenever there's a home run. In Little Giants Park, kids can hit softballs or whiffle balls thrown by a pitching machine or a pitcher, and their parents can watch over them from the seats in the grandstand. Older kids will want to test their arms at the Speed Pitch section. And everyone can take their own pictures in the Fan Lot Photo Booth. Telescopes also help make the game up close and personal.

● Golden Gate Railroad Museum

Hunters Point Shipyard, Building 809, 3rd and Evans Streets (Mail: P.O. Box 881686), San Francisco 94188. (415) 822-8728. Weekends, 10–5 except major holidays and when excursions are in progress. Groups by appt. Events. Rent a locomotive and streamliner car for a party. Adults, $5; children, $3. **Ages 5 & up.** *W. www.ggrm.org*

An 80 plus-year-old Southern Pacific Delmonte steam engine and excursion train headlines this collection of a dozen or more trains of various vintage, all in varying stages of restoration. The Coast Daylight used to travel between San Francisco and Los Angeles. The Pullman sleeper, the lounge car, the three-unit lounge/diner with its own kitchen, and little dormitory for the crew are all fun to explore.

● Basic Brown Bear Factory

444 DeHaro Street, at Mariposa Street on Potrero Hill, San Francisco 94107. (800) 554-1910/(415) 626-0781. Daily, 10–5. Factory does not operate on weekends. Free hour-long tours on the hour. Reserve for groups of eight or more. Parties. Field trips and kits are available. **Ages 2–10.** *W. www.basicbrownbear.com*

While learning about the history of the teddy bear, from spats to safety eyes, visitors can see 30 kinds of teddy bears cut and stuffed right in front of them—and even stuff their own. After the teddy bear is out of the "teddy bear bath" machine, children pull a handle that shoots the bear through a tube of air jets and onto the floor. Usually, another child gets to catch the bears, which fly about. Afterward, children can buy their own bear and stuff it themselves, working the pedal on the stuffing machines, which shoot plastic beads and soft polyester fluff into the bear. A helper will expertly sew your bear closed by hand. Then you or a bearmaker will brush your bear's hair to fluff up the seams. Clothes and accessories are available for personalizing your teddy bear. We were torn between choosing Baby Bear ($12), Basic Brown Bear ($28), and Beary Godmother ($65).

● San Francisco Museum of Modern Art

151 3rd Street, at Mission Street, San Francisco 94103. (415) 357-4000. TDD: (415) 357-4154. Fri.–Tues., 11–6; Thurs., 11–9 (Thurs., 6–9 half price). Audio tours. Museum Store: daily, 10:30–6:30; Thurs. until 9:30 P.M. Closed holidays. Caffe Museo: Tues.–Sun., 10–6; Thurs. until 9. Adults, $10; seniors, $7; students, $6; children under 13 with adult, free. First Tues. of the month, free. Groups by appt. Events. **Ages 9 & up.** W. *www.sfmoma.org*

SFMOMA offers constantly changing exhibits of paintings, sculpture, works of art on paper, photography, and media arts, architecture, and design. The permanent collection includes works by Matisse, Jackson Pollock, Franz Kline, San Franciscans Wayne Thiebaud and Clyfford Still, and an in-your-face sculpture self-portrait by Robert Arneson, *California Artist.* There are many who feel that children are best able to view modern art, because they're open to everything, with no preconceived ideas about what art should be. We are inclined to agree. There is a small interactive CD-ROM computer section for school groups and kids of all ages. Educational programs include "Making Sense of Modern Art."

SFMOMA is the centerpiece of the **Yerba Buena Gardens,** an urban park with theaters, restaurants, cafés, gardens, and galleries including the **Yerba Buena Center for the Arts,** where themed exhibits of fine art and photographs change every three months (701 Mission Street. 415-978-2787. Tues.–Sun., 11–6; until 8 on the first Thurs. of the month—admission free after 6. Adults, $4; seniors and students, $2; kids, free; seniors, free on Thurs., 11–3. **Ages 10 & up.** W. www.yerbabuena.org).

● California Historical Society

678 Mission, at 3rd Street, San Francisco 94105. (415) 357-1848. Tues.– Sat., 11–5. Adults, $3; seniors and students, $1; under 6, free. Bookstore. **Ages 8 & up.** W. *www.californiahistoricalsociety.org*

The California Historical Society's research library and gallery are located in the historic Hundley Hardware Building. Exhibits change three or four times a year and range from "California's Quilts, 1840–1940" to "Alaska Gold," "Interpreting California" to "Sunset Magazine," to an exhibit on the city's firefighters. Lectures, walking tours, educational outreach programs, and a research library are available.

● Cartoon Art Museum

655 Mission Street, San Francisco 94105. Tues.–Sun., 11–5. Adults, $5; seniors and students, $3; ages 6–12, $2; first Tues. of the month is Pay What You Wish Day. Groups by appt. Parties. **Ages 6 & up.** *W. www.cartoonart.org*

This museum exhibits, collects, and studies original art from cartoon strips, comic books, animation, magazines, and editorial cartoons. Here cartoon art is treated as fine art in the only museum west of the Mississippi dedicated to Cartoon Art. Visitors will see a variety of works from Charles Schulz's *Peanuts,* Jim Davis's *Garfield,* the underground art of Robert Crumb and Art Spiegelman plus dozens of favorite cartoon artists from the past and present. With half the gallery dedicated to an overview of cartoon art and half dedicated to rotating exhibitions, there's always something new and interesting to experience. The animation room, with its "samples" of Disney art from movies such as *Sleeping Beauty* and *The Lion King* will attract youngsters.

● Metreon

A Sony Entertainment Center. 4th and Mission Streets, San Francisco. (415) 369-6000. The center is open 10–10, but attractions within Metreon have varying times. Events. Parties. Group rates. **All ages.** *www.metreon.com*

Metreon has put it all together: it's a place to play, shop, eat, catch a movie in one of the 15 theaters, shoot pool, learn, and enjoy. The IMAX theater offers an eight-story view of the world, with natural history shows and special attractions. The Action Theatre, the only one of its kind outside Japan, is home to an ever-changing lineup of animated entertainment and action features. The shop next door features one of the Bay Area's largest assortments of animated products, toys, games, television and movie collectibles, and gear.

Kids will want to shop at the Discovery Channel Store; the PlayStation, a totally interactive video game store; and Digital Solutions for the best, latest, and easiest-to-use technology.

At Portal One youngsters can Hyperbole down the streets of San Francisco, through the trees of Yosemite, or across the deck of a rocking pirate ship. Dance Dance Revolution is an interactive dancing game. The Extreme Sports Adventure Room challenges gamers to go to the limit with Air Table Hockey, Super Shot Basket, and Rolling Extreme. (Two-hour unlimited gaming passes: Mon., Wed., Thurs., Fri., $20; Tues. $10. Hours are from 10 A.M.–10:30 P.M.)

The youngest will head for **Where the Wild Things Are** where they become characters in Maurice Sendak's beloved story. They can wend their way through the goblin kitchen and a mirror maze, swoosh down a tree slide, make a giant Wild Thing dance, and have a scary good time in this hands-on, feet-on world of discovery (Mon.–Thurs., 10–5; Fri. and Sat., 10–7; Sun., 10–6. $6 per person ages 4 and up. Family rates). The store next door offers creations from the characters in Sendak's books, the coolest new toys, and a special fantasy playspace. Also next door is the Night Kitchen, a family-oriented restaurant set in a dreamy world of giant bakers, massive milk bottles, and planes made of dough all set against a backdrop of twinkling stars (Tues.–Thurs., 12–4; Fri.–Mon., 12–5).

● Seymour Pioneer Museum

300 4th Street, near Mission Street, San Francisco 94107. (415) 957-1849. Wed.–Fri. and first and third Sat., 10–4. Adults, $3; seniors and students, $1. Groups. **Ages 8 & up.** *W. www.californiapioneers.org*

California history lives in constantly rotating exhibits of photographs, ephemera, artifacts, and memorabilia run by the Society of California Pioneers. The upstairs gallery focuses on California in the 19th and early 20th centuries. Schoolteachers will be happy to take classes to this museum, which also specializes in California's fourth-grade California history curriculum. There are always interactive exhibits, CD-ROMS, and DVDs to go along with each show.

● Zeum

Zeum at Yerba Buena Gardens, 4th Street at Howard across from the Metreon, 221 4th Street, San Francisco 94103. (415) 777-2800. Adults, $7; seniors and students, $6; youth, $5. Wed.–Sun., 11–5 in summer. Weekends, 11–5, and by appt. Groups; field trips; parties; rentals. Store. **Ages 5 & up.** *W. www.zeum.org*

Young people and their families experience and explore creativity and innovation through the arts and media. Build It! consists of hands-on stations for creating almost anything you can dream up in real three-dimensional space. Children can build robots and send them on "space missions," create designs on the Lego Wall, design and fly innovative paper airplanes, and create paddleboats or sailboats and then sail them in the patio pool. Exhibits and adventures change regularly, but one favorite is the chance to build a play, a dance, a piece of music, and an animation with a giant metal Venus's-flytrap. Daily performances and workshops in music, puppetry, dance, filmmaking, animation, and other challenges. Would your youngster like to build a folk song? Or a comic book?

Zeum is in the Rooftop at Yerba Buena Gardens, which also includes an ice-skating rink and bowling center, a child development center, and gardens. The Carousel at Yerba Buena Gardens is the historic 1906 Charles

Looff Carousel from San Francisco's former amusement park Playland-at-the-Beach (415-247-6500. Daily, 11–8. $2 per ticket for two rides). This gem from the past is housed in a glass pavilion and offers sweeping views of the city as you ride in a menagerie of giraffes; camels; rams; regal, jeweled jumping horses; and gilded chariots.

● Federal Reserve Bank

101 Market Street, San Francisco 94105. (415) 974-3252. Mon.–Fri., 9–4. Tours by reservation for eighth-graders and older. Free. **Ages 12 & up.** *www.federalreserveeducation.org*

"The World of Economics," a classy, block-long permanent exhibit in the lobby of the Federal Reserve Bank, teaches all about money and the economy in exciting, up-to-the-minute, interactive, dynamic display. A new exhibit, which has taken over a year to mount, opened in mid-2003.

● Asawa Fountain

Grand Hyatt Hotel, 345 Stockton Street, between Sutter and Post Streets, San Francisco 94108. Free. **All ages.**

Ruth Asawa, artist and creator of the Mermaid Fountain in Ghirardelli Square, has given the people of San Francisco a one-stop tour of the people and places that make up the city. This fountain, 14 feet in diameter, on the steps of the plaza of the Grand Hyatt on Union Square, was molded in bread dough—the same dough children use for sculpting—and cast in bronze. And the little people, trees, Chinese dragon, Painted Ladies, and school buses demand to be touched. At the bottom of the fountain is the Ferry Building; as you go around it, you'll see Coit Tower, Broadway, Aquatic Park, the Cannery, the zoo, and the Mission District. Everything is laid out in the same general direction as it is in real life. A group of Noe Valley schoolchildren created one of the fountain's 41 plaques, which depicts the children of San Francisco. Your kids will enjoy figuring out which one it is.

● Bank of California Museum

Union Bank of California, 400 California Street, downstairs, San Francisco 94104. (415) 291-GOLD/765-3254. Mon.–Fri., 9–5. Free. **Ages 8 & up.** *W (by arrangement).*

This tiny but nicely mounted collection of money and gold provides a glimpse of banking and mining in the Old West. Each coin is a piece of history. Privately minted coins from Utah, Colorado, and California show the kind of money used before the U.S. Mint was set up in San Francisco. Ingots, gold bullion, currency, and early bank drafts are here, along with counterfeit coins and counterfeit detectors. One method of counterfeiting, "the platinum menace," used hollowed-out coins filled with platinum, then worth much less than gold. Is that why an Oregon two-ounce copper-alloy coin reads, "In Gold We Trust"?

● Wells Fargo History Museum

420 Montgomery Street, San Francisco 94104. (415) 396-2619. Weekdays except bank holidays, 9–5. Group guided tours by appt. Free. Gift shop.
Ages 5 & up. *W. www.wellsfargo.com/about/museum_info*

Ever wanted to bounce along in a stagecoach? Or send a telegraph message? Or rock a gold-panning cradle? The youngsters can relive the romance of the West in this beautifully designed bilevel museum. Here you'll find gold, money, treasure boxes, art, tools, photos, a map of Black Bart's 28 stagecoach robberies, iron doors from a Wells Fargo office in the Gold Country, Pony Express memorabilia, and a rocking Concord Stage Coach with an audiotape of one young man's trip from St. Louis to San Francisco.

● Chinatown

A visit to San Francisco would not be complete without a visit to Chinatown, along Grant Avenue from Bush to Broadway and along Stockton Street from Sacramento to Vallejo. For the curious, there are fortune-cookie factories, fish stores, and temples, as well as shops and restaurants.

The **Golden Gate Fortune Cookie Factory** (415-781-3956. Weekdays, 10–noon) on Ross Alley, between Washington and Jackson Streets, above Grant Avenue, sometimes leaves its doors open so you can see the row of tiny griddles revolving under a hose that squirts dough onto each pan. The pans cook the dough on their way to the cookie maker, who picks up each browned wafer, pushes it onto a spur for the first fold, inserts the paper fortune, presses the final fold, and puts the cookie in a muffin tin to harden.

One of our favorite lunchtime meals is dim sum, which means "heart's delights." With dim sum, also called Chinese tea or tea lunch, there's always something to entice every palate. Dim sum are simply little bites of good things. You choose small plates of delicacies such as shrimp rolls, taro cakes, beef dumplings, spareribs, mushroom turnovers, custard pies, or steamed barbecued-pork buns, *bao*. Sometimes, you pay by the number of plates you have piled on the table. So if there are only two of you, and what you want is, for example, scallop dumplings, and they're presented on two plates, ask for a half order. That way you only get two dumplings on one plate—and have room for more tastes. In Chinatown, we recommend family-friendly **Lychee Garden** on Powell Street, between Broadway and Stockton Street.

At **Harbor Village** (4 Embarcadero Center. 415-781-8833. http://harborvillage.net) you can get a peek at the bay and the Bay Bridge, along with good food, then shop in the four buildings that make up Embarcadero Center.

Cultural, historical, and artistic exhibitions are presented in the **Chinese Culture Center,** the forum for the Chinese community (750 Kearny Street, 94108, in the Holiday Inn, third floor. 415-986-1822. Tues.–Sun., 10–4. Gallery, ages 7 and over, free. W. www.c-c-c.org). The center is especially popular during the Chinese New Year celebration in February. The Culinary Walks offered are fun for whole families and school groups who want to learn more about Chinatown—and they always end with a dim sum lunch.

● Chinese Historical Society of America Museum and Learning Center

965 Clay Street, San Francisco 94108. (415) 391-1188. Tues.–Fri., 11– 4; Sat. and Sun., 12–4, and by appt. Adults, $3; seniors and students, $2; ages 6–17, $1. First Thurs. of the month, free. Groups. Learning center, Tues. and Thurs., 2–4, and by appt. Gift shop. **Ages 6 & up.** *www.chsa.org*

Located in the historic Julia Morgan YWCA in San Francisco Chinatown, this gorgeously designed museum is devoted to sharing the history, culture, and legacy of Chinese Americans from the 1850s to the present. Permanent and changing panels and exhibits illuminate their lives and times. Famous Chinese Americans such as skater Michelle Kwan, author Jade Snow Wong, cellist Yo-Yo Ma, architect I. M. Pei, and director Wayne Wang are in spotlights. Ceremonial swords, printing blocks, an altar, porcelain pillows, clothes worn by 19th-century laborers and the highborn, opium pipes, photographs, and documents are on view in themes such as the Cold War, medicine, the voyage, fashion, even the musical *Flower Drum Song.* Art shows change every four to six months with renowned Chinese American artist Dong Kingman the very first one so honored.

● Pacific Heritage Museum

608 Commercial Street, between Montgomery and Kearny Streets, San Francisco 94111. (415) 399-1124. Tues.–Sat., 10–4. Free. **Ages 8 & up.** *W. www. pacificheritage.citysearch.com*

The Bank of Canton has integrated the historic 1875 U.S. Subtreasury Building, once the U.S. Branch Mint, into its architecturally acclaimed world headquarters in San Francisco's Financial District. Exhibits of Pacific Rim culture and history change every 12 to 18 months. During one visit, we were fascinated with "Wings Over the Pacific," which re-created the colorful history of flight throughout the Pacific Rim with hundreds of artifacts, models, engines, and rare photographs. "Shining Stars: Four Cultural Vision-aries of Contemporary Painting" showed the kinetic exchange of philosophi-cal ideas and approaches, transcending each into a new level of expression and vision.

● Cable Car Barn Museum

1201 Mason Street, at Washington Street, San Francisco 94108. (415) 474-1887. Daily, 10–5 in winter; 10–6 Apr.–Sept. Closed holidays. Free/donation. Museum shop and bookstore. **Ages 4 & up.** *W. www.cablecarmuseum.com*

All three cable car lines in San Francisco are run by the huge revolving wheels in the brick cable car barn, built in 1887. Visitors can watch the wheels from a gallery, where there are samples of the cable itself and charts explaining how the cable cars work. You can see scale models, earthquake mementos, old cable car seats, photographs, and the cable cars on display, including the first one to operate in San Francisco, in 1873. An underground viewing room lets you see the cables running under the streets from the car barn at nine and a half miles an hour. A 16-minute video offers more information.

● North Beach Museum

1435 Stockton Street, upstairs in Bayview Bank, San Francisco 94133. (415) 391-6210. Mon.–Thurs., 9–5; Fri., 9–6; Sat., 9–1. Free. **Ages 9 & up.** *www.sfnorthbeach.com*

Photographs and artifacts in changing thematic exhibits celebrate the city's, and especially North Beach's, colorful past, from the Gold Rush to the 1906 earthquake and fire, to the growth of the neighborhood as the center of the city's Italian community, to the Beat Generation.

● San Francisco Performing Arts Library and Museum

War Memorial Veterans Building, 401 Van Ness Avenue, San Francisco 94102. (415) 255-4800. Wed.–Fri., 11–5; Sat., 1–5. **Ages 10 & up.** *W. www.sfpalm.org*

What did Enrico Caruso sing the night before the earthquake? What did Lola Montez wear while dancing the tarantella? What were Michael Smuin's favorite ballets at the San Francisco Ballet Company? How did *Flower Drum Song* come to be made? Visitors can find the answers here. Posters, sheet music, photographs, costumes, and audio visual material are used in the three to four changing exhibits each year with focus on performing arts, particularly the performing arts of the Bay Area. "San Francisco in Song" and "San Francisco 1900: On Stage" are permanent exhibits. For school tours, contact Brad Rosenstein, director of education and outreach.

● Asian Art Museum of San Francisco

200 Larkin Street, San Francisco 94102. (415) 379-8800. TDD: (415) 752-2635. **Ages 5 & up.** *W. www.asianart.org*

For 35 years, the Asian Art Museum has served as one of San Francisco's premier arts institutions, offering visitors groundbreaking exhibitions as well as fascinating and innovative public programs for all ages. At the museum's core is a permanent collection of more than 13,000 objects spanning 6,000 years of history and representing the countries and cultures of Asia. The museum is still being installed in redesigned space at the old San Francisco Library. Call or see the website for hours, fees, and programs.

● Haas-Lilienthal House

2007 Franklin Street, San Francisco 94109. (415) 441-3000. Tours Wed. and Sat., 12–3; Sun., 11–4, and by appt. Pacific Heights Walk, Sun. at 12:30. Adults, $5; seniors and students, $2. **Ages 10 & up.** *www.sfheritage.org*

"We would like to thank you for our tour at the Haas-Lilienthal House. We learned so much about the family that used to live there, the utensils and furniture they used, and what they did in the rooms we visited. Thanks again!" wrote middle schoolers Jennifer and Wendy. Forty-five-minute docent-led tours will show you this glorious Queen Anne Victorian, built in 1886, a completely furnished memory of yesterday.

Victorian Home Walks are available from Jay, (415) 252-9485, www.victorianwalk.com. These 2 ½-hour tours are daily at 11 A.M., $20, and include a trolley ride to great views of the Golden Gate Bridge and low-impact walking while you see more than 200 Victorians.

● Octagon House

2645 Gough Street, at Union Street, San Francisco 94123. (415) 441-7512. Open on the second Sun. and second and fourth Thurs. of each month, 12–3. Groups for fifth-graders and up, by appt. Closed on holidays and in Jan. Free/donation. **Ages 7 & up.** *W (first floor).*

Built in 1861, this unusual eight-sided home is the headquarters of the National Society of the Colonial Dames of America in California as well as a gracious museum of the decorative arts of the Colonial and Federal periods. A framed pack of Revolutionary War playing cards, a 13-star flag, dishes taken in battle from the USS *Constitution* (Old Ironsides), and a 1789 leather fire bucket from Massachusetts make this a pleasantly educational stop. In one room is a display of documents featuring signatures of 54 of the 56 signers of the Declaration of Independence. The child's room with its old toys, a 1750 child's walker, and a framed 1840s doll wearing pantaloons is especially popular with the young set. Paper models of the house, 50¢, are popular with young visitors as is the "Simple History of the Octagon House," 50¢. Next door is Allyne Park, a lovely picnic spot. Did you know that the house was originally across the street, on a hill, and that you could see the ships in the Golden Gate from the cupola on top?

● Ghirardelli Chocolate Manufactory

Ghirardelli Square, 900 North Point, at Larkin Street, San Francisco 94109.
(415) 771-4903. Daily, 10:30–10; later in summer. Parties: 474-3938.
All ages. *W. www.Ghirardelli.com*

Since the beginning of the century, Ghirardelli Chocolate has been a popular trade name throughout the West. This red brick, aromatic ice cream and candy shop invokes that name in a nostalgic corner of the old Ghirardelli factory. After filling out an order form and paying the cashier, you claim a table, then take turns watching the chocolate-making machinery in the back of the room until your order is ready. We always dream of diving into the big vats where the chocolate is conched after the beans are roasted, cracked, husked, ground, and mixed with other ingredients. Instead, we dive into a hot fudge sundae, or a delicious extravaganza such as the Emperor Norton, with bananas, or the Chocolate Decadence. Or we could have a soda or cone.

The square itself is three stories full of shops and restaurants, often with great views of the bay. Here you can find shoes, popcorn, cookies, crafts, books, perfume, clothes, jewelry, gadgets, and gifts galore. Jugglers and street entertainers perform on weekends and in summer in the flower-bedecked plazas, free. Ruth Asawa's mermaid fountain is wonderful. Say "Gear-ar-delly."

The **Cannery**, a block away (2801 Leavenworth Street, at Beach Street, San Francisco 94133. W. www.thecannery.com), was once the biggest peach cannery in the world. Like Ghirardelli, it is now a shopping complex, with gift and crafts stores and restaurants to browse through. Spectacular views from the third-floor walkway extend from the Golden Gate Bridge to the Berkeley hills. Kids can test their skills on a didgeridoo or try their hand at any of the exotic musical instruments found at the world-renowned music store **Lark in the Morning** (415-922-4277). Toddlers will certainly enjoy the **Basic Brown Bear Factory** where they can stuff and dress their very own teddy bear (second floor. 415-931-6670. www.basicbrownbear.com). **Toy Symphony** (415-775-7893) offers a huge selection of art and educational toys for creative minds of all ages. Events, such as the California State Yo-Yo championships, are staged, free, in the plaza.

● Maritime Museum (San Francisco Maritime National Historic Park)

*900 Beach Street, at the foot of Polk Street, San Francisco 94109 (Mail: P.O. Box 470310, 94147). (415) 561-7100. TDD: 556-1843. Daily, 10–5. Call for calendar of events. Lesson Plans: www.nps.gov/safr/lesson.html. School groups: www.nps.gov/safr/local/sgroup.html. Free. **Ages 5 & up.** W. www.maritime.org*

The Maritime Museum, housed in a historic art-deco streamline modern building that resembles a cruise ship, is a mecca for ship lovers of all ages. The maritime history of San Francisco lives on here in models of clippers, iron ships, schooners, barkentines, cutters, and cod fishers; and in photos, figureheads, tools, scrimshaw, whaling guns, harpoons, diaries, maritime paintings, and ships' logs. The 19-foot sloop *Mermaid*, which one man, Ken-Ichi Hori, sailed from Osaka to San Francisco, is on the veranda. The Radio Room from the freighter Rider Victory is now on the museum's second floor. An interactive exhibit documenting the history of communication at sea is on the third floor. The Steamship Room presents the history of West Coast steam navigation.

The **J. Porter Shaw Library** is part of San Francisco Maritime National History Park, located near park offices at Building E, Fort Mason Center (415-561-7030. Tues., 5–8; Wed.–Fri., 1–5; Sat., 10–5. Free. www.maritime.org). One of the world's largest collections of maritime records including maps, logbooks, ship plans, photographs, and oral histories, this is the place to track down a sailing grandfather, find historic plans for a ship model project, or peruse binders full of fascinating one-of-a-kind daguerreotypes.

● Hyde Street Pier (San Francisco Maritime National Historic Park)

Hyde Street Pier, at Hyde and Jefferson Streets, San Francisco 94109 (Mail: P.O. Box 470310, San Francisco 94147-0310). (415) 561-7100. TDD: 556-1843. Daily, 10–5. Tours, events, and Environmental Living Programs. Adults, $6; seniors, $4; ages 12–17, $2; under 12, free. Store. **All ages.** *W (limited). www.maritime.org*

At Hyde Street Pier, the only "floating" national park and home of the world's largest collection of historic ships by tonnage, visitors can board several National Landmark vessels, including the 1886 square-rigger *Balclutha*, the three-masted 1895 schooner *C. A. Thayer*, the 1891 scow schooner *Alma*, and the 1890 ferryboat *Eureka*.

On the *Balclutha*, one of the last surviving square-rigged Cape Horners, you can spin the wheel, visit the "slop chest" and galley, check out the captain's quarters with its swinging bed, ring bells, and read sea chanties and rousing tales of the Barbary Coast below decks, while the movement of the boat on the water stimulates the imagination.

This steel-hulled, 301-foot three-masted ship was launched in 1886. It rounded Cape Horn 17 times and, after technology made shipping less profitable, starred in the original movie version of *Mutiny on the Bounty*.

Go below decks on the 1895 schooner *C. A. Thayer*, a logging and salmon packet, to see the captain's family cabin. There are antique cars waiting for the next docking on the 1890 ferry Eureka. Hyde Street Pier also offers regular ranger-guided tours, chantey sings, special programs, and hands-on demonstrations for all ages as well as classes, movies, and videos.

● USS *Pampanito* SS383

Pier 45, Fisherman's Wharf, San Francisco (Mail: San Francisco Maritime National Park Association, P.O. Box 470310, San Francisco 94147-0310). (415) 561-6662. Daily, 9–6; later in summer. Adults, $7; seniors, $5; ages 6–12, $4. Family tickets and combination Pampanito/*Hyde Street Pier tickets available. Self-guided audio tours included. Store.* **Ages 6 & up.** *www.maritime.org/index.html*

Experience what life was like for submariners during World War II by stepping aboard this fully restored floating exhibit. Now a National Landmark, *Pampanito* saw heavy duty during the war, rescuing 73 prisoners of war from the Pacific Ocean in one particularly heroic effort in 1944. Explore the torpedo room, crew's quarters, control room, and fully operational galley while listening to the voices of *Pampanito* veterans describing daily life aboard the submarine, the tension of being on war patrol, and the dramatic rescue of POWs in the Pacific. A museum is in the works.

● Museum of the City of San Francisco and Musée Mécanique

As of this writing, the Museum of the City of San Francisco was planning to join with the Musée Mécanique in a new, 9,000-square-foot establishment on Pier 45. Call 415-255-9400 or log on www.sfmuseum.org for up-to-date hours, fees, and programs. Both museums are scheduled to move to more permanent quarters in 2006.

San Francisco treasures will capture the imagination in this "temporary" museum space. One section might focus on the earthquake and fire of 1906 and the earthquake of 1989. Photographs and memorabilia such as dishes and letters that survived will help tell the story. A favorite artifact is the supersized head of the Goddess of Progress, which crowned City Hall before 1906. We hope a use will be found for the hand-carved wooden ceiling from a 13th-century Spanish palace purchased by William Randolph Hearst. Dioramas featuring the Gold Rush era and a 1913 player piano delights young and old.

Fans of the old Musée Mécanique will greet old friends like Laughing Sal, a huge freckled animatron and San Francisco native that lets out peals of hysterical laughter, and the palm-reading Bocca de la Verita (the Mouth of Truth). My favorite is the Carnival Scene that moves all its parts at the drop of a quarter.

● *Jeremiah O'Brien* **Liberty Ship**

Pier 32, San Francisco (Mail: P.O. Box 470310, San Francisco 94147-0310). (415) 544-0100. Daily, 9–5. Adults, $7; seniors, $5; ages 6–14, $4. Rentals. Guided tours by appt. **Ages 6 & up.** *www.ssjeremiahobrien.org*

The last intact liberty ship carried food and ammunition to England, ferried troops during the Normandy invasion, and transported supplies to the South Pacific. Volunteers, who are always welcome, have restored the ship and enjoy showing visitors around. On the third weekend of each month, they show the kids how a 50-year-old triple-expansion steam engine works. In 1994, volunteers sailed the ship on a five-month voyage to reenact the World War II invasion of Normandy. In 1996, they sailed to the Pacific Northwest.

● **Ripley's Believe It or Not! Museum**

175 Jefferson Street, at Fisherman's Wharf, San Francisco 94133. (415) 771-6188. Sun.–Thurs., 10–10; Fri. and Sat., until midnight. Adults, $10.95; ages 5–12, $7.95; seniors, $8.50. School tours by appt. **Ages 8 & up.** *W. www.ripleysf.com*

This two-story collection of oddities and puzzles is almost unbelievable. Here you'll find the tallest, smallest, funniest, yuckiest oddities and puzzles, videos and films, and interactive challenges. Where else could you see a cable car made from 270,836 matchsticks? A stegosaurus made of chrome car bumpers? Here you can walk through an animal kaleidoscope and a rotating tunnel and over a disappearing bridge. Wonder at the man with two pupils in each eye. The museum is always on the lookout for new unbelievable facts or unusual items, so if you send one in, you too can become part of the legend of Robert Ripley's Believe It or Not!

● **Wax Museum at Fisherman's Wharf**

145 Jefferson Street, at Fisherman's Wharf, San Francisco 94133. (800) 439-4305/(415) 202-0400. Weekdays, 9 A.M.–11 P.M.; weekends until midnight. Adults, $12.95; seniors and military, $10.55; children, $6.95. Group rates. Parties. One-price tickets available for Wax Museum, Ripley's Believe It or Not, Blue and Gold Fleet, and Rainforest Café. **Ages 8 & up.** *W (limited). www.waxmuseum.com*

Meet Prince Charles and Princess Diana, Abraham Lincoln, Mona Lisa, Michael Jackson, King Tut with his treasures, Elvis Presley, General MacArthur, Joe Montana, the Phantom of the Opera, and other heroes and villains. There are 250 wax figures in 70 scenes re-creating the past, the present, and the world of the future. You may choose to take the "chicken walk" to bypass the Chamber of Horrors, which is "not recommended for cowards, sissies, and yellerbellies." That includes us.

● Rainforest Café

145 Jefferson Street, San Francisco 94133. (415) 440-5610. Sun. and Thurs., 11–10; Fri. and Sat., 11–11. **All ages.** *W. www.rainforestcafe.com*

This "wild place to shop and eat" is a three-story restaurant with a spectacular two-story waterfall and unique aquariums. Wander in a tropical wonderland with cool mists and cascading waterfalls, continuous tropical rain storms, animation featuring butterflies, crocodiles, snakes and frogs, trumpeting elephants and entertaining gorillas, all within the surroundings of larger than life banyan trees and the sounds of a tropical rain forest. Then dine on "planet pasta," "volcanic cobb salad," "flying dragon pizza," steaks, and appetizers.

● Alcatraz Island Cruise and Tour (GGNRA)

Pier 41, San Francisco 94133. (415) 561-4700. Frequent departures on the Blue and Gold Fleet daily. Advance ticket purchase by phone (415-705-5555) or website (www.telesails.com) with a credit card is strongly suggested. Once docked, you can walk with the self-guided audio tour available, for an extra charge, when you purchase your ticket. Call for up-to-date schedules and prices. Bookstore and mini-museum. **Ages 6 & up.** *SEAT (Sustainable Easy Access Transport) is available for wheelchair users and those unable to walk the quarter-mile 12%-grade hill.*

Wear walking shoes and take a sweater on this educational, fascinating-yet-depressing, self-guided walking tour of Alcatraz. One friend calls the two- to two-and-a-half-hour trip a surefire way to stop juvenile delinquency. Try spending time in a five-by-nine-foot cell, all alone, just for a few minutes. Alcatraz is part of the Golden Gate National Recreation Area, a nationally protected parkland along the coast. The National Park Service presents ranger programs, a captioned orientation video with historical footage, and an award-winning audio tour of the prison Cellhouse with actual interviews of former guards and inmates.

The Blue and Gold Fleet offers Alcatraz Excursions from Pier 41, (415) 705-5555. Call for schedule information. Adults, $9.95; seniors, $7.50; ages 5–11, $6 ($13.25/$11.50/$8 with audio). **Ages 5 & up.** W. www. blueandgoldfleet.com

Alcatraz After Dark Excursions feature sunset and cityscape views of San Francisco after dark (adults, $20.75; seniors and ages 12–17, $18; ages 5–11, $11.50), which include westside island viewing with narration by Alcatraz guides from Dock to Cellhouse and specialty tours. Wear warm clothing!

Alcatraz-Angel Island "Island hop" combines two sites in one six-hour trip. On Angel Island you enjoy a one-hour narrated Tram Tour. Call (415) 705-8200 for ferry, (415) 561-4630 for GGNRA, and (415) 897-0715 for

Angel Island TramTours. Adults, $35.25; seniors, $32.50; ages 5–11, $21. Food service is available on the ferry and at the Cove Café on Angel Island.

● Bay Cruises

On a sunny day in San Francisco, there's nothing nicer for the family than getting out on San Francisco Bay. You can take a ferry that goes to Sausalito, Angel Island, Tiburon, or Marine World, or simply take a guided-tour cruise of the bay, under the Golden Gate and Bay Bridges. **All ages.**

The **Red and White Fleet** offers a one-hour cruise with audio tours in English, German, Japanese, Mandarin, Spanish, and French. Daily commuter trips to Sausalito and Tiburon leave from Pier 41 and Pier 43½. Call (415) 447-0597 for fares and schedules. www.redandwhite.com

The **Blue and Gold Fleet** has a one and a quarter-hour Bay Cruise looping under the Golden Gate Bridge, past Alcatraz, under the Bay Bridge, and back to the sea lions at Pier 39. For schedules and prices, call (415) 773-1188. Advance tickets: (415) 705-5555. Group rates. W. www.blueandgoldfleet.com

Three-hour dinner-dance or holiday cruises from May to December are also available. Blue and Gold Fleet also operates the Alameda/Oakland and Vallejo ferries with frequent daily departures. Special ferry packages are available to destinations such as Angel Island, Six Flags Marine World, and the Napa Valley Wine Train and Wine Tour.

San Francisco Seaplane Tours take off from a walk-up dock on Pier 39, hourly, 10 to dusk, and from Sausalito. Call (415) 332-4843 for reservations. www.seaplane.com. Adults, $129; under 12, $99. The Canadian-built seven-passenger de Havilland Beaver, a beautiful, rugged bush plane, has bubble center windows and enlarged rear windows for easy, fun sightseeing on 45-minute tours.

Hornblower Cruises and Events offers Dinner Dance cruises, Sunday Champagne Brunch cruises, and Monte Carlo Casino cruises on three worthy vessels. For reservations and information, call (415) 788-8866 ext. 7. www.hornblower.com. Rentals and Groups: (415) 788-8866 ext. 6. Pier 3, on the Embarcadero, San Francisco 94111. We spent one wonderful Fourth of July evening on a Hornblower Cruise.

● Pier 39

Beach Street and the Embarcadero. (415) 981-PIER. The Pier 39 Garage is across the street, and many restaurants partially validate the parking fee. **All ages.** *W. www.pier39.com*

Pier 39 is a shopping-restaurant complex set right on the water. Shops are open daily from 10:30 until 8 and may have extended hours in summer. Most restaurants open at 11:30. Some, like the historic Eagle Café (415-433-3689)

open earlier for breakfast. Pier 39 boasts the most popular tourist attraction in town—and it's free: a huge, barking colony of smelly, splashing, or sleeping sea lions that have made their home at the end of the West Marina. It's fun to watch them push each other off the floats.

On the pier, stop at the Information Center for the **Marine Mammal Center** (the M. M. Center is in the Marin Highlands) for the free flyer, "39 Fascinating Facts," about the California sea lion. Parties at the Stuff-A-Teddy Store (second level, 415-397-1090) can be "very beary." Choose your style of teddy, stuff it, then dress it with the costume of your choice. Fun! The California Welcome Center, upstairs next to the theater, provides half-price tickets along with information. There's even a one-hour photo shop.

Youngsters will head for the colorful two-tiered, twinkling San Francisco carousel, the only one in the country with artistic, hand-painted renderings of its home city, including the Golden Gate Bridge, Coit Tower, Chinatown, Lombard Street, Alcatraz, and the sea lions (415-705-5500. Sun.–Thurs., 10–8; Fri. and Sat., 10–9. $2). Middle-graders will prefer the Namcoland Arcade, the Turbo Ride Simulation Theater, or the Riptide Arcade, with its more than 100 video games, virtual reality games, bumper cars, and an Old West–style shooting gallery (415-955-1600). Frequent Flyers, a trampoline bungee jumping game, is nearby in the West Park. Entertainers perform on the two stages and on the boards. Sailing sessions and lessons and buggy and rickshaw rides are available. Pacific Marine Yachts (415-788-9100) offers charters and dining cruises. AdventureCat (415-777-1630) offers catamaran excursions. There's even a bed-and-breakfast aboard a yacht!

● **Great San Francisco Adventure**
Pier 39, San Francisco 94133. (415) 956-3456. Daily, every 45 minutes, 10–10 in summer; 10:30–8 in winter. Adults, $7.50; seniors, $6; under 12, $4.50. **All ages.** *W. www.pier39.com*

The Cinemax Theatre presents a thrilling new half-hour giant-screen tour of San Francisco that captures the historical and cultural wonders, the myth, magic, and beauty of San Francisco. There's lots of aerial photography and vignettes of local personalities. The Chinese New Year's Parade, the Bay to Breakers race, windsurfing on the bay, and a high-speed chase on San Francisco's hills are highlights.

● **Aquarium of the Bay**
Pier 39, the Embarcadero at Beach Street, San Francisco 94133. (888) SEA-DIVE/(415) 623-5300. Daily, 9–8 in summer; 10–6 in winter. Closed on Christmas. Adults, $12.95; seniors and ages 3–11, $6.50. Groups, family rates. School tours by appt., free. (415) 705-5500. Gift shop. **All ages.** *W. www.aquariumofthebay.com*

Aquarium of the Bay is a brand-new way to discover the bay. Explore the wonders of San Francisco Bay as you walk through crystal-clear tunnels surrounded by sharks, eels, octopuses, and thousands of marine animals indigenous to its waters. This is your chance to go face-to-face with the Pacific's most fascinating residents. Reach out and touch a beautiful sea star, a prickly purple urchin, or a leopard shark. It's a touch-and-learn experience with live animals the kids will never forget.

● Hard Rock Café

Pier 39. (415) 885-1699. Gift shop. Call or check online for hours. **All ages.** *W. www.hardrock.com*

The Hard Rock Café is just as much a rock-and-roll shrine as it is a restaurant. It's a mecca for rock fans of all ages. Sounds of the great rockers greet you as you walk into a large, two-level room, the walls of which are covered with posters, gold and platinum records, and the guitars of rock stars. The room has a California openness punctuated by a "dodge 'em" car, a motorcycle, and a standard Hard Rock fixture: half of a Cadillac over the entranceway. The menu's California touches lighten the load of affordable golden oldies such as ribs, fries, hamburgers, shakes, and banana splits. Expect a wait most of the time.

Justin wrote, "My favorite restaurant is Hard Rock Café. Why I like this particular place so much is because of the food and what there is to look at. While I'm waiting for my food I can just look around and keep myself entertained. I also like the pinball games they have there. . . . They also play loud rock-and-roll music which you can sit in your comfortable seats and listen. . . . Hard Rock Café is a great and fun place to eat."

● Fort Mason Center

Once a lonely barracks with deserted piers, Fort Mason (www.fortmason.org), at the foot of Marina Boulevard and Laguna Street, is now a flourishing center for the arts. Nonprofit organizations from the Endangered Species Society or the Golden Gate Raptor Observatory to Western Public Radio are based here, and performing arts groups give shows in the three theaters. The **Oceanic Society** (Building E, second floor, 415-441-1106, www.oceanic-society.org) offers Whale Watch and Farallon Islands day cruises as well as national and international trips for wildlife enthusiasts. **Sailing Education Adventures** (Building E, second floor, 415-775-8779. www.sailsea.org) offers sailing camps, lectures, and field trips featuring marine environment or maritime history topics.

Greens, a fine vegetarian restaurant, has a phenomenal view of the docks, the bay, and the Golden Gate Bridge (415-771-6222 for lunch and dinner reservations. W. www.greensrestaurant.com).

The **San Francisco Museum of Modern Art**'s rental wing is in Building A (415-441-4777). The **City College of San Francisco Fort Mason Art Campus** is in Building B. Call (415) 441-3400 or check www.fortmason.org for a list of events each week.

The following five galleries are of special interest to the young. On Free Museum day, the first Wednesday of each month, they are open late, until 7, and admission is free.

Museum of Craft and Folk Art, *Building A. (415) 775-0991. Tues.–Fri., 11–5; Sat., 10–5. Adults $3. seniors, $1. $5 for families. First Wed., 11–7, free.* **Ages 10 & up.** *W. www.mocfa.org.* Changing shows on wearable and unwearable art and folk art themes can educate and amuse. A past favorite show, "Sirens and Snakes: Water Spirits in Folk Art and Legend," was devoted to our enduring enchantment with mermaids, sirens, nixies, and other water spirits from countries such as Haiti, Indonesia, West Africa, Australia, Panama, the Caribbean, and New Guinea. Family activities on mermaids were then held at the Children's Art Center so the kids could make their own mermaids.

Museo ItaloAmericano, *Building C. (415) 673-2200. Wed.–Sun., 12–5, and by appt. Adults, $3; seniors and students, $2; under 12, free. Gift shop. W. www.museumitaloamericano.org.* This museum preserves and displays Italian and ItaloAmerican art, history, and culture in changing exhibits. Classes, community activities, and films are presented.

San Francisco African-American Historical and Cultural Society, *Building C. (415) 441-0640. Wed.–Sun., 12–5. Adults, $2; children, $1. Gift shop.* **All ages.** The society features changing exhibits or photos, art, and artifacts that portray the history and culture of African Americans.

Mexican Museum, *Building D. (415) 202-9700. Wed.–Sun., 12–5. Adults, $3; students, $2; under 10, free. Tours by appt. Gift shop. www.mexicanmuseum.org.* The Mexican Museum's vision is to generate new perspectives of American culture that shape the way we perceive ourselves as a nation. It collects, preserves, exhibits, interprets, and promotes the artistic expression of Mexicano and Latino people through the visual arts and other multi-disciplinary media. Six Sundays a year, the museum invites families to come together, to create crafts projects connected with Mexican cultural and religious holidays.

Children's Art Center of San Francisco, *Building C, first floor. (415) 771-0292. Party facilities available.* Children ages two to 10 draw, paint, sculpt, and print in small classes with individual attention, exploring the organized freedom of the studio.

● Japan Center

With stores and restaurants, the Japan Center (*Nihonmachi*) can really be another world. The Peace Plaza with its reflecting pools and five-tiered Peace

Pagoda is the center of entertaining festivals and celebrations during the year. You can see music and dance programs as well as judo, karate, and kendo matches. Inside the center, you can fish for an oyster with a pearl in it, or have a Japanese fish-shaped *tai yaki,* a warm, filled, wafflelike pastry. Kids like the Mikado store, which sells Sanrio Hello Kitty products.

Introduce friends and youngsters to sushi at **Isobune** (1737 Post Street, San Francisco 94115. 415-563-1030. W. www.isobune.com). Here you sit in front of a running stream. Boats float by you carrying little plates of sushi. You take off what looks good and pay by the plate. Start with *maki,* cucumbers in rice wrapped in crunchy seaweed, or *tamago,* a slice of omelet, or *ebi,* cooked shrimp, for the wary. My 10-year-old nephew, Alan, was hooked by the *unagi,* broiled eel with barbecue sauce. A friend prefers all the salad sushis—sushi made of shrimp salad, crab salad, mushroom salad, even seaweed salad. **Mifune,** across the way in the Kintetsu Mall (415-922-0337), is noted for its many nourishing, inexpensive noodle soups and dishes. It's okay to slurp!

● San Francisco Fire Department Museum

655 Presidio Avenue, between Pine and Bush Streets, San Francisco 94115. (415) 563-4630. Thurs.–Sun., 1–4, and by appt. Free. **All ages.** *W. www.sffiremuseum.org*

Awe-inspiring photos of today's firefighters mingle with uniforms, bells, trophies, and mementos of men and machines, the silver speaking trumpet, leather buckets, a buffalo-leather fire hose, and other relics of yesteryear. Lillie Coit, the darling of the San Francisco Fire Department, has her own case full of mementos. Two American LaFrance Steam Fire Engines and other machinery fill the room.

● Mission Dolores

Dolores at 16th Street, 3321 16th Street, San Francisco 94114. (415) 621-8203. Daily, 9–4 in winter; 9–4:30 in summer. Adults and group tours for those 10 and older, adults, $3; children, $2; seniors and students, $1; free Wed. 11–7 and Sat. 10–12. Audio tour, $5. **Ages 6 & up.** *www.missiondolores.citysearch.com; www.ca-missions.org*

Established in 1776, the Mission San Francisco de Asis, as it is properly named, is the city's oldest structure. Ohlone Indians built the existing mission church in 1788. The unique Corinthian and Moorish architecture is not at all like that of other California missions. Inside, two elaborate late-18th-century *reredos* flanking the altar have been restored, as have the Indian designs painted on the ceiling. The three bells in the facade came from Mexico in the 1790s and Bret Harte wrote a famous poem about them in 1863. The gardens wind around one of the two cemeteries left in San Francisco. It contains the remains of some of the city's first settlers, from the first Mexican governor, Louis Arguello, who died in 1830, to Francisco de Haro, first *alcalde* (mayor) of the city, to James Casey, a fireman mistakenly hanged for murder by the 1856 Vigilance Committee. To young Juan, "The best part was when we got to see the cemetery and the cowhide stuff was cool. It was great when we heard the bells. I liked the graves in the church. That was really fantastic."

● Randall Museum

199 Museum Way, San Francisco 94114. Off Roosevelt, from 14th Street, west of Castro. (415) 554-9600. Tues.–Sat., 10–5. Animal Room, 10:30–1 and 2–5. Free. Classes, workshops, nature walks. **All ages.** *www.randallmuseum.org*

On a 16-acre hill overlooking the city and the bay, the Randall Museum is a place where children, youth, and adults can explore the arts, the sciences, and the environment through a wide variety of hands-on classes, exhibits, and programs. The museum features live animals, special events, and classes for all ages. A model railroad exhibit is open every Saturday from 11 to 4. Low-cost drop-in family classes are held on most Saturdays at 10 and 1. The museum hosts performances, presentations, and lectures.

● Golden Gate Park (GGNRA)

From Fulton and Stanyan Streets, west to the ocean. The park office is in McLaren Lodge, John F. Kennedy Drive, at Stanyan Street, San Francisco 94117. (415) 831-2700. www.nps.gov/goga/index.htm

There are more than 1,000 acres of lakes and greenery in San Francisco's Golden Gate Park and at least 100 things to see and do. You can go boating or feed the ducks, cheer model boat races, picnic, ride horses, play tennis, golf, or handball, go lawn bowling, watch the grazing bison, bicycle, skate, watch soccer and polo matches, pitch horseshoes, shoot arrows, play cards or chess, fly cast, or make water rings in the fountains. Stow Lake is the place to rent rowboats, motorboats, and pedal boats (415-752-0347). Visit the magical, silvery Golden Gate pavilion from China, located on Stow Lake's island.

The **Children's Playground,** located on the Lincoln Avenue side of the park, features the slide with the fastest ride in the West, plus three other slides, geometrical shapes to climb (handicapped accessible), and swings.

The nearby **Herschel-Spillman 1912 Carousel** (Wed.–Sun., 10–4:15. $1) has been perfectly and wonderfully restored, with 62 menagerie animals, mostly in sets of two—cats, dogs, zebras, tigers, roosters, storks, giraffes, reindeer, frogs, pigs, goats, and beautiful horses—like Noah's Ark, plus a love-tub and a rocker.

Older children might enjoy a walk through **Shakespeare's Garden** to identify the plants he wrote about. You can climb a drum bridge in the splendidly peaceful **Japanese Tea Garden** (Tours, 415-752-1171/

754-4227. Daily, 9–5. Adults, $3.50; seniors and children, $1.25) and then sit down to tea and cookies in the Tea House (daily, 10–6:30. $2.95. School tours: 415-666-7024) and watch the birds.

Visit the restored spun-sugar Victorian **Conservatory of Flowers** on Kennedy Drive to see displays of flowers (501 Stanyan Street, Golden Gate Park, 94117. 415-750-5105. www.conservatoryofflowers.org).

Ring the Mexican Bell in the **Strybing Arboretum's Garden of Fragrance,** where you can test your sense of smell, touch, and taste (415-661-1316. Weekdays, 8–4:30; weekends and holidays, 10–5. Tours, theme walks, plant sales, and bookstore. Free).

Gaze at the **Portals of the Past,** the marble columns that are all that was left of a Nob Hill mansion after the 1906 earthquake and are now the guardians of a duck-filled lake. Don't forget to say thank you to John McLaren—whose statue is tucked in a dell of rhododendrons across from the conservatory, though he hated statues in parks—for turning former sand dunes into an oasis of greenery gracing the city.

● **M. H. de Young Memorial Museum**
75 Tea Garden Drive, Golden Gate Park (north side of Music Concourse), San Francisco 94118-4501. (415) 750-3614. Information Hotline: 863-3330. www.thinker.org

The West Coast's best collection of American painting, sculpture, and decorative arts, including Georgia O'Keeffe's *Petunias,* Frederick Church's *Rainy Day in the Tropics,* and the John D. Rockefeller 3rd Collection of American Art with several works by the Ash Can school, and art from pre-Columbian Latin America and Africa are now under wraps. A new state-of-the-art museum will open in 2005.

● **California Academy of Sciences**
Golden Gate Park (south side of Music Concourse), San Francisco 94118. Taped information: (415) 750-7145; switchboard: 750-7000. Daily, 10–5 in winter and 9–6 in summer. Adults, $8.50; seniors and ages 12–17, $5.50; ages 6–11, $2. First Wed. of the month, free. Rates for groups by appt. Special programs and lectures. Gift shop. **Ages 3 & up.** *W. www.calacademy.org*

Earth, Ocean, and Space, all in one place! Wander through the innovative Wild California Hall and the Hall of Gems and Minerals. The African Safari Hall teems with sights and sounds of Africa. Don't miss the Hohfen Hall, with the Earth-Quake, a ride that simulates an earthquake. The Far Side of Science Gallery features the work of cartoonist Gary Larson. In the Life Through Time hall, you'll discover facts about the evolution of life on Earth and find out how our planet's remote past affects our world today. Robotic saber-toothed cats, woolly mammoth, giant sloths, and a bucktoothed, long-snouted Platybelodon are some of the Ice Age animals re-created in unique sound-and-movement exhibits. The African Play Space is a hands-on touch-and-learn room for tiny explorers.

The whale fountain courtyard leads to the academy's **Steinhart Aquarium**'s swamp, inhabited by crocodiles and alligators. Thousands of fish and reptiles live in 243 colorful tanks, all low enough for children to see into easily. Sea horses, black-footed penguins, deadly stonefish, piranhas, and shellfish of all colors, shapes, and sizes are here. Upstairs, the Fish Round-about puts you in the middle of a huge tubular tank where fish swim quickly around you. The penguins are fed at 11:30 and 4. For information, call (415) 750-7145. www.calacademy.org/aquarium

In the **Morrison Planetarium,** the unique Sky Theater with a 65-foot hemispherical dome presents simulations of the heavens as seen from earth at any time in history. Special-effects projectors take the audience through space into whirling galaxies and black holes. Shows change regularly. For daily shows, call (415) 750-7141. There are shows on weekdays at 11, 12:30, 2, and 3:30; on weekends at 11, 12, 1, 2, 3, and 4. Adults, $2.50; seniors and ages 6 to 17, $1.25; under 6 by special permission. "Exploring the Skies of the Season," $1 for all, is shown at noon on weekends and holidays. www.calacademy.org/planetarium

The academy will close in December, 2003, for renovation and will reopen in 2008.

● Beach Chalet

Golden Gate Park Visitor's Center and Beach Chalet Brewery and Restaurant. Visitor's center and store: daily, 9–6. 751-2766. Restaurant: 415-386-8439. 1000 Great Highway. on the ocean. Breakfast, 9–11; lunch, 11–5; dinner, 5–10; and Sunday brunch. Jazz on Tues., 6:30; live music on Sat., Call 753-5260 for groups. **All ages.** *W. www.beachchalet.com*

Downstairs, exhibits on park history and ecology are complemented by restored 1930s WPA-style murals. Upstairs, burgers, both beef and veggie, good meals, and salads are made more enjoyable by the fabulous view of the ocean.

● Exploratorium

Palace of Fine Arts, 3601 Lyon Street, between Marina Boulevard and Lombard Street, San Francisco 94123. (415) EXP-LORE. Tues.–Sun., 10–5; Wed. until 9. From Memorial Day to Labor Day: daily, 10–6; Wed. until 9. Closed Thanksgiving and Christmas. Also closed Mon., except open on holiday Mon. Adults, $10; seniors and students, $7.50; people with disabilities,

$6; ages 6–17, $6. For Tactile Dome reservations, call (415) 561-0362. Groups: (415) 561-0308. Parties. Café. Gift shops. **All ages.** *W. www.exploratorium.edu*

This touchingthinkingpullingsplashingblinkingspinningamazing museum of science, art, and human perception contains more than 650 exhibits. It's the best combination of learning while playing in California. At the "seeing" collection, you'll swear that an object is white, only to discover that it is practically black. In the "Traits of Life" section, see a roundworm glow with the implanted genetic luminescence of a jellyfish or harvest your own cheek cell and compare it to the cells of a tomato. You can blow a two-foot bubble, learn about light, language, patterns, vision, color, motion, and more. Shrink your mom. Play a game of basketball wearing perception altering glasses. Laser beams, stereophonic sound testers, tornadoes, geysers, and 100,000 dangling straight pins are here to play with. PlayLab is an interactive environment for toddlers and their parents. In the sensory journey into total darkness of the Tactile Dome, you crawl, slide, and climb in and through a black maze of strange textures.

Karen from Morrill Middle School, wrote, "Exploratorium is really a great place for people to understand how fun science is. This wonderful museum will let us touch and experience how it feels to be a scientist. Exploratorium is the best museum on the planet."

● Presidio Officer's Club Exhibition Hall

Main Post, 50 Moraga Avenue, the Presidio (Mail: P.O. Box 29052), San Francisco 94129. (415) 782-9528/561-5500, Tues.–Sat., 12–4. Gift shop. Classes. Events. **Ages 10 & up.** *W. www.presidiotrust.gov*

The Presidio Officer's Club Exhibition Hall has become a small museum offering changing shows that are little jewels. We loved the exhibit showing how early Russians helped colonize California. And the show of modern Mexican art, showcasing Mexican artists who emerged in the nineties and who use imagery to document the way they live and interact with their surroundings.

Now that San Francisco's former military base has become part of the Golden Gate National Recreation Area, the public has a new playground. There's a golf course, a bowling center, a gymnasium and swimming pool, tennis courts, hiking and biking trails, a chapel for weddings and concerts, picnic areas, and Inspiration Point for the best views of the bay. The Presidio Visitor Center (415-561-4323) offers directions, maps, and up-to-date information. Herbst International Exhibition Hall (415-921-7854) offers changing exhibits from museums around the country such as the U.S. Holocaust Museum and shows on such things as inscribed Armenian rugs.

The National Trust, the Presidio Trust, and the Golden Gate National Parks Association are teaming up to preserve and restore the natural resources within the Presidio. For information and to volunteer at, for example, the Presidio Native Plant Nursery or the Habitat Restoration Programs, call (415) 561-4755 or e-mail volunteer@ggnpa.org. The Park Archives and Records Center, Presidio Building 667 (415) 561-4807, will help you access your old records, photos, maps, or books.

● Fort Point National Historic Site

San Francisco 94129. Foot of Marine Drive, on Presidio grounds, under the San Francisco end of the Golden Gate Bridge. (415) 556-1693. Fri., Sat., Sun., except holidays, 10–5. Guided tours and demonstrations throughout the day. Gift shop. Free. **Ages 5 & up.** *Partially W. www.nps.gov*

Nestled below the underpinnings of the Golden Gate Bridge, Fort Point, the guardian of San Francisco Bay, was built before the Civil War and is the only brick coastal fort in the West. With the icy Pacific slamming into the retaining wall and the wind whistling around the point, this is one of the coldest spots in the city. Two exhibits housed in the fort feature the contributions of women in the military as well as the history and achievements of black soldiers in the army. Roam throughout the officers' and enlisted men's quarters and walk through the huge casemates where once were mounted more than 100 huge cannons. Ask one of the park rangers to demonstrate how to load and fire a cannon. You may end up earning a cannoneer certificate. Cannon demonstration at noon. Videos on the history of Fort Point and on the construction of the Golden Gate Bridge are shown throughout the day.

Fifth-grader Michael wrote, "The special thing I liked very much is the top of the fort because you can see the bay and Alcatraz. Besides I like the wind blowing in my face and the waves crashing against the walls. There is another thing I liked about the fort. I liked the museum because it leads all the way to the middle of the fort."

● California Palace of the Legion of Honor

34th Avenue and Clement Street, Lincoln Park (Mail: Fine Arts Museums of San Francisco, 75 Tea Garden Drive, San Francisco 94118-4501). (415) 863-3330 Tues.–Sun., 9:30–5. Adults, $8; seniors, $6; ages 10–17, $5; college student annual pass; Muni transfers, $2 off admission fee. Tues., free. Lectures, classes, events, organ concerts on weekends, free. Self-paced audio tours. Saturday afternoon drop-in art classes for children, docent tours. Store. Café. **Ages 5 & up.** *W. www.legionofhonor.org*

San Francisco's ancient and European art museum includes a major collection of sculpture by Rodin, a Cycladic figure dated 2500 B.C., medieval tapestries and jeweled objects, and paintings by El Greco, Rembrandt, Rubens, Watteau, Seurat, and Picasso. Begin your tour by walking under a 15th-century Spanish carved and polychromed ceiling and finish in an impressionistic world of Monet's *Water Lilies* and works by Van Gogh, Renoir, and Pisarro.

The Ceramics Gallery and the Achenbach Foundation for Graphic Arts also offer study centers available to the public. For information on "Doing and Viewing Art" for ages 7–12 and "Big Kids/Little Kids" for ages 3½–6, call (415) 750-3658.

● Cliff House

1090 Point Lobos Avenue, San Francisco 94121. Geary Boulevard and Great Highway. (415) 386-3330. **All ages.**

"A drive to the 'Cliff' in the early morning . . . and a return to the city through the charming scenery of Golden Gate Park tends to place man about as near to Elysian bliss as he may hope for in this world," wrote B. E. Lloyd in 1876. A drive to and from the Cliff House can still place you in Elysian bliss. At certain times of year, seals bask on the Seal Rocks. There are restaurants with great views.

A **Visitor Center** downstairs (415-556-8642. Daily, 10–5. www.nps.gov/goga/clho) shows the Cliff House in its various incarnations throughout the years, along with rotating natural history displays. Here you can also find information about Farallon Islands tours, whale watching, and other adventures.

● Polly Ann Ice Cream

3142 Noriega Street, between 38th and 39th Avenues, San Francisco 94122. (415) 664-2472. Daily, 11–10. **All ages.** W. *www.pollyann.com*

In 1955 a wonderful man named Ted Hanson retired and went into the ice-cream-making business, creating more than 400 exotic flavors and plastering his tiny stand-at-the-counter store with funny signs and jokes. New owners have retained the signs and flavors and added a few of their own from the Far East, such as jasmine tea, mung green bean, lychee, durian, ube, and other Thai and Filipino fruits. With so many flavors, such as American rose petal, ginger (that bites back!), Batman (grape vanilla with lemon swirl), lemon chippee (lemon with chocolate chips), strawberry rocky road, and cinna-mint, it's really hard to choose. The pure-of-heart may choose the vegetable, made with 14 kinds of veggies, including parsley, beets, and corn.

● San Francisco Zoo

One Zoo Road, Sloat Boulevard at Great Highway, San Francisco 94132. (415) 753-7080. Daily, 10–5. Adults, $10; seniors and youth, $8; ages

3–11, $4. Additional charge for Carousel and Little Puffer miniature steam train. Adopt-an-Animal programs. Summer junior volunteer programs. Group tours. Strollers and wheelchairs for rent. Gift store. Picnic areas. Café and snack bars. **All ages.** *W. www.sfzoo.org*

Do you have an urge to pet a tarantula? Walk about an Australian setting? The San Francisco Zoo, located near the Pacific Ocean, provides a natural, open-air setting for a variety of rare, endangered, and exotic animals. A premier education and conservation facility, the zoo offers children a chance to see and learn about wild animals from all over the world.

Animal highlights include black rhinos, cassowary birds, ring-tailed lemurs, kangaroos and koalas, a green anaconda, polar bears, domestic and Native American animals in the Children's Zoo, and big cats, such as African lions, Sumatran and Siberian tigers, fed daily (except Mondays) at 2 P.M. (They don't eat every day in the jungle, either.)

Visitors can observe endangered snow leopards in the tranquil Feline Conservation Center, see the antics of five species of lemurs in the lush and naturalistic Lipman Family Lemur Forest, and see playful North American river otters at Otter River. Gorilla World, one of the nation's largest exhibits for gorillas, is a serene setting for a group of Western lowland gorillas. Koala Crossing, patterned after an Australian outback station, allows visitors to see koalas both outdoors in a peaceful eucalyptus yard and indoors through a glass viewing window. Australian Walkabout is a two-acre retreat for many marsupial species and emus. The Primate Discovery Center features large open atriums housing some of the world's most endangered primates. Other highlights include Penguin Island, home to a colony of Magellanic penguins, and the Children's Zoo where you can see meerkats and prairie dogs up close in an exhibit simulating their native habitats, visit rare breeds of farm animals in the Family Farm, see more than 30 different arthropod exhibits in the Insect Zoo, and see magnificent raptors stationed in front of the Koret Animal Resource Center, home to a variety of animals used for educational outreach programs. The 1921 Dentzel Carousel has been restored to its original splendor and the 1904 Little Puffer miniature steam train runs daily on a three-mile track. The Connie and Bob Lurie Education Center offers bright, airy classrooms for interactive learning, and the Koret Animal Resource Center is a unique training ground for hundreds of youth volunteers who meet you throughout the zoo and on the Nature Trail.

■ Marin County

Marin County is a land of mountains and seashore just north of the Golden Gate Bridge. Most of the "places to go" with children in Marin are natural wonders. You can drive to the top of Mount Tamalpais and walk the trails overlooking miles of ocean, land, and city. You can explore the silent redwood groves of Muir Woods, then travel on to Stinson Beach or one of the lesser-known beaches for picnicking by the seaside, collecting driftwood, or wading in the icy sea. Muir Beach is best for tide pooling, Bolinas Beach attracts bird-watchers, and Tennessee Valley Beach and Heart's Desire Beach beckon hikers. You can also spend hours fishing in the Marin lakes or hiking the beautiful Point Reyes National Seashore. And when you feel the need for civilization, you can head for the bayside villages of Tiburon or Sausalito, which will enchant the children as much as they do you.

And you don't have to have a car to get there. **Golden Gate Transit Bus Route 63** starts at the Golden Gate Bridge Plaza and takes the Panoramic Highway out to Stinson Beach, stopping at the Discovery Museum, Tam Junction, Mountain Home, the Boot Jack trailhead, and the Pan Toll ranger station in Mount Tamalpais State Park on the way (415-453-2100. Varying schedules weekends and holidays, Mar.–Nov., $3.50).

Another bus service is the West Marin Stagecoach of Whistlestop, which goes back and forth into San Francisco. Call (415) 454-0964, www.marin-stagecoach.org

Golden Gate Ferry Transit operates daily from San Francisco's historic Ferry Building to Larkspur and Sausalito. Call (415) 923-2000 from San Francisco or (415) 455-2000 from Marin for fares and schedules.

● Marine Mammal Center

1065 Fort Cronkhite, Sausalito 94965. From San Francisco, cross the Golden Gate Bridge, take the first exit after Vista Point, and follow signs to park entrance and beach. Located on the Marin Headlands of the Golden Gate National Recreation Area, near Rodeo Beach. (415) 289-SEAL. Daily, 10–4. Group programs, for a fee, require a reservation. Free. Gift store. Picnic tables. **All ages.** *W. www.marinemammalcenter.org*

The Marine Mammal Center is where we finally learned the difference between sea lions and seals. Sea lions have outer ear flaps; seals have small holes for ears. Sea lions walk on all four flippers, and seals move on their bellies, like inchworms. The purpose of this center is to rescue, rehabilitate, and then release marine mammals stranded on the beach. Orphan pups are fed herring milkshakes and eventually whole fish; injured animals' wounds are treated, and in the process much is learned about marine mammals. (Please remember that just because a seal appears on the beach it doesn't necessarily need rescuing. Don't approach or scare them. If you think a marine mammal is hurt, call the center.) At the center, there are critters in cage-tanks to see, and informative illustrated panels to learn from. Volunteers are always needed. Inquire about new opportunities for youth ages 14 to 18.

After a visit, one third-grader sent this poem as a thank-you:

Dolphins are pink
whales are red
and seals blue and green like the ocean where they live.

The **Pacific Energy and Resources Center in the Marin Headlands** (415-332-8200) has a small informational museum on the property.

● Point Bonita Lighthouse

Marin Headlands Visitors Center, Fort Cronkhite. (415) 331-1540. Daily, 9:30–4:30. Free. Reserve for sunset or full-moon tours. **Ages 5 & up.** *www.nps.gov/goga/mahe/pobo*

Called one of the "Guardians of the Golden Gate," Point Bonita lighthouse is open to the public. Built in 1877, the lighthouse has been meticulously renovated and restored, replacing a century of rust with aluminum and shiny stainless steel. The 1,000-watt lightbulb is surrounded by a magnificent Fresnell lens, built in Paris in the 1850s and shipped to California around Cape Horn. Today, the light is controlled by computer. The trail across the rocks has also been strengthened and restored. Nonetheless, while walking through a tunnel and over seven small footbridges, you'll understand why one lighthouse keeper's wife kept her children tied to ropes, so they wouldn't fall off the yard into the sea. To stay in the hostel, call the YMCA, (415)-331-9622.

● Sausalito

After stopping for a moment to look back at the Golden Gate Bridge from Vista Point, spend a few hours in Sausalito, the Riviera by the Bay. Noted for years as an artists colony, the village of Sausalito is now a mecca for tourists and young people. There are clothing and toy stores, ice cream parlors and coffeehouses, art galleries and restaurants for every age, taste, and budget. www.sausalito.com

● San Francisco Bay-Delta Model

2100 Bridgeway, Sausalito 94969-1764. (415) 332-3870. Tues.–Sat., 9–4; weekends and holidays, 10–6. Free. **Ages 6 & up.** *W. www.spn.usace.army.mil/bmvc*

Cheryl wrote, "Dear Ranger Suzette, Thank you for taking us on the tour. I learned about the tides . . . that movie was great. I hope I can come again.

Thank you." And Hannah wrote, "Dear Ranger Bob, Thank you for showing us that the water in the bay is really shallow and that pollution spreads quickly into the bay. I wish we could have stayed longer."

The U.S. Army Corps of Engineers has constructed a huge hydraulic scale model of San Francisco Bay and the Sacramento—San Joaquin Delta. The model shows the action of the tides, the flow and currents of the water, and the mixing of seawater and freshwater. Guided tours take an hour, or you can use the self-guided written information or the tape-recorded audio program, which provides extensive information about the model and its operation. The model only operates when testing is scheduled, but there's so much to see—pictures, slides, models, and more—you won't be disappointed. Robert wrote, "I liked learning the word 'estuary,' salt and fresh! I especially liked exploring the ship display."

● Bay Area Discovery Museum

557 East Fort Baker, Sausalito 94965. From San Francisco, take Highway 101 north to Alexander Avenue exit and follow signs. (415) 487-4398. Tues.–Fri, 9–4; Sat, Sun., 10–5. Adults, $7; children, $6; seniors, $4; under 1, free. Second Sat. of the month, 1–4, free. Parties. Discovery Café. Gift shop. At this writing, the museum is closing for reconstruction, so call before heading out. **Ages 2–13.** *W. www.badm.org*

"The Bay Area Discovery Museum: A boppin' jammin' dancin' happenin' place to be!" So wrote Jez. And Fran called it a "Cool Place! Best museum in the world!" This hands-on museum for children and families is located in a spectacular setting at the foot of the Golden Gate Bridge. Its six historic buildings house the permanent "San Francisco Bay" and "Building the City" exhibitions, the Art Spot, a science lab, a media center, the Maze of Illusions, the Tot Spot, and a café. The museum features ever-changing activities and workshops focusing on the arts and sciences. The surrounding area provides picnic spots, hiking trails, and tide pools for the entire family to enjoy. A not-to-be-missed attraction is the handmade carousel created especially for the museum by master carousel maker Bill Dentzel.

● Tiburon

Named Punta de Tiburon, or Shark Point, by Spanish explorers, Tiburon (www.Tiburon.CitySearch.com) is a nice place to spend a sunny afternoon. Having lunch, indoors or out, while enjoying the view of the city from one of the restaurants on the bay can be heaven. Nautical shops, a Swedish bakery, and the bookstore are all fun to browse through. Our favorite restaurant is right next to the Blue and Gold Fleet ferry landing: **Guaymas** (5 Main Street. 415-435-6300) for the kind of grilled fish and fowl you'd have in a seaside Mexican village.

The Landmarks Society (415-435-1853) maintains three historic sites. Hardy walkers can head up the hill to **Old St. Hilary's Church** (Juanita Lane off Esperanza, Apr.–Oct., Sun. and Wed., 1–4, and by appt.; donation) to see a changing photo exhibit and 217 species of plants that grow nowhere else in the world. The **China Cabin Maritime Museum** (Wed. and Sun., 1–4, and by appt.; free), on the cove in nearby Belvedere, is the restored 20-by-40-foot Victorian social saloon, from the SS *China Cabin,* a steam side-wheeler. It looks exactly as it did when it left New York for San Francisco in June 1867 on its first voyage. The **Railroad-Ferry Depot** (Mon.–Fri., 9–4; free) at 1920 Paradise Drive in Shoreline Park displays photos of Tiburon during its heyday as a railroad town from 1884 to 1964.

● Richardson Bay Audubon Center and Sanctuary

376 Greenwood Beach Road, Tiburon 94920. (415) 388-2524. Daily, 9–5. Lyford House, Oct.–Apr., Sun. only. Donations. Call for program information. **Ages 5 & up.** *www.audubon-ca.org/centers.htm*

Richardson Bay Audubon Center and Sanctuary provides a habitat for wildlife and is an environmental education center, a "window on the bay." Youngsters can explore sea life and observe birds on nature trails. Programs, films, and classes help make visitors aware of the wonders around them. Lyford House is a Victorian mansion with period furnishings and Marin County history displays.

● Angel Island State Park

(Mail: P.O. Box 866, Tiburon 94920) For special events and tour information, call the Angel Island Association, (415) 435-3522. For disabled access contact, Angel Island State Park (415) 435-1915. For ferry schedules from San Francisco, call (415) 773-1188. Ferry from Tiburon daily in summer; on weekends or by arrangement in winter. Call (415) 435-2131. State Park entrance fee of $1 included in price of ferry ticket. **All ages.** *www.angelisland.com*

Most visitors ride the ferries to Ayala Cove, where lawn, beach, and barbecue pits beckon. Hikers and bikers (helmets required) are welcome. The visitors center has interpretive nature and history displays, a free video, and a gift shop. Tram tours take visitors to the other side of the island (daily in summer, on weekends, Apr.–Oct., fee. 415-897-0715). Camp Reynolds, a Civil War site; Fort McDowell, a site from World War I and World War II; and the Immigration Station barracks museum are staffed by volunteer docents waiting to give tours and tell stories. The Military History Tram Tour is a new attraction. The U.S. Immigration Station on Angel Island was built to enforce the 1882 Chinese Exclusion Act. Young Alexis wrote, "When you first set foot on Angel Island you see the green of the trees and the yellow of the houses but what you really see is the gray of the people . . . even though the colors may be of joy—you can feel the sorrow." Angel Island is a wonderful place to spend the day or camp overnight (for reservations, call Reserve America, 800-444-PARK).

Angel Island can be reached by ferry from San Francisco, Tiburon, Oakland, Alameda, and Vallejo. For rates and schedules, call:

San Francisco Blue and Gold Fleet, (415) 705-5444, blueandgoldfleet.com

Tiburon Angel Island Ferry, (415) 435-2131, angelislandferry.com

Oakland/Alameda Ferry Co., (415) 705-5444, eastbayferry.com

Vallejo Blue and Gold Fleet, (707) 643-3779, baylinkferry.com

● San Quentin Museum

Highway 580 at the Richmond–San Rafael Bridge. San Quentin Prison. (415) 454-1460 ext. 5817. Sat. and Sun., 10–4. Volunteers staff the place so call that day to be sure someone is there. Adults, $2; seniors and students with ID, $1. **Ages 7 & up.** *www.turnpike.net/~mystery/tmg/san_quentin.html*

If your kids still think about living the life of a criminal after visiting Alcatraz, a visit to San Quentin should put them on the straight and narrow. Artifacts, memorabilia, photographs, and records trace the history of the state's oldest and best-known prison, founded in 1852. One display board shows the weapons the staff used from 1860 to the 1970s. A contraband board shows different things the inmates have manufactured illegally in prison, such as a tattoo gun and a 32-caliber bolt action semiautomatic made with no gun parts. This history of capital punishment includes mock-ups of a gallows and a gas chamber and the last noose used to hang someone in the state of California, in 1942.

● Marin History Museum

Boyd Park, 1125 B Street, off 3rd Avenue, San Rafael 94901. (415) 454-8538. Tues., Thurs., Fri., 9–12; Wed., 12–3; third Sat. of the month, 1–4, and by appt. Gift shop. Research and photographic records room. Free. **Ages 6 & up.** *W. www.marinhistory.org/museum.htm*

Designed to "stir the imagination and bring back panoramas of the past," this newly refurbished museum reflects themes in Marin's history. The changing displays range from transportation that once served Marin to the once extensive dairy industry, to portraits of the founders of Marin County. Others may focus on the Miwok Indians, Mission San Rafael, and military history. Exhibits, such as one on filmmaking in Marin, are changed regularly. A favorite with youngsters is the entrance bell from the ferryboat *Donahue*.

Down the block is the **Mission San Rafael Archangel** (1104 5th Avenue. 415-456-3016. Daily, 11–4; gift shop; free. www.marinhistory.org/articles/mission.htm). Inside this replica of the original mission built in 1817, the six flags under which the mission has served still fly: Spain, Mexico, the California Republic, the United States of 1850, the Vatican, and the United States of America.

Budding architects may wish to tour the Frank Lloyd Wright–designed **Marin County Civic Center** (3501 Civic Center Drive, off Highway 101. 415-499-6646. Business days, 8:30–5. Tours on Wed. at 10:30 from the Civic Center Gift Shop. Free). Said the architect: "We know that the good building is not one that hurts the landscape, but is one that makes the landscape more beautiful than it was before that building was built. In Marin County you have one of the most beautiful landscapes I have seen and I am proud to make the buildings of the County characteristic of the beauty of the County."

● Wildcare: Terwilliger Nature Education and Wildlife Rehabilitation

76 Albert Park Lane, off B Street, San Rafael 94915. (415) 456-SAVE/453-1000. Daily, 9–5. Donation. **All ages.** *W. www.wildcaremarin.org*

This volunteer-run wildlife rehabilitation hospital cares for and releases back into the wilderness more than 4,000 birds and mammals each year. The center operates a Living With Wildlife Hotline to answer questions about how to live harmoniously with wildlife. Summer and holiday camps, field trips, and nature walks are offered throughout the year. A small interpretive center houses native birds and mammals unable to survive in the wild because of injuries. A museum with hands-on activities for children is open all year.

● China Camp Village

China Camp State Park, off North San Pedro Road from Highway 101. Museum is in a shed on piers over the water. (800) 444-7275/(415) 456-0766. Daily, 10–5. Parking, $3; camping by reservation. **Ages 7 & up.** *www.cal-parks.ca.gov*

In 1889, nearly 500 Chinese processed about 200,000 pounds of shrimp a year on the beach near this 1,400-acre park. Today, the caretaker considers 10 pounds a day a good catch. The little museum displays photographs of Chinese fishermen along with some of the simple furnishings and fishing gear that were part of life in the village. Boilers and a shrimp sheller still toil in the nearby processing shed. The old diner-style bait and snack shop is open on sunny afternoons at the foot of a pier where old-timers still catch bass and perch. Birding and bike trails are excellent in this protected, critical wildlife habitat.

● Muir Woods National Monument

Muir Woods Road, off Highway 1, Mill Valley 94941. (415) 388-2595. Daily, 8 to sunset. School groups and special events by reservation. Adults over 17, $3. Visitors center. Café. Gift shop. **All ages.** *W. www.nps.gov/muwo*

This lovely forest of giant coast redwoods, some more than 200 feet high, is a breathtaking place to start the day. Among these magnificent trees, you'll encounter many other species of plant life, as well as an occasional black-tailed deer, Sonoma chipmunk, or stellar's jay. Naturalist John Muir wrote, "This is the best tree-lover's monument that could possibly be found in all the forests of all the world." There are several self-guided trails starting at the second bridge. During a fall visit, we spent a long time just counting all the ladybugs coming awake on the fence posts. Junior-ranger packs are offered free to young naturalists. Short ecology talks are given throughout the day.

● Audubon Canyon Ranch

4900 Highway 1, Stinson Beach 94970. From Stinson Beach, north 3 miles. (415) 868-9244. Mid-Mar.–mid-July, weekends and holidays, 10–4, and by appt. School programs. Bookstore. Picnic areas. Donations. **Ages 5 & up.** *W. www.egret.org*

This 1,000-acre wildlife sanctuary bordering on the Bolinas Lagoon is a peaceful spot to view birds "at home." From a hilltop, you can watch the nesting activities of the great blue heron and the great egret. The ranch's pond, stream, and canyon are a living demonstration of the region's ecology—the delicate balance between plant and animal life and their environment. The display hall/museum shows local fauna and flora and offers information on the San Andreas fault. Ranch guides will explain all.

Erica enthused, "The mountains, the ocean, the trees. It's like the whole world was changing into a whole new world. All the flowers and trees were interesting. When I came to the Ranch my whole life had changed . . . I am coming back soon."

In nearby Bolinas, the **Bolinas Museum** (48 Wharf Road, 94924. 415-868-0330. Fri., 1–5; weekends, 12–5, and by appt. Free. **Ages 8 & up.** www.bolinasmuseum.org) exhibits the work of local and national artists and photographers and commemorates the historic events and accomplishments that shape the life of the area. Historic photos, documents, and objects portray shipwrecks, notable boats, the local stagecoach, and early settlers.

● Point Reyes National Seashore

National Park Service, Point Reyes 94952. On Highway 1 near Olema. (415) 464-5100. Beaches close at midnight, lighthouse area by 10 P.M.; no overnight parking is allowed unless you're camping. Free. **All ages.** *www.NPS.gov/PORE*

When Francis Drake landed here in 1579, his chaplain wrote of a "Faire and Good Baye, with a good wind to enter the same." Today's visitors will agree. The beauty of the cliffs, the surf (swimmable in some places), the tide pools, lowlands, and forest meadows make you wonder why he went back to England. You can follow nature trails, bird-watch, backpack, picnic, rent horses, and camp (with fee, by permit only). We like Drake's Bay best, and before we set out, we call the ranger's office there (415-669-1250) to check the weather. The café at Drake's Bay is nicely protected and even serves fresh oysters.

Start your visit at the **Bear Valley Visitors Center** (415-464-5100. Weekends, 8–5; weekdays, 9–5). You can get maps with suggested itineraries and all the information you may need while the kids watch a movie or slide show or explore the beautifully designed "walk-through diorama" of the world of Point Reyes. Our favorite of the interactive exhibits is a large log attached to a handle. When you press down, the log lifts up to show all the creepy-crawlies living underneath. Classes and special programs are listed on the schedule. Here's where you can pick up tide schedules, if you're planning to hike to Secret Cave.

From Bear Valley, you can walk to the Morgan Horse Ranch (415-663-1763. Daily, 9–4:30), along the Earthquake Trail, or to **Kule Loklo,** the replica of a coastal Miwok village. A granary, sunshade, sweat house, and *kotcas,* "the place where real people live," have been reconstructed with authentic materials by volunteers. On weekends there are demonstrations on skills such as hunting, sewing, weaving, and preparing acorn mush (sunrise to sunset; interpretive programs on request; 415-464-5100).

The **Ken Patrick Visitors Center** at Drake's Beach has displays on marine paleontology, 15th- and 16th-century exploration, Native Americans, and the marine environment. A saltwater aquarium has critters collected from the bay (415-669-1250. Weekends, 10–5).

The **Point Reyes Bird Observatory's Palomarin Station,** located at the southern entrance to Point Reyes National Seashore, is open to the public for bird-banding demonstrations, nature walks, and educational field trips. More than 400 species have been spotted and banded in a network of 20 mist nets, which net and release birds unharmed. Visitors Center and Nature Trail, 99 Mesa Road, Bolinas. (415) 868-0655. Daily, dawn to 5. **Ages 5 & up.** www.prbo.org

The **Point Reyes Lighthouse** is open Thurs.–Mon., 10–4:30; (415) 669-1534. You have to walk down 300 steps to get there, because the light was meant to shine below the fog line on Marin's rocky coast. The first wreck occurred here when the Spanish galleon *San Agustin* sank in a storm on November 30, 1595. The beacon finally went into service in 1870 and has been saving ships ever since. The lens room itself is open 2:30 to 4, Thurs.–Sun. Because whale watching is increasingly popular, and the best place for viewing is the lighthouse, the park supplies a weekend shuttlebus service ($4; kids, free), January to March, from Drake's Beach to the Point Reyes Lighthouse.

Tomales Bay State Park (415-669-1140. Daily, 8–8 in summer; until 6 in winter. Adults, $2; seniors, $1. Camping, $5 per car) has beaches for swimming and picnic facilities. The tide pools—rocky pockets that retain seawater when the tide goes out—provide endless hours of fascination, as long as you watch very quietly as the tide pool's occupants move through their daily routines. Seaweeds, anemones, barnacles, jellyfish, sand dollars, tiny fish, and flowery algae can hide if they want to!

● Johnson's Drake's Bay Oysters

Sir Francis Drake Boulevard, on the way to Drake's Bay in Point Reyes National Seashore (Mail: P.O. Box 69, Inverness 94937). (415) 669-1149. Mon.–Sat., 8–4:30; Sun. 9–4:30. **All ages.**

Follow the crushed-oyster-shell driveway to the "farm" to see how oysters are raised, and buy a small succulent sample to taste in the sea air. Signs tell you interesting facts about oyster farming. For example, did you know that it takes 18 months for an oyster to grow?

● Tomales Bay Oyster Company

115479 Highway 1, Marshall. (Mail: P.O. Box 296, Point Reyes Station 94956). (415) 663-1242. Daily, 8–6. Picnic area and barbecue. **All ages.**

Families are welcome and, if the tide is out, rubber boots and old clothes are suggested for the kids who want to catch crabs and "slosh" in the mud while looking at intertidal life. The farm is bordered by state parkland that is open for hiking and exploring. Founded in 1909, TBOC is the oldest aquaculture facility in the state. Its many "fields" of stakes are spread out in the bay, each stake holding about 100 oysters. Different holding tanks contain seed, juvenile, and harvest-size oysters. Bay mussels are also grown on the farm. Kids love the bags of "empties." And the staff loves answering questions.

● Hog Island Oyster Company

Highway 1 (Mail: P.O. Box 829), Marshall 94956. (415) 663-9218. Wed.–Sun, 9–5. Picnic areas. Groups by reservation. Free. **Ages 6 & up.** *www.hogislandoyster.com*

Oysters, clams, and abalone are farm raised and sold alive and in the shell. Built in the late 1860s on the site of Marshall's original general store and railway station, Hog Island welcomes picnickers and provides shucking knives and BBQ kettles for your use. The staff offers "Day on the Farm" educational programs in schools and loves to share oyster lore and shucking tips on-site.

● Marin Museum of the American Indian

Miwok Park, 2200 Novato Boulevard (Mail: P.O. Box 864), Novato 94948. (415) 897-4064. From Highway 101 take San Marin Drive west to Novato Boulevard. Tues.–Fri., 10–3; weekends, 12–4. Docent tour Sun., 1:30. Free. **Ages 5 & up.** *www.marinindian.com*

"Thank you so much for being our guide! I would love to come back! . . . I loved your visitors exhibit. I have been using my crow call a lot and wearing my arrowhead necklace a lot too. I learned a lot about the artifacts and boat materials, clothing, food, money, and their religious ceremonies. I loved the diorama. I also enjoyed grinding acorns and drilling holes into the soapstone. I was fascinated about what they wore for religious ceremonies. It was so very interesting examining their money, blankets, and games. Hope to see you soon!" This was from Kylie, fifth grade.

The hands-on education room downstairs in the museum invites visitors to explore coastal Miwok Indian culture through replicas of clothing, tools, animal skins, mortars and pestles, shell bead money, basketry, and hunting implements. Changing exhibits focus on other aspects of Indian cultures of the western United States. Classes, lectures, films, and docent-led field trips, summer day camps, and weekend programs are offered, so call for fees and schedules. A newly refurbished California Native Plant Garden including a tule pond with miniature replica tule *kole kotka* (house) flank the museum building.

To walk in the world of the Miwok, drive north on Highway 101 a mile past the Marin Airport to San Antonio Road, and cross west off the highway to the **Olompali State Historic Park and Gardens,** the former site of an old Miwok Indian village (Mail: P.O. Box 1019, Novato 94948. 415-892-3383. 10–5 in winter; 10–7 in summer. www.cal-parks.ca.gov).

The Olompali people and volunteers are trying to restore the historic adobes that were saved in 1863, when Maria Black married Dr. Galen Burdell. They've built models of original coastal Miwok structures on their original site. They include a redwood bark roundhouse; *kotkas,* houses made of tule and redwood bark; an acorn granary; and a dance circle. Pitted grinding rocks are also on the site.

● Novato History Museum

815 DeLong Avenue. (415) 897-4320. Wed., Thurs., Sat., 12–4, and by appt. Free. **Ages 8 & up.** *W. www.ci.Novato.ca.us/prcs/museum.cfm*

The **Novato History Museum,** in the home of the town's first postmaster, focuses on the history of northern Marin County. Children enjoy the hands-on activities created just to entertain and educate. There are bells to ring and costumes to try on. And people of the town's history to meet. The children's table is a special favorite. They'll also learn about the farms, horses, and cows that are so much a part of Novato history.

● Dollhouses, Trains & More

*300 Entrada Drive, Novato 94949. (415) 883-0388. Mon.–Fri., 9:30–6;
weekends, 10–5. Classes.* **All ages.** *www.dollhouses-trains-more.com*

Special playrooms bring fans into this combination store and crafts
center. You'll find an 800-square-foot dollhouse village, a Christmas Village
up all year round, a "lake with waterfalls" for floating boats, a Lego room, a
train room with its own miniature drive-in theater playing a real movie, and
other playrooms for fun and classes.

● Marin French Cheese Company

*7500 Red Hill Road, Petaluma–Point Reyes Road, .25 mile south of Novato
Boulevard, Petaluma 94952. (800) 292-6001 ext. 11. Daily, 8:30–5.
Tours on the hour, 10–4. Cheese made Wed. and Thurs. Student programs.
Free. Picnic areas. Snacks.* **Ages 5 & up.** *W. www.marinfrenchcheese.com*

Situated next to a pond in the rolling, cow-speckled hills between Novato
and the coast, this is a perfect destination for an afternoon outing or picnic.
Four generations of the Thompson family make this America's oldest
operating cheese factory, since 1865. And it's the winningest cheese factory
in the American Cheese Society. A 15-minute tour begins with the 4,000-
gallon tank of milk and takes you through the different stages of cheese
making—heating the milk, adding the three "cheese" ingredients (culture,
enzymes, and starter), and aging. You pass shiny steel tubes and tanks and
different aging rooms, each with its own smell. Kids like the cheese, but they
love the duck pond.

■ The East Bay: Alameda and Contra Costa Counties

Mount Diablo crowns the East Bay, which ranges along the east shore of San Francisco Bay. There's even a visitors center and observation platform near the top of Mount Diablo (Wed.–Sun., 11–5; free). The places of interest in the East Bay are some distance from each other, so plan ahead and call for up-to-the-minute times and prices. Boaters, fishermen, picnickers, hikers, and nature lovers of all ages will find public parks to visit here.

A life-size statue of Jack London greets visitors to Jack London Village, now being restored as a center for shopping, dining, play, and the arts. Heinold's First and Last Chance Saloon, where London hung out, is still open. Nearby is the log cabin London supposedly lived in when in the Yukon and a tiny Jack London Museum. To take advantage of the estuary, rent a boat at California Canoe and Kayak, which also offers classes and rentals (510-893-7833). Jack London Village can be reached by Amtrak and the Alameda/Oakland Ferry (510-522-3300).

● TJ's Gingerbread House

741 5th Street, Oakland 94607. Take the Broadway exit from Highway 880. (510) 444-7373. Breakfast, 8–10; lunch, 11–3; dinner (by reservation), 6–8:30, Tues.–Sat. Gazebo and Pink House downstairs are available for parties. **All ages.** *Partially W.*

Hansel and Gretel's wicked witch would be envious of this restaurant, which looks good enough to eat. In a tiny shop downstairs, you'll find gingerbread cookies, puppets, dolls, T-shirts, soaps, tea—even gingerbread bubble bath. Upstairs, in a fantasy land of dolls—"a dream come true!"—TJ Robinson serves copious Cajun-Creole breakfasts, lunches, and dinners. Prices range from $23, for vegetarian rice and beans, to $39.95, for Pheasant "Bon Temps." Try Bayou Spiced-Baked Catfish and "Spoon" Jambalaya, or Pick-Your-Heart-Out-Chicken. Each meal comes with fruit salad, Cajun come-back dirty rice, vegetables, sassy corn bread, beverage, and ice cream with a gingerbread cookie. For a nominal price, children can order just their own fruit salad, rice, and dessert.

● Museum of Children's Art (MOCHA)

538 9th Street, Suite 210, Oakland 94607. (510) 465-8770. Tues.–Sat., 10–6; Sun., 12–5. Free. **Ages 2-12.** *www.mocha.org*

MOCHA's mission is to ensure that the arts are a fundamental part of the lives of all children. For ages 18 months to five years, the Little Studio provides young artists an art exploration space created just for them. Upstairs, MOCHA features a gallery exhibiting original work done by children from local national and international communities, from story quilts by second-graders to clay sculptures by fifth-graders. In the Big Studio, MOCHA provides field trips, classes, workshops, camps, and drop-in art for grades K–6 and kids of all ages. MOCHA is the place for families to come Draw! Paint! Spill Stuff!

● Ebony Museum

1034 14th Street, West Oakland 94607. (510) 763-0141. Tues.–Sat., 11–6. Donation. Gift shop. Guided tours by appt. **Ages 5 & up.** *W www.museumusa.org*

This grassroots museum specializes in African and African-American arts and artifacts. Benin royal tribal busts, 300-year-old Lobi ancestor figures from Zaire, and chieftain headdresses mingle with graceful wooden statues and rows of weathered masks. The "Degradation" collection of early racist art is an eye-opener, but the owner, Aissatoui Vernita, believes in waking kids (and adults) up. The "soul" jewelry—necklaces of gold chitlins, fatback earrings, peanut pendants—is fun.

● African American Museum and Library

659 14th Street, at Martin Luther King Jr. Way, Oakland 94612. (510) 637-0200. Tues.–Sat., 12:30–5:30, and by appt. Free. **Ages 6 & up.** *W. www.oaklandlibrary.org/AAMLO*

California's African Americans and their history are the theme of this lovingly put together collection that focuses on local families and recalls especially African-American athletes, musicians, scientists, politicians, gold miners, cowboys, farmers, business leaders, and early settlers. There are almost 10,000 books and biographies in the library and archives. Changing exhibits will introduce youngsters to the first Africans who lived in California from 1535, when the land was still under Spanish and Mexican rule. Photos, artifacts such as cowboy ropes and canteens, and maps will bring to life people like Pio Pico, an early governor of California; black mountaineer James Beckworth; and "Mammy" Pleasant.

● Oakland Museum of California

1000 Oak Street, Oakland 94607-4892. (510) 238-2200. Wed.–Sat., 10–5; Sun., 12–5. First Fri. of the month until 9 P.M. Closed holidays. Adults, $6; seniors and students, $4; 5 and under, free. Second Sun. of the month, free. Café. Gift shop. **Ages 5 & up.** *W. www.museumca.org*

The Oakland Museum of California is actually three first-rate museums in one: California art, California natural sciences, and California history. You can always be sure of finding an afternoon's worth of interesting things for children of all ages. One level concentrates on art from the days of the Spanish explorers to the present. Panoramic views of San Francisco and Yosemite, cityscapes and landscapes, and contemporary jewelry, ceramics, photos, paintings, and sculpture create a historic continuity in the visual arts.

The natural sciences gallery takes you across the nine zones of California, from the coast to the snow-capped eastern Sierra with its ancient bristlecone pines. Dioramas and displays of mammals, birds, rodents, and snakes in their native habitats provide fascinating replicas of the real thing.

Kids will like the California history level best of all. Begin with the Native Californians, the many Indian tribes, and walk through the superbly furnished "rooms" of the state's history, from the Spanish explorers and *Californios* to the gold miners and cowboys, the pioneers, the Victorian San Franciscans, and on to the California dream, from *Beach Party* to *American Graffiti* and the "Summer of Love."

We always head for the 1890s shiny red fire pumper and the pioneer kitchen with the chair outside the glass—to bring the visitor into the picture. The "information TV centers" provide instant answers to kids' questions with demonstrations and discussions by noted authorities.

Concerts, films, and special exhibits are scheduled regularly. One young visitor wrote in the guest log, "I think that using junk to create art is very ingenious." Another third-grader wrote, "The Oakland Museum allows everybody to learn about history, experience the beauty of being around art, learn about animals and how they live, and see special exhibits. The Oakland Museum is a lovely building."

● Paramount Theatre

2025 Broadway, Oakland 94612. Take Highway 980 to the Downtown exit. (510) 893-2300. Public tours, first and third Sat. of the month, 10 A.M., $1. Groups by appt. $50 for up to 30 people; over 30, $100. Not advised for those under 10. Call for performance schedule and prices. **Ages 10 & up.** *W. www.paramounttheatre.com*

The Paramount is the best example of art-deco architecture on the West Coast. A metal grillwork ceiling teeming with sculpted life, gold walls with sculpted motifs from the Bible and mythology, and elegant embellishments almost compete with what's on stage.

● Camron-Stanford House

1418 Lakeside Drive, Oakland 94612. (510) 836-1976. Tours Wed., 11–4; Sun., 1–5; and by appt. Donation. Children 12 and under, free. **Ages 8 & up.** *www.oaklandhistory.com*

This 1876 Italianate-style Victorian, once the Oakland Museum, shows life in the days of horse cars and gas lighting. Museum displays on the first floor show local history as well as the restoration of the mansion. The video of the Academy Award–winning documentary *Living in a House,* inspired by the life and letters of Franklina Gray Bartlett, shows what it was like to live in a house in Oakland from 1876 to 1936. Upstairs, the elegant rooms have been restored to gracious splendor and include a portrait by F. B. Carpenter of Franklina as a 14-month-old bacchante, as well as newspaper stories about her wedding here. Special exhibits and engaging docents add to the young visitor's enjoyment.

● Pardee Home

672 11th Street, near Castro Street, in Preservation Park, Oakland 94607. (510) 444-1287. One-hour tours Fri. and Sat. at noon and by appt. Adults, $5; under 12, free. **Ages 8 & up.** *www.pardeehome.org*

Youngsters who want to step back in time will also enjoy visiting Governor George C. Pardee's art-laden family home, water tower, carriage house, and barn. Built in 1868 at a cost of $12,000, the home is one of the finest remaining examples of the bracketed Italianate villa style in the area and still stands on the original lot. Pardee's daughters, Madeline and Helen, lived in the house until 1980–81. They maintained their mother's extensive collections of candlesticks, minerals, teapots, ceramic pottery, glassware, rocks, scrimshaw, art, and textiles from Asia, Africa, North America, and South America just as she'd left them. Scholars will be interested in the extensive archive of photographs and documents related to the Pardee family. Somehow, children are fascinated by all of the collections in this home.

Another historic home in downtown Oakland is the **Cohen-Bray House,** which is a perfect example of "fly in amber" preservation. A representation of the 1884 Anglo-Japanese style, the house was a wedding gift to Emma Bray and Alfred Cohen on February 28, 1884. Their daughter Emelita lived there—and never redecorated—until she died in 1991. Today the house serves as a study center of late-19th-century decorative arts. For tours, call the Victorian Preservation Center at (510) 532-0704 (1440 29th Avenue, Oakland 94601). $5. **Ages 8 & up.**

● Fortune Cookie Factory

261 12th Street, at Harrison, Oakland 94607. (510) 832-5552. Mon.– Fri., 10–3. Self-guided tours, $1; groups by appt. Free cookies. **Ages 5 & up.**

Fortune cookie machines are huge and black and make a lot of noise. You can see the flames inside them. Small round pans march relentlessly in and out of the flames. A giant dipper drops cookie batter into each pan, and by the time the rounds emerge, they are browned and just soft enough to bend. A worker grabs the soft round, puts a fortune in the cookie, and folds it over a small metal bar, then sets it on a cooling rack. The fortune cookies also come in flavors. And you can write your own fortune.

● Lake Merritt Wildlife Refuge and Rotary Center

Lakeside Park, off Grand Avenue at Lake Merritt, Oakland 94612-4598. Nature Center: 600 Bellevue Avenue, Oakland 94610. (510) 238-3739. Daily, 10–5. Free. Parking, $2 on weekends and holidays. **All ages.** *W. www.Oaklandnet.com*

A narrow strip of grass around Lake Merritt creates a peaceful oasis in the center of a busy city. The refuge is the oldest in the nation, started in 1870, and is on the path of migrating birds on the Pacific Flyway. In the Kiwanis Kiddie Korner, children can slide down double and triple slides and play on swings or climb on rocks in the Astro Circle, which looks like the Jetsons' home or a UFO rocket/spaceship.

The **Rotary Nature Center** offers an educational exhibit of native reptiles, mammals, and birds as well as turtle ponds and an observation beehive. One young visitor wrote, "I enjoy your animals. The toad felt like mashed potatoes. I want to come back soon."

Sailboats, houseboats, and paddleboats are available for renting in the Lake Merritt Boating Center.

● Children's Fairyland

Lakeside Park, at Grand and Bellevue Avenues, Lake Merritt, Oakland 94610. (510) 452-2259. Spring and fall, Wed.–Sun., 10–4; winter, Fri.– Sun. and school holidays, 10–4; daily in summer, 10–4:30. Adults, $6; children, $1.75. Under 1, free. Gift shop. Parties by reservation. **Ages 2–13.** *www.fairyland.org*

Duck through the Old Woman's Shoe to meet Alice, the Cheshire Cat, and the Cowardly Lion. Then slide down a dragon's back or sail on a pea-green boat with the Owl and the Pussycat. Pinocchio, Willie the Whale, slides, mazes, rides, and enchanted bowers come to life. A magic key opens wee audio storybooks in spiffed-up Farm Country, Adventureland, and Fantasyland. Young children can explore, play, and let their imaginations run free with rides, puppet shows, animals, and storybook settings.

● Junior Center of Art and Science

558 Bellevue Avenue, Oakland 94610. (510) 839-5777. Tues.–Fri., 10– 6; Sat., 10–3. Weekends, groups, and outreach programs by reservation. Free. **Ages 3–12.**

Changing art and cultural exhibits on subjects such as "a child's garden," California Native Americans, and African-American heroes greet the drop-in visitor and those scheduled for weekend or after-school art classes. In the In Touch With Nature Room, visitors will enjoy child-size displays of nine animal habitats at their eye level. Then they can use the Drawing Surface to make their impressions of the leopard geckos, the seven-inch-long African millipede, the Canadian garden snake, fish, turtles, bugs, fire belly toads, and the hissing cockroaches. Betty, the miniature lop-eared rabbit, is a family favorite.

● Oakland Zoo

9777 Golf Links Road, Oakland 94609. At 98th Avenue off Highway 580. (510) 632-9525. Daily, 10–4, except Christmas and Thanksgiving, weather permitting. Park admission: $3 per car. Zoo: daily, 10–4, later on summer weekends. Adults, $7.50; ages 2–14 and seniors, $4.50; group discounts. Rides: 75¢ and $1.50. **All ages.** *W. www.oaklandzoo.org*

This beautifully arranged zoo is one of the nicest in the state. Glide over the African veldt and up into the hills on the 1,250-foot Skyfari Ride, or ride a miniature train for a breathtaking view of the bay. More than 330 animals from around the world make their home in 525 acres of large natural habitats. The new replica of an East African village, with three thatched huts typical of the Kikuyu tribe of Kenya, centers a rolling grasslands habitat for lions and elephants, gazelles, and buzzards. The Children's Petting Zoo will make tots' barnyard tales come alive. Picnic, barbecue, and playground facilities are located throughout the park.

● Western Aerospace Museum

8260 Boeing Street, Oakland Airport North Field (Mail: P.O. Box 14264), Oakland 94614. Near Doolittle Drive and Hegenberger. From Highway 880, west until you reach Earhart, right on Earhart to Hangar 6, Alaska Airlines, then right onto Cook. (510) 638-7100. Wed.–Sun., 10–4. Adults, $7; seniors, $6; ages 6–12, $3; 6 and under, free. Gift shop. Parties. **Ages 6 & up.** *W. www.westernaerospacemuseum.org*

Twenty-two antique and retired airplanes can be seen in this exciting museum. Among the aircraft you'll find a navy jet A-3 bomber, a navy A-7 fighter, a navy A-6 attack aircraft, a NASA "jump jet," a Lockheed 10E like Amelia Earhart's (without the camera modifications), a Yugo trainer, an aerobatic flyer, and a F-14A Tomcat. The pride of the fleet is the Short Solent, a large flying boat used in *Raiders of the Lost Ark*. Twelve exhibit rooms show flying photos and memorabilia on subjects such as Jimmy Doolittle, early Oakland aviation, African-American aviators, and women pilots. Special video screenings are run in the theater, and there are regular guided "climb aboard" tours for groups.

● Dunsmuir House and Garden

2960 Peralta Oaks Court, Oakland 94605. Take the 106th Avenue exit from Highway 580. (510) 562-0328. Mar.–Sept. Grounds open Tues.–Fri., 10–4. Drop-in mansion tours, Weds., 11 and 12. Adults, $5; seniors and ages 6–12, $4; under 6, free. Call for group rates and box lunch reservations.

Special Family Sundays throughout the season, such as Easter, Father's Day, Fourth of July, Scottish Highland Games, "Music on the Meadow" concert series, and annual December Holiday Faire. Admission varies for special events. Call (510) 615-5555. **Ages 7 & up.** *www.dunsmuir.org*

This 37-room Colonial Revival mansion is set in a 40-acre estate in the East Oakland foothills. A visit will provide an enlightening sense of another way of life through architecture, photos, and garden strolls. Dunsmuir is the site of movies, weddings, and private events.

● Chabot Observatory and Planetarium

1000 Skyline Boulevard, Oakland 94619. Joaquin Miller Road exit from Highway 13. (510) 336-7300. Sept.–May: Tues.–Sun., 10–3; June–Aug.: Tues.–Sun, 10–5. Additional hours for planetarium, theater, and observatories: Fri. and Sat., 7 P.M.–10 P.M. Adults, $8; children under 12, $5.50. Theater and planetarium additional. Group rates. Gift shop. Café. **Ages 8 & up.** *W. www.chabotspace.org*

Hang out with the stars in this high-tech facility majestically situated in the Oakland hills. Chabot features a world-class planetarium, dome-screen 3-D theater for large format films, powerful telescopes, and exciting hands-on exhibits. State-of-the-art lasers, fiber optics, and sound technology surround you in stunning celestial displays. Kids can travel on an orbiting space station or discover stars with a 36-inch refractor telescope (one of the largest in the world accessible to the public) or tour an Envirogarden and a Moongarden (where plants bloom only at night) in one of the premier astronomy and space museums in the country. The youngest will love the Discovery Center of changing hands-on exhibits and the "Icy Bodies" exhibit. And everyone, including parents, will thrill going through the mock-up Habitation module to be used by NASA astronauts in 2005.

● Crab Cove Visitor's Center

1252 McKay Avenue, Alameda 94501. (510) 521-6887. Wed.–Sun., 10–4:30. Tours by reservation. Free. **All ages.** *www.ebparks.org/parks/crab.htm*

This East Bay Regional Park District center is where the old Coast Guard Station was, on Crown Beach. The museum displays marine life and San Francisco bay animals such as a saltwater hawk, a turtle snake, and a mountain toad.

● USS *Hornet* Museum

Pier 3 (Mail: P.O. Box 460), Alameda Point, Alameda 94501. (510) 521-8448. Daily except Tues. and holidays, 10–4. Adults, $12; seniors, students, and military, $10; ages 5–18, $5. Open on Tues. until 1:30 for $5. Groups, parties, conferences, concerts, and events: (510) 521-8448 ext. 234. Big-band dances. Snack bar. Ship store. **Ages 5 & up.** *Limited W. www.uss-hornet.org*

One of the proudest aircraft carriers in the U.S. Navy is now at home as a vast floating museum in an abandoned former naval air station. And even while volunteers paint and polish, you can explore the ship itself, the ready rooms, officers' quarters, engine room, and navigation bridge. Aircraft of various eras, including TBM Avenger, A-4 Skyhawk, F9F Panther, and F-8 Crusaders are on board. Youth groups can live aboard (510-521-8448 ext. 232) and follow the painted footsteps of Neil Armstrong, Buzz Aldrin, and Michael Collins on their return from the moon on July 24, 1969. The USS *Hornet* can be reached by BART/AC Transit (510-817-1717) and Alameda/Oakland Ferry (510-522-3300).

● Alameda Historical Museum

2324 Alameda Avenue, Alameda 94501. (510) 521-1233. Wed.–Sun., 1:30–4; Sat., 11–4. Free. Walking tours. Groups by reservation. **Ages 6 & up.** *W. www.alamedamuseum.org*

The Alameda Museum houses the archives of the city of Alameda and provides information to homeowners about structures built before 1909. Its historical gallery offers exhibits on Neptune Beach, the former gala bathing resort; Victorian era toys; Ohlone artifacts; and other displays. Vivian wrote, "I especially liked the key. When we visited the rooms I especially liked the Victorian Room, the Barbershop, and the dollhouse. They were all great. In the dollhouse, all the dolls were so pretty I wished I could keep one of them. And in the Victorian Room the thing I liked most was the Chinese cupboard. With thanks."

● UC Berkeley Art Museum and Pacific Film Archive

2626 Bancroft Way (Mail: 2625 Durant Avenue), Berkeley 94720-2250. (510) 642-0808. Wed.–Sun., 11–7; Thurs. until 9. Ages 18–64, $6; ages 12–17 and over 65, $4; under 12, free. Free admission Thurs., 11–12 and 5–9. Café. Gift shop. **Ages 7 & up.** *W. www.bampfa.berkeley.edu*

The UC Berkeley Art Museum is a natural for children, not so much for the art but for the building itself. Its unique multileveled, concrete-slab construction enables a young visitor to see its spacious interiors from any of the many corners and balconies. The outdoor sculpture garden is fun and strikes a chord with young people. Special family days offer art making and art touring, music, storytelling, and free screenings at the Pacific Film Archive, part of the museum, show classic, international, and children's films for all ages. Call (510) 642-1124 for schedules.

● Lawrence Hall of Science

Centennial Drive, University of California, Berkeley 94720. Take Highway 80 to University Avenue until it ends at Oxford. Left on Oxford, then right on

Hearst Avenue. Take Hearst to the top of the university, then left on Rim Way and left on Centennial Way to the top of the hill. (510) 642-5132. Daily, 10–5. Summer hours 1:30–4:30 daily. Adults, $8; seniors and students, $6; ages 3–6, $4. Galaxy Snack Bar. Parties. **Ages 4 & up.** *W.* *www.lawrencehallofscience.org*

There are young scientists who'd rather spend a day here than anywhere else in the world. The Lawrence Hall of Science has an outstanding variety of exhibits, science workshops, tests of your mathematical and logical ability, tests of knowledge, computers to play with, visual oddities, and a hundred different things to tantalize and amuse. That brightly colored structure on the outdoor plaza isn't just something to climb on, it's a replica of a DNA molecule. Tots love the growling apatosaurus. Many kids are fascinated by "Within the Human Brain," in which visitors step inside a simulated "rat cage" of learning activities. "Math Rules!," a collection of hands-on math challenges, sweeps others away. The Biology Lab is the place to investigate the world of living things (weekdays and holidays, 1:30–3:30; weekends, 1:30–4; daily in summer). In the building lab, kids can learn how to build a house without nails or a Mongolian yurt and design a doghouse. Holt Planetarium shows, the Science Discovery Theater, and special events offer ever-changing inducements to learning. The Amazing Maze is 1,000 square feet of wonder. And the New Idea Lab is a floor of changing exhibits and experiments.

As one visitor wrote, "The LHS is the best science place to visit in the world. I learned a lot!! Have a good day!!" Another simply said, "This place is cool!"

● Phoebe Hearst Museum of Anthropology

Kroeber Hall, Bancroft Way, at College Avenue, University of California, Berkeley 94720. (510) 643-7648. Wed.–Sat., 10–4:30; Sun., 10–4:30. Adults, $2; seniors, $1; children, 50¢. Thurs., free. Groups by reservation (510 642-3682). Museum store. **Ages 6 & up.** *W.* *http://hearstmusuem.berkeley.edu*

Ten-year-old Mary wrote, "This place is really cool and interesting. I especially liked the rock statue of Phoebe Hearst. It was beautiful. I liked looking at the pottery too. P.S. How did you get all this stuff here?" Gena wrote, "I liked the headphones, the cows, and the baby carrier from Borneo." Many of the museum's rotating exhibits are developed from its vast holdings of ethnographic, archaeological, and archival materials. On occasion, the museum hosts traveling exhibits related to anthropology and ethnic studies. A visit will help children understand other peoples' worlds, past and present.

School groups may request tours of all major exhibitions, and the museum will provide children's activity sheets. Although the Ishi exhibit is now in the permanent collection, a special presentation on Ishi and the invention of Yahi culture is given for school groups. In addition, a limited number of teaching kits that complement state-mandated social science curricula are available for loan at no charge. Lectures, movies, and slide presentations are also available.

● The Campanile

Sather Tower, University of California, Berkeley 94720. (510) 642-5215. Mon.–Sat., 10–3:30; Sun., 10–1:45. 50¢. **Ages 6 & up.** *www.berkeley.edu/visitors*

From the top of this tower, you can see San Francisco, Alcatraz, Mount Tamalpais, the Golden Gate and Bay Bridges, and the entire campus while, above you, 61 bronze bells, the largest weighing 10,000 pounds, ring out melodies three times a day. Sather Tower is being renovated, so call to be sure it's open.

● Habitot Children's Museum

2065 Kittredge Street, at Shattuck Avenue, Berkeley. (510) 647-1111. Mon. and Wed., 9:30–1; Tues. and Fri., 9:30–5; Thurs., 9:30–7; Sat., 10–5. Adults, $4, for the first child, $6; for siblings and guests under 7, $3. Groups. Art studio. Gift shop. Toy lending library, party room, and classes. Parenting classes, too. **Ages 1–7.** *W. www.habitot.org*

This hands-on discovery museum offers developmentally appropriate interactive experiences for the youngest children from a pint-size grocery store and café, a wind tunnel for experiments, and a water-play exhibit, "Waterworks."

● Hall of Health

2230 Shattuck Avenue, lower level, Berkeley 94704. (510) 549-1564. Tues.–Sat., 10–4. Groups by appt. Drop-in visits encouraged. Free. **Ages 5 & up.** *W. www.hallofhealth.org*

"Your body is yours for life . . . take care of it yourself" is the motto here. The Hall of Health, sponsored by Children's Hospital and Research Center at Oakland, is a free hands-on health museum full of interactive exhibits that encourage you to learn with all your senses. Kids can ride an exercycle that counts calories burned, put together a life-size magnetic bone puzzle, look at cells in microscopes, watch films, and much more. Younger children can listen to their heart beat, visit the organ cut-out table, and draw their insides on a human-shaped chalkboard. There are interactive exhibits on safety, drugs, addiction, and the heart and circulatory system. On the third Saturday of each month, the Hall of Health sponsors Kids on the Block puppet shows to promote acceptance and understanding of physical, mental, medical, and cultural differences. The puppet characters represent diverse cultures and have conditions such as cerebral palsy, Down's syndrome, and blindness.

A seven-year-old wrote, "I liked all of the computers and the junk food man. The eyeball looks funny. The bladder sounds funny. I could not put the brain together." One second-grader reported, "I never knew so much about the body. Doesn't it seem kind of impossible for 206 bones to fit in a body?"

● Magnes Museum at Berkeley

2911 Russell Street, one block north of Ashby off Pine, Berkeley 94708. (510) 549-6950. Sun.–Thurs., 10–4. Tours by appt. Donation, $5. Children, free. Gift shop. **Ages 6 & up.** *(combined with the Magnes Museum in San Francisco; see p. 15).* *W. www.magnesmuseum.org*

Prints, photographs, maps, prayer books, and ceremonial and folk art from the museum's collections illuminate the city's place in Jewish, Christian, and Muslim traditions. The changing exhibits of art and artifacts always include something that is of special interest to children. Afterward, they can picnic in the garden.

● Tilden Regional Park

Canon Drive, off Grizzly Peak Boulevard, Berkeley 94708. (510) 525-2233. Nominal prices for rides. Daily, 10–5. The Little Farm is open daily, 8:30–5. Free. **Ages 2–13.** *www.ebparks.org/parks/tilden.htm*

Tilden Park has a pony ride, historic merry-go-round, and 50-year-old miniature steam train. A 12-minute ride through hill and tunnel costs $1.75 or five rides for $7. Under 2, free. Native California botanical gardens, an environmental educational center, wooded hiking trails, and swimming in Lake Anza are also popular. But the chief attraction for youngsters is the Little Farm in the Nature Area. Here they can meet barnyard animals such as sheep, goats, cows, pigs, chickens, geese, and rabbits.

● Pixieland Amusement Park

2740 East Olivera Road, in Willow Pass Park, Concord 94519. (925) 381-0359. Daily in summer, and Wed.–Sun. in spring and fall, 10:30–6; weekends Feb., Mar., Apr., Oct., Nov., Dec.; closed Dec. 15–Feb. 2. Rides, $1.25, 10 for $11. Unlimited weekday pass, 10:30–4, $12. Season pass, $80. **Ages 2–10.** *www.pixieland.com*

This small amusement park is strictly for very young children. Spinning tea cups, a Red Baron airplane ride, a frog hopper, and a flying dragon roller coaster are new additions to this sweet little park. Old favorites such as the merry-go-round, train, boat ride, car ride, and airplane are still there. There's a game section, where every kid wins, a little concession stand, and a picnic area reserved for birthday parties.

● The Jungle

1975 Diamond Boulevard, Box 20, Willows Shopping Center, Concord 95420. (925) 687-4FUN. Sun.–Thurs., 10–9, Fri., 10–10; Sat. and holidays, 9–10. Admission prices vary depending on time of day and age of children. Parents always play free and are required to stay on the premises with their children. Groups by appt., discount for 10 or more. Socks are required. Parties. Café. **Ages 1–12.** *W. www.junglefunandadventure.com*

The Jungle is a 20,000-square-foot jungle-themed entertainment center where kids can crawl in tubes, romp in foam forests, soar through the air on track glides, climb on cargo nets, and slide and jump on special equipment designed to build social and physical skills. Parents have unlimited viewing of their children at play on all three levels. Infants and toddlers have their own special play area and playhouses.

The Jungle in San Jose is at 950 El Paseo de Saratoga, (408) 866-4FUN.

● McConaghy Estate

18701 Hesperian Boulevard, Hayward 94541. Off Highway 880 between Bockman and A Streets. (510) 276-3010. Fri.–Sun., 1–4. Last tour at 3:30. Groups: (510) 278-0198. Adults, $3; seniors, $2; ages 6–12, 50¢. Classes, $10. Special Christmas program and rates. Closed holidays, Thanksgiving week, and January. **Ages 7 & up.** *www.haywardareahistory.org*

This elegant 1886 farmhouse is so completely furnished it looks as if the family still lives here. One bedroom is filled with toys, games, books, and clothes used by a turn-of-the-century child. The dining room is lavishly decorated for each holiday. A tank house (which used to store water) and a buggy-filled carriage house adjoin the house, handily located next to Kennedy Park with its picnic tables, merry-go-round, and train.

● Hayward Area Historical Society Museum

22701 Main Street, at C, Hayward 94541. (510) 581-0223. Tues.–Sat., 11–4; Closed holidays. Adults, $1; children, 6–12, 50¢. School and group tours by appt. Summer walking tours. **Ages 6 & up.** *W. www.haywardareahistory.org*

The large brick 1927 post office is now a lovingly presented album of Hayward area history including photographs and artifacts, a hands-on interactive area for children, and a temporary exhibits gallery that changes every three months to keep visitors returning. A favorite is the holiday collection of toys, trains, dolls, Christmas ornaments, and cards.

● Sulphur Creek Nature Center

1801 D Street, Hayward 94541. (510) 881-6747. Tues.–Sun., 10–5. Free. Animal-lending library, 10–3, $8. E-mail: SlphrCreek@aol.com. Picnic tables. **Ages 3 & up.** *W. http://hard.dst.ca.us/index.html*

Sulphur Creek Park is a charming spot in which to introduce children to wildlife native to Northern California. Coyotes, opossums, foxes, rabbits, hawks, owls, song and garden birds, a variety of reptiles and amphibians, and invertebrates are displayed in natural habitats. There are changing exhibits and a wildlife garden. Nature study classes, wildlife rehabilitation, and volunteer opportunities are available. A fan wrote, "I liked the opossum, when you brought it out! I like the crow. While you were with the other group the crow said 'hellow.' I learned that there are more animals and bigger habitats. Thank you for talking to us."

● Hayward Shoreline Interpretive Center

4901 Breakwater Avenue, Hayward 94545. (510) 670-7270. Weekends, 10–5, and by appt. Free. E-mail: Hayshore@aol.com. Gift store. Volunteer opportunities. Summer day camps. **Ages 3 & up.** *www.hard.dst.ca.us*

Located on the Hayward shore of San Francisco Bay, this center displays exhibits of local estuary animals and is the hub of a 1,800-acre marshland park. You can explore marine life in a hands-on Wet Lab, search for animal life under the microscope, see a variety of exhibits on the shoreline area, check out a free family discovery pack or binoculars, and hike on eight miles of trails. Public naturalist programs on weekends. Sam wrote, "We ate some plants. They taste good. We learned how some plants live in salt water. We also found out that a female plant looks more beautiful than the male. We went fishing for fish and plankton. But we found a lot of crabs under rocks. I found one and I put it in the water and I saw it eat plankton. On the way back we found out how many bugs are in a kind of plant."

● Ardenwood Farm

Ardenwood Regional Park, 34600 Ardenwood Boulevard, at Highway 84, Fremont 94555. (510) 796-0663/796-0199. Christmas events and holidays. Tues.–Sun., 10–5. Adults, $5; ages 4–17, $3.50; seniors and disabled, $4. Special events, extra. When the Patterson House tours, horse-drawn train rides, and blacksmithing demonstrations are available; the admission is adults, $5; seniors, $4; children 4–17, $3.50. Wagon rides. Rain may close the park. Food service available. Café. Picnic tables. **All ages.** *W. www.ebparks.org/parks/arden.htm*

Ardenwood Farm leaped onto our "top 11" list on the first visit. The 205-acre farm is a look into the Bay Area's farming past. Its motto:

May learning, science, useful art,
Adorn thy life, improve thy heart.
May kind affection, love so dear,
Hereafter bless, and guide you here.

At Ardenwood, kids of any age can visit a remarkably well restored Victorian farmhouse, built in 1857 by George Patterson, a forty-niner who found gold in the land. Costumed docents tend the Victorian flower garden, demonstrate Victorian crafts such as lace making, and show off farming skills. Farm produce and flowers can be purchased.

The Deer Park train is fun. There are lots of animals in the farmyard. There are lectures, slide shows, and demonstrations in the Granary and cooking demonstrations in the Country Kitchen. The Haybarn and Horse Corrals are working today as they were yesterday. There are also picnic and party areas, and concerts are given in the gazebo. Amy said, "I learned that history can be real fun by the way you girls made it." Juliane expounded, "I learned that women were very fancy. They wore corsets laced very tightly, which rearranged their internal organs. They wore swimsuits which you couldn't swim in. They wore a hatpin and always carried an umbrella. They had small beds. I learned this from your presentation. When some of my classmates got to put something on, I found it really hilarious."

● Mission San Jose

43300 Mission Boulevard, Fremont 94539. (510) 657-1797. Daily, 10–5. Closed holidays. Donation: adults, $2; children 12 and over, $1. Group tours by reservation. Gift shop. **Ages 7 & up.** *W. www.californiamissions.com/cahistory/sanjose.html*

"Dear Mission San Jose, I appreciated you letting us come to your mission. It was fun and exciting to see how the missioners lived and I liked the slide show about the mission and the church. I had a good time. My favorite thing was the fountain and the olive trees. Thank you very much. Sincerely, Lakisha."

Founded in 1797, Mission San Jose holds an exciting place in California history. A highlight of the museum tour is an exhibit on the Ohlone, the native people of the Bay Area. Father Duran, who arrived in 1806, taught some of the 2,000 Ohlone neophytes to play the original mission bells and musical instruments now on display. Original mission vestments, the original baptismal font, a pioneer cradle, and the sanctus bells are housed in the adobe living quarters of the mission padres. The mission church has been carefully reconstructed from hand-hewn beams and more than 180,000 adobe bricks.

● San Francisco Bay National Wildlife Refuge

Highway 84, Fremont 94536. At the east end of the Dumbarton Bridge, near the toll plaza, off Thornton Avenue. (510) 792-0222. Visitors center, Tues.– Sun., 10–5. Free. **Ages 5 & up.** *http://desfbay.fws.gov*

Weekend interpretive programs, nature study walks, slide and film presentations, and a self-guided trail through the marsh and diked ponds help introduce youngsters to the world around them. Discovery packs are available free for checkout and further exploratory fun.

Henry and James wrote, "Dear Rangers, We had a good time at the wild life refuge. We went to Salty's house and we tasted his pickleweed. We saw salt crystals. We liked your slide show. We saw mud creatures. We saw the great egret and snowy egret. We saw the California claperal. The beaks and feet were cool. The spider in the salt sand was walking on the water. We hope you had a good time. Sincerely."

● Wind Farms of Altamont Pass

On windy days you can often hear them before you see them—the more than 7,500 giant wind turbines, perched on towers, on either side of Interstate 580. The world's largest "wind farm" produces electricity from the wind. A seven-mile drive just north of and paralleling I-580, begun either from Greenville or Mountain House Road, east of Livermore, tours the heart of the wind farms.

● Livermore History Center

2155 3rd Street, Livermore 94550. (925) 449-9927. Wed.–Sat., 11–3. Free. **Ages 8 & up.** *www.carnegie-libraries.org*

This exhibit on the history of the Livermore Valley from prehistoric times to the present is housed in the old Carnegie Library. Pictures, maps, artifacts, and mementos from local families, businesses, and groups are on display. A 19th-century drugstore exhibit has been installed. The museum members are currently working on the restoration of the historical Duarte Garage/Lincoln Highway Museum in Livermore at North L Street and Portola. Early-day fire trucks, wagons, and other apparatus can be viewed by appointment.

Ravenswood, the Victorian-era home and gardens of San Francisco's "Blind Boss" Christopher Buckley, is open to the public (2647 Arroyo Road, Livermore 94550; 925-443-0238. Second Sun. of the month and by appt. Groups: 925-373-5708. Donation. Gift shop. www.larpd.dst.ca.us). Costumed docents show visitors the cloisonné chandeliers, ornate billiard table, clothing, pictures, and mementos of the Buckley family.

● Amador-Livermore Valley Museum

603 Main Street, Pleasanton 94566. (925) 462-2766. Wed.– Sat., 11–4; Sun., 1–4. Donation. **Ages 8 & up.** *W.*

Housed in the 1914 Pleasanton Town Hall, this museum features yesteryear exhibits including a sitting room, 1900s kitchen, blacksmith shop, beauty shop, and dentist's office. Rotating cultural exhibits feature a variety of topics. A gallery exhibits heritage photos of the Tri-Valley area. An archives/reference library is available for research, and educational programs are offered by reservation.

● Clayton Historical Museum

6101 Main Street (Mail: P.O. Box 94), Clayton 94517. (925) 672-0240. Groups and reservations: (925) 672-4786. Wed. and Sun., 2–4. Free. Gift shop. **Ages 8 & up.** *www.94517.com/chs*

Located at the base of Mount Diablo, this city of 12,000 owes its existence to a fear of developers—it's a small, quaint old town. The museum, the home of the town founder, miner Joel Clayton, is one of several older buildings that occupy the downtown district and whisper about yesteryear. It's a small, two-story clapboard farmhouse. Period furnishings, photos, coal mining artifacts, and British family memorabilia bring this 1860s home to life. Clayton was so wealthy that he loaned money to William Randolph Hearst's father, George, but he died in 1872 of pneumonia and was never repaid.

● Blackhawk Museum

3700 Blackhawk Plaza Circle, Danville 94506. (925) 736-2280. Wed.– Sun., 10–5. Adults, $7; seniors and students, $5. Lectures and programs. Tours by appt. Events: (925) 736-2277 ext. 249. Gift shop. **Ages 7 & up.** *W. www.BlackhawkMuseum.org*

This is where old cars dream of ending up when they die, in a lavishly designed modern museum set in a beautifully landscaped shopping center. The Blackhawk Museum, in association with the Smithsonian Institution, showcases ever-changing exhibitions organized and developed by the Smithsonian. The **Car Collection** displays rare, classic, automobiles as works of art. It showcases Kenneth Behring's $100 million collection of custom-built and one-of-a-kind automobiles created during the years between the two world wars. There are rotating exhibits of the 120 autos as well as video interactive presentations with the designers of the Tucker, Duesenberg, 1955 Ford Thunderbird, and other classics. The 1897 Leon Bollee three-wheeler, the oldest existing GM automobile, the nickel-silver-bodied Daimler built for the Maharaja of Rewa, the 1948 Tucker, the 1901 "Merry Oldsmobile" Model R, and the 1929 Isotta Fraschini are favorites. My mother remembered the 1930 Cord Convertible and my nephew thought the 1945 215 from Moscow was the best.

Shows on Broadway, spiders, and the Gold Rush are just a few that have appeared this year in collaboration with the Smithsonian.

● Museum of the San Ramon Valley

West Prospect and Railroad Avenues, Danville 94526. (925) 837-3750. Tues.– Fri., 1–4; Sat., 10–1. Donation. **Ages 8 & up.** *W. www.MuseumSRV.org*

A restored 1891 Southern Pacific depot contains artifacts, pictures, flags, and drawings commemorating the valley's past. There are rotating exhibits including "Agriculture in the San Ramon Valley, 1850–1950" with photographs and artifacts demonstrating how farmers, ranchers, and businesses worked together in the past. Special children's programs and puppet show are given regularly. The little Tassajara One Room Grammar School has been moved to the museum land and visitors step back in time, playing 19th-century games, and learn to cipher, recite, and use pen and ink. An Indian life program is offered to fourth-graders.

● Richmond Museum of History

400 Nevin Avenue at 4th Street (Mail: P.O. Box 1265), Richmond 94802. (510) 235-7387. Wed.–Sun., 1–4, except holidays, and by appt. Free. **Ages 8 & up.** *W. www.ci.richmond.ca.us/~library*

Life in the Richmond area up to the mid-1940s is portrayed in the history gallery with the aid of room re-creations, photographs, panel displays, and text. Old-time vehicles such as a peddler's wagon and a Model A Ford are a thrill to young and old alike. In addition to the permanent history gallery, changing exhibits draw on a wide variety of topics of local interest.

● Diablo Valley College Museum and Planetarium

321 Golf Club Road, Pleasant Hill 94523. Off Willow Pass Road from Highway 680. (925) 685-1230 ext. 2330. Open only when the college is open; hours change each semester. Museum open Wed., 1–4. Groups by appt. A van can take people up to the planetarium. **Ages 8 & up.** *W. www.dvc.edu*

Here, youngsters can see a seismograph, a Foucault pendulum swinging, and changing oceanography and anthropological exhibits on Native Americans. Local animals, especially the nocturnal moles, weasels, and owls, are fun to see, as are the star shows.

● Lindsay Wildlife Museum

1931 First Avenue in Larkey Park, Walnut Creek 94596. Highway 680 to Geary/Treat exit, west on Geary. From Geary, turn left onto Buena Vista, right onto First Avenue. (925) 935-1978. Tues.–Sun., call for hours. Adults, $6; seniors, $5; ages 3–17, $4; under 3, free. Wildlife Rehabilitation training for ages 12 and up. Classes, tours, field trips. **All ages.** *W. www.wildlife-museum.org*

Lindsay Wildlife Museum is a unique natural history and environmental education center where live wild animals are just inches away. Visitors can listen to the cry of a red-tailed hawk and watch a bald eagle eat lunch. The exhibit hall features more than 50 species of live, native California animals, encounters with unique wildlife, a hands-on discovery room for youngsters, and changing exhibits. Storytelling helps connect people with wildlife. The museum is the oldest and one of the largest wildlife rehabilitation centers in the United States, treating nearly 6,000 injured or orphaned wild animals each year.

Alexa, a first-grader, wrote, "My favorite part was when you showed us the live Barn Owl. It was so beautiful. I loved the way its wings fluttered without a sound. My second favorite animal was the gopher. It was so cute in its little habitat. I know they eat your garden but still I don't see why anyone would want to kill them. One of the neatest animals was the snake. I really liked the way it felt and it had such a beautiful pattern on its scales. Thanks again."

Every once in a while, the Walnut Creek Model Railroad Society runs its Diablo Valley Line in Larkey Park across the street. The miniature handmade models in the "mining town" make this fun for everyone (510) 937-1888; the office is not open every day).

● Old Borges Ranch

1035 Castle Rock Road, near Northgate High School and Shell Ridge Open Space, Walnut Creek 94596. (925) 934-6990. Daily, 8–dusk. Visitors center, Sat., 1–4; first Sun. of the month, 12–4. Free. Group tours by reservation. **All ages.** *www.ci.walnut-creek.org*

Visitors to this 1899 working cattle ranch can see goats, lambs, pigs, chickens, geese, and cattle; check out the antique farm machinery; peek in the farm buildings; and draw water at the windmill. Or they can fish or hike the many trails.

● Shadelands Ranch Historical Museum

2660 Ygnacio Valley Road, Walnut Creek 94598. (925) 935-7871. Wed., 11:30–4; Sun., 1–4. Adults, $2. Picnics and parties. **Ages 9 & up.** *W. www.ci.walnut-creek.ca.us/wchs.html*

History buffs will also want to visit this restored time capsule in town, a turn-of-the-century Colonial Revival farmhouse with a gazebo in back. There are nine rooms with many original Penniman/Johnson-period furnishings. The museum also features changing exhibits and archives.

● Eugene O'Neill National Historic Site, Tao House

(Mail: P.O. Box 280, Danville 94526) Visits by reservation only on a guided tour, Wed.–Sun. at 10 A.M. and 12:30 P.M., 14 people at a time. (925) 838-0249. Free. **Ages 13 & up.** *www.nps.gov/euon*

Eugene O'Neill, the only Nobel Prize–winning playwright from the United States and the architect of modern American theater, lived at Tao House in the hills above Danville from 1937 to 1944. It was here that he wrote his final and most successful plays: *The Iceman Cometh, Long Days Journey Into Night,* and *A Moon for the Misbegotten.* Since 1980, the National Park Service has been restoring Tao House, its courtyard and orchards, and telling the story of O'Neill, his work and his influence on the American theater.

The ceilings and doors are blue and red, and the house has many Chinese accents. "Rosie's Room" houses a replica of O'Neill's 1910 garish pea-green Nickelodeon player piano, bedecked with loud pink roses. As he said, "This is a final home and harbor for me." Today, the house offers student days for aspiring writers, artists, and photographers.

● Niles Canyon Railway

Boarding area: the corner of Main Street and Kilkare Road, Sunol. Along Highway 84, just west of Interstate 680. (Mail: P.O. Box 2247, Fremont 94545-0247) (925) 862-9063. See website for operating days and times. Adults, $8; seniors, $7; ages 3–12, $4. **Ages 5 & up.** *www.ncry.org*

Volunteers with the Pacific Locomotive Association operate 18 vintage steam and diesel locomotives, and passenger and motor cars over more than six miles of sun-dappled curves of Niles Canyon. A 1924 steam locomotive and a "skunk" car, with its trademark yellow sides, silver room, and skunk logo, are favorites. The association continues to expand its operation and restore railroad tracks and cars. Niles is best known for the more than 400 Charlie Chaplin, Ben Turpin, and Zasu Pitts silent movies filmed here at the Essanay Film Manufacturing company. Chaplin's cohort, Bronco Billy, would be right at home here today.

● Waterworld

1950 Waterworld Parkway (two blocks east of Interstate 680 off Willow Pass Road), Concord. (925) 609-9283. Adults, $24.99; seniors and children under 48 inches tall, $17.99; under age 3, free. Parking, $4. Season pass, $45. Rentable walkers and tubes. Picnic areas outside; no food allowed in park. Snack bars. **All ages.** *www.sixflags.com*

The old swimming hole was never like this! There are free-fall slides, rubber-tube wars, river-runs, double-tubing in total darkness, and splash landings sure to cool you off fast. Always call ahead for discount deals, schedule updates, picnic possibilities, and health considerations. Wear waterproof sports sandals or watersocks.

● Alvarado Adobe and Blume House Museum

1 Alvarado Square, San Pablo 94806. Near San Pablo Avenue. (510) 215-3046. Each house is open on alternate Sundays, 12–4. Free. Open third Sun. of the month and by appt. Donation. **Ages 7 & up.** *W. www.ci.san-pablo.ca.us*

The Alvarado Adobe has been precisely reconstructed on its original site by the San Pablo Historical Society and Recreation Dept. Service. The owner, Juan Bautista Alvarado, husband of Martina Castro, was the Mexican governor of Alta California from 1836 to 1842 and lived here from 1848 to

1882. The house was built in the early 1840s by the Castro family. Furnished in a mix of rancho and early California styles, it offers visitors showcases of artifacts including *cascarones*—painted eggshells that were filled with confetti or cologne and cracked open on party-goers. And from local Indian mounds there are Indian shell games and samples of amole, the soap plant, which was roasted and eaten; boiled for glue; pounded into a paste that stupefied fish when thrown into a stream; used for twine, shampoo, and soap; and dried to stuff mattresses.

The Blume Museum (510-215-3046) is a 1905 farmhouse now refurnished to look as it did then, with oak furniture, early plumbing fixtures, and an iron stove in the kitchen.

● Crockett Historical Museum

900 Loring Avenue, Crockett 94525. At the foot of Rolph Avenue, in the old Southern Pacific Depot alongside the railroad tracks. (510) 787-2178. Wed. and Sat., 10–3. Free. **Ages 7 & up.** *W. www.museumstuff.com*

Exhibits of C&H Sugar Refining Co., a world-record sturgeon, an eight-foot model of the National Cathedral, pictures of Crockett and the Carquinez Strait, ship models, and artifacts of 20th-century life in Crockett are part of this exhibit. Visitors can see the "N" track model railroad display with the small trains in action.

● John Muir National Historic Site

4202 Alhambra Avenue, off Highway 4, Martinez 94553. (925) 228-8860. The house is open for self-guided tours Wed.–Sun., 10–4:30. Guided tours and Environmental Living Programs by reservation. Adults, $3; children under 16, with an adult, free. **Ages 6 & up.** *Visitors center, First floor of Muir house and the grounds are wheelchair accessible. www.nps.gov/jomu*

"I hold dearly cherished memories about it [the house] and fine garden grounds full of trees and bushes and flowers that my wife and father-in-law and I planted 'fine things from every land. . . ."

The book John Muir wrote these words in is still in his "scribble den." After a beautiful film narrated with John Muir's words and scenes of the natural wonders that inspired it, visitors tour Muir's large 19th-century ranch house, one of the most authentically presented houses you can visit. The closets are still filled with clothing. Muir's suitcase is on the bed, ready for travel; his glasses and pencils are on the desk in his "scribble den." Pictures of his friends President Theodore Roosevelt and naturalist John Burroughs are on the walls, and you can look through some of the scrapbooks in the parlor. You can go up to the attic and ring the ranch bell in the bell tower.

The **Martinez Adobe,** built in 1849 by the son of the Mexican don for whom the town was named, is in the garden, where you can wander at will. Muir's daughter and her family lived there. Muir also advised, "Climb the mountains and get their good tidings. Nature's peace will flow into you as sunshine flows into trees. The winds blow their open freshness into you, and the storms their energy, while cares will drop off like autumn leaves." This is a great place to start.

● Black Diamond Mines Regional Preserve

5175 Somersville Road, Antioch 94509. Take Highway 4 to Somersville Road and head south on it toward the hills. Park open 8 to dusk. Center open 10–4:30 weekends, Mar.–Oct. (925) 757-2620. Free. **Ages 8 & up.** *www.ebparks.org/parks/black.htm*

Black Diamond Mines Regional Preserve was the site of 19th-century coal mining and 20th-century sand mining. There are six public-access mine openings that are available for exploration by older children, with adults, during park hours. Prospect Tunnel, 200 feet deep, was named by miners prospecting unsuccessfully for coal. Two of the other tunnels are powder magazines that were created by miners to store explosives.

The surrounding 4,000-acre preserve was once home to three thriving towns. Now, only Rose Hill cemetery, ghosts, and trails remain. Historic photographs and videotapes on the area's history are available for viewing daily, 8 to 4:30. There are weekday and weekend naturalist programs and hikes and talks on the natural and cultural history of the area. Most are free.

● Pittsburg Historical Society

515 Railroad Ave Avenue, Pittsburg 94565. (925) 439-7501. Wed. and Sat., 1–4, and by appt. Donation. **Ages 8 & up.** *W. www.museumsusa.org*

"Were it not for the preservation of memorabilia, the history of this area would fade and pass without record." This is the motto of the Pittsburg Historical Society.

Gifts from local families have helped make this a fine collection. Visitors will enjoy the barbershop and the little schoolroom, the kitchen with the collection of old irons, and the World War II army camp with mannequins in uniform. Displays honor the commercial fishermen of the area, as well as the Indian, Mexican, and ranching eras. Outside, the 1909 Biplane is fun. The mural of the chronology of the area, from Native Americans to coal mining and farmers, is where talk-tours of the museum start. Films and presentations keep kids coming back.

■ The Peninsula and San Jose Area

The Peninsula and the San Jose area offer many days of happy "attraction" hunting. Here one can explore the past, at the historic town that is the San Jose Historical Museum, and the future, at Silicon Valley's finest Tech Museum. You can dig beneath the sea at Coyote Point or search the skies at Lick Observatory. For sheer pleasure, there's a gentle "tree-themed" amusement park, Bonfante Gardens, and a screaming one, Great America. Since the area grows ever more crowded and less suburban, city street maps are especially helpful.

● Sanchez Adobe

1000 Linda Mar Boulevard, off Highway 1, Pacifica 94044. (650) 359-1462. Tues.–Thurs., 10–4; Sat. and Sun., 1–5, and by appt. Free. Groups. **Ages 7 & up.** *www.sanmateocountyhistory.com*

In 1842, the *alcalde*, or mayor, of San Francisco, Señor Francisco Sanchez, built his home in the farm that once produced food for San Francisco's Mission Dolores. The adobe still stands. Today's youngsters can participate in hands-on programs that take place in the historic garden. Activities include adobe brick making, junior archaeology workshops, Native American games, and Native American skills workshops put on by the San Mateo County Historical Association, including storytelling with One-eyed Charlie.

● Mary Vallejo History Center

505 Johnston Street (Mail: P.O. Box 62), Half Moon Bay 94019. (650) 726-7084. Self-guided tours on the third Sat. of the month. Call for hours. Guided tours, by appt. Adults, $3; free for schoolchildren. **Ages 7 & up.** *W. www.spanishtownhs.org*

The Spanishtown Historical Society is restoring the little 1850s Half Moon Bay jail cell as a photo-packed museum. Behind it, near the blacksmith shop, the 1877 barn built by Thomas Johnston displays old farm equipment, and docents give hands-on tours of early coastside farming. The society uses the old Ocean Shore Railroad depot as a meeting place.

The nearby **James Johnston House** (the White House, Higgins Purissima Road, just south of downtown. 650-726-7084. Guided tours the third Sat. of the month, by appt. Partially W. www.JohnstonHouseHMB.org) is the society's sweet interpretive house museum, with a community garden. James Johnston came west in the Gold Rush and made his fortune with a store in San Francisco. He bought 160 acres. Then he went home to Ohio and, with his three brothers, herded 900 dairy cows to California. Historical walking tours of this gallery-filled beach town are also available. There are beaches, redwood parks, and perfumed nurseries to walk through as well as Pescadero State Marsh for free weekend bird walks (650-879-2170).

● Phipps Country

2700 Pescadero Road (Mail: P.O. Box 349), Pescadero 94060. (415) 879-0787. Daily, 10–6 in winter; until 7 in summer. Closed Christmas week. Free. Tours, by appt. **All ages.** *www.phippscountry.com*

This working farm, with a roadside stand, nursery, barnyard, gardens, and picnic areas, makes a very pleasant outing. Pick your own berries in season. While parents buy fresh produce, herbs, an intriguing selection of dried beans, and plants in the nursery, kids can explore out back. There are several aviaries filled with colorful, exotic birds. In the barnyard is Eeyore the donkey, a family of potbellied pigs, and momma goats with babies. There is a large poultry enclosure with chickens and other exotic birds and a pond for the ducks and geese to play in. Kids of all ages will enjoy looking at the antique farm equipment. Take a picnic and enjoy the country.

Little Loryn wrote, "Dear Phipps Ranch Friends, I liked picking strawberries at your ranch. I also liked it when the donkey (Eeyore) yelled at us. I also liked that big black pig. I got to touch the goat's horn, too, and I liked that. Thank you very much!"

● Pigeon Point Light Station State Historic Park

210 Pigeon Point Road, Highway 1, Pescadero 94660. (650) 879-2120. Grounds and light station: Daily, 8 to sunset; a 45-minute guided tour of the tower, including the lens room, on weekends. **Ages 8 & up.** *www.parks.ca.gov*

The fog signal building houses a small but intriguing museum of local history. The point was called Punta de las Ballenas ("whale point") until the clipper ship *Carrier Pigeon* ran aground here in the fog in 1853. The 115-foot light tower, built in 1872, still has its original first order Fresnel lens (the largest made) at the top of a 136-step, iron spiral stairway. The light is now automated.

● Coyote Point Museum for Environmental Education

1651 Coyote Point Drive, San Mateo 94401. Coyote Point Park, off Poplar Avenue from Highway 101. (650) 342-7755. Information: (650) 342-9969. Tues.–Sat., 10–5; Sun., 12–5. Closed Christmas, New Year's Day, and Thanksgiving. Adults, $4; seniors, $2; ages 12–17, $2; ages 4–12, $1. First Wed. of the month, free. Gate fee for park, picnic areas, playgrounds, and beach, $4 per car. **Ages 5 & up.** *W. www.coyoteptmuseum.org*

The Environmental Hall takes visitors on an imaginary trip from San Francisco Bay over the Santa Cruz Mountains and down to the Pacific shore. Six ecological zones of the Bay Area are interpreted. The display emphasizes the need to preserve and protect nature's resources and creatures. Models, exhibits, hands-on games, and computers serve as educational tools. The adjacent Wildlife Habitats house more than 40 live mammals, amphibians, birds, and reptiles native to the Bay Area. River otter feeding at noon, daily. Theme gardens are planted to attract hummingbirds and butterflies. One area shows how Native Americans used plants, trees, and shrubs. First-grader Jestina wrote, "Thank you for letting us touch the animals. The one I like is the 'possum and the mice or rat or whatever, but I thank you."

● Burlingame Museum of PEZ Memorabilia
214 California Drive, Burlingame. (650) 347-2301. Tues.–Sat., 10–6. Free. Gift shop. **Ages 4 & up.** *W. www.spectrumnet.com/pez*

Gary Doss proudly shows off his more than 280 kinds of Pez candy dispensers from as far back as the fifties. Invented in 1927 to help those who wanted to stop smoking, peppermint-flavored Pez were named after the German word *Pfefferminz*. Dispensers appeared in 1950 and cartoon heads were introduced in 1952. Miss Piggy, space aliens, Daisy Duck, the Pez clown, the 1960s blue astronaut, Santa Claus, Davy Crockett, the "Luv" eyeball from the '60s, and the Simpsons are displayed along with Tweety Bird, German subway vending machines—all on kids' eye level. There's a $1.39 Peppermint Patty and a $25 vintage Road Runner on sale. The "Make-a-Face Pez," made in 1972 for an Austrian bank giveaway and worth $5,000, is not for sale. The original patent for the dispensers is wonderfully tongue-in-cheek. Star Wars heroes and Wonder Women are on hand, as well.

● Japanese Tea Garden
Central Park, Parks Dept., 330 West 20th Avenue, San Mateo 94403. (650) 522-7400. Mon.–Fri., 10–4; Sat. and Sun., 11–4. Free. **Ages 6 & up.** *W.*

This proper, gracious Japanese garden is a soothing spot in the midst of city bustle. Quaint bridges and rock pathways take the visitor past a waterfall, a pond thick with water lilies and koi (carp), and in the springtime, pink cherry blossoms. The teahouse is open, irregularly, in summer.

● San Mateo County History Museum
777 Hamilton, Redwood City 94063. (650) 299-0104. Tues.–Sun., 10–4. Adults, $2; seniors and ages 6–12, $1. **Ages 7 & up.** *W. www.sanmateocountyhistory.com*

A walk through this museum is a walk through history. You begin with the Pleistocene epoch—14 million years ago—and view bones and fossils from that age found in San Mateo. Then on to the Costanoan Indians of 3,000 years ago, and the description of their magic dances, boats, tools, and food. The Mission Rancho period is well represented. Exhibits of lumber mills, an old general store and bar, settlers' wagons, and unicycles recall the past. Galleries change exhibits to focus on subjects such as 19th-century firefighting, the many mansions of San Mateo County, and transportation. There are also lectures, audiovisual programs, and community events such as "California in the '20s: Bootlegging and Moonshine," and a Victorian picnic.

● Lathrop House

627 Hamilton Street, Redwood City 94063. (650) 365-5564. Tues.– Thurs., 11–3. Closed August and the last two weeks of December. Donation. **Ages 7 & up.**

In 1863, Benjamin G. Lathrop, the county's first clerk, built this handsome Carpenter Gothic mansion, "Lora Mundi," on a lot bought from the Arguello family. The house has survived the earthquakes of 1906 and 1989, has been relocated twice, and has been restored—right down to the top hats on the hall rack—by the Redwood City Heritage Association. The servant's parlor is equipped with a wood-burning stove and butter churn. Naturally, kids like the upstairs bedrooms (with chamber pots!) best.

● Marine Science Institute

500 Discovery Parkway, Redwood City 94063. (650) 364-2760. Mon.– Sat., 8–5. Call for prices of the Shoreside and Discovery Voyage programs. **Ages 5 & up.** *www.sfbaymsi.org*

"I enjoyed geo/chem—using the VanDorn bottle to get water samples and sticking your fingers in 'Benthic Ooze'! I liked putting out the otter net and catching the fish and giving birth to some fish. I thought that looking at Phytoplankton, Zooplankton, and Circumplankton was fun." This is one San Jose student's response to the four-hour Discovery Voyage on the 90-foot research vessel *Brownlee.* Groups of 40 to 60 learn about marsh and marine life and the sea around us in more than a dozen programs, on land and sea.

● Filoli House and Gardens

Canada Road, Woodside 94062. Filoli Nature Hikes: Individual and group house and garden docent-led and self-guided tours, and nature hikes by reservation. (650) 364-8300 ext. 507. Feb. 12–Oct. 26, 10–2:30. Guided tours at 10 and 1, Tues.–Sat. Self-guided tours Tues.–Sat. Guided tours, self-guided tours and nature hikes, $10 per adult. Children 7–12 are $1; student discount with ID, $5. Children must be accompanied by an adult. Garden shop, café, visitors center. **Ages 12 & up.** *Limited W access. www.filoli.org*

Explore the many trails in the remote areas of Filoli. You can learn about the Indians who lived here many years ago and touch the San Andreas fault line. Learn about the animals, plants, ecosystems, and history of a fascinating place in the Bay Area. The two-hour hikes are two to three miles long.

Gustavo wrote, "I had a real good time. . . . My favorite part was when we went to the wildlife center. I also liked the Indian dig. Even if we didn't really see a turkey vulture or a red-tailed hawk, the turret spider was pretty amazing!"

● Woodside Store Historic Site

Kings Mountain and Tripp Roads, Woodside 94062. (650) 851-7615. Tues. and Thurs., 10–4; Sat. and Sun., 1–4. Tours by appt. Free. **Ages 7 & up.** *www.sanmateocountyhistory.com*

The San Mateo Historical Society has preserved, stocked, and opened the 1850s lumber/general store that started in 1854 as a stage stop. A slide show explains more of the site's history.

● Hiller Aviation Museum

601 Skyway Road, San Carlos 94070. Daily, 10–5 Adults, $5; seniors and children ages 12–17, $4; under 12, free. Classes. Library. Restoration shop. Theater. Gift shop. **Ages 8 & up.** *W. www.hiller.org*

A collection of technological advancements related to flight—past, present, and future—highlighting Northern California's unique role in the field of aviation, "where inspiration takes flight." More than 50 aircraft, mostly restored originals, include a steam-engine gasbag with two cloth props, a one-of-a-kind Lincoln Beechey's 1913 "little Looper" (the first plane built for aerobatics), and the first plane to land and take off from a ship, 1911 Curtiss Pusher. Stanley Hiller, the Bay Area helicopter pioneer, is represented by several creations including a one-man flying platform and a helicopter with rotor-tip jets. Some of the airplanes are "could-have-beens" and others are futuristic. Some planes are on loan from the Smithsonian and other museums, so things will change regularly. I wouldn't mind having one of the yellow "Hiller-copters" (smaller than most cars) myself.

● NASA Ames Research Center

Moffett Field 94035. Off Highway 101. (415) 650-6274. Visitors center open Mon.–Fri., 8–4:30. Free. Closed federal holidays. Exhibits and gift shop, 10–4:30. **Ages 9 & up.** *W. www.arc.nasa.gov*

There are many artifacts on display, including wind tunnel models, a Mercury spacecraft, a moon rock, space suits, and several research aircraft. Ongoing research programs are highlighted with displays, models, and interactive computer software. The newest exhibit explores Ames's exciting astrobiology research. The exhibit included lighted scale globes of Earth, Mars, and Europa, our solar system's "water world." A collection of photographs of exotic life-forms inhabiting Earth's open oceans is on display.

Ames Aerospace Encounter, created for fourth- through sixth-graders, is a unique interactive program designed to stir young people's enthusiasm for science, math, and technology (650-604-1110).

As NASA's "Center of Excellence" for information technology, Ames conducts the cutting-edge research and development that makes NASA's aeronautics and space missions possible. Ames is also NASA's lead center for astrobiology, conducting research on the origin, evolution, distribution, and destiny of life in the universe.

● Computer History Museum

Moffett Field, Building 126, Moffett Field 94035. (650) 604-2579. Tours Wed. at 1:30; Fri. at 1 and the first and third Sat. of the month at 1 and 2. Free. By reservation. **Ages 10 & up.** *www.computerhistory.org*

Lots of human stories mingle with the tons of cold metal, miles of wire, buttons, switches, and everything else that can be expected from a museum devoted to the short history of computers. An original APPLE 1, a MITZ Altair 8800 for which Bill Gates wrote an early version of his programming language, and a computer the size of PacBell Park are just three of the fascinations on exhibit. The museum will move into a state-of-the-art building nearby in 2005.

● West Bay Model Railroad Association

1090 Merrill Street, Menlo Park 94025. (650) 322-0685. Fourth Wed. of the month, 7–10 P.M. Free. **Ages 5 & up.** *home.earthlink.net/~pesce/westbay.htm*

Three different-size trains run on the club's 2,000 feet of track, whistling past miniature towns and painted scenery and over tiny bridges and turntables. Adding to the effectiveness of the show is a tape of special sound effects interspersed with the story of how the club came about. The club also has a railroad-stationery display, a library, and a workshop. The members' special Christmas show on the second weekend in December is a favorite with local youngsters.

● Stanford University

Stanford University Campus, Stanford 94305. Highway 101 to Stanford exit. (650) 723-2300. Stanford Guide and Visitors Service, (650) 723-2560. Visitor's Information Center: Weekdays, 8–5; weekends, 9–5. Hoover Tower Observation Platform, Mon.–Sun., 10–4. Adults, $2; seniors and children, $1. **Ages 7 & up.** *www.stanford.edu/dept/ccva*

In addition to the breathtaking view from the 250-foot-high observation platform at the top of the Hoover Tower, the **Hoover Exhibit Rooms** (daily, 9–4:30) display some of the treasures collected by Herbert Hoover and his wife, Lou Henry Hoover, and document some of their remarkable accomplishments. Among the items on display are a priceless gold Peruvian mask, one of Hoover's fishing rods, a model of the Hoover Dam, Lou Henry's Stanford diploma, and the original copy of one of the earliest Soviet-American agreements (1921).

The visitors center will also provide information on the following attractions of interest to teens and older: **Stanford Linear Accelerator Center** (650-926-2204; tours by appt., free), **Jasper Ridge Biological Preserve** (650-327-2277; tours by appt., free), and **Stanford campus walking tours** (650-723-2560; Mon.–Sun., 11 and 3:15, free).

The **Iris and Gerald Cantor Center for the Visual Arts** (Lomita Drive and Museum Way, Wed.–Sun., 11–5; Thurs. to 8. Closed holidays. Free. 650-723-4177, www.stanford.edu/dept/ccva), offers 27 galleries with many different focuses, from ancient times to the present. In addition to European and American art, works from Oceania, Africa, Asia, the ancient Mediterranean, and the ancient Americas have individual galleries, as does Native American art. There are 20 Rodin sculptures. Leland Stanford Junior's collections, begun in his early teens, are particularly interesting.

● **Baylands Nature Interpretive Center**

2775 Embarcadero Road, at the eastern end, Palo Alto 94303. (650) 329-2506. Tues.–Fri., 2–5; weekends, 1–5. Free. Groups by appt. **Ages 6 & up.** *www.city.palo-alto.ca.us*

This bayside nature center is on pilings out in a salt marsh, handy for the nature walks and ecology workshops it excels in. The exhibits show local birds, plants, and a saltwater aquarium. On weekends, there are nature movies and slide shows, as well as nature and bird walks; bike tours; wildflower shows; fish, pond, and geology programs; and workshops.

● **Palo Alto Junior Museum and Zoo**

Rinconada Park, 1451 Middlefield Road, Palo Alto 94301. (650) 329-2111. Tues.–Sat., 10–5; Sun., 1–5. Free. **Ages 4 & up.** *W. www.city.palo-alto.ca.us*

This beautifully constructed museum has one major changing exhibition yearly to keep kids coming back for more. Outside, in the poured concrete shelters are snakes and reptiles, ravens, owls, bobcats, raccoons, and an evian aviary. Ducks nest under the bridge that curves over the pretty pond. The exhibition's program focuses on physical, biological, and cultural themes. Last year's "Take Shape" interactive museum included "Go Fish," a simulated pond where kids could fish out shapes and then create art.

● **Museum of American Heritage**

351 Homer Avenue, Palo Alto 94306-1731. (650) 321-1004. Fri.–Sun., 11–4. Free. Gift shop. **Ages 8 & up.** *W. www.moah.org*

Frank Livermore decided to share his love of gadgets, so he created this "celebration of mankind's technical ingenuity of the past as an inspiration for the future." Displays of machinery, appliances, and mechanical items in use during the 100 years before the advent of solid state electronics are combined with special exhibits, featuring items on topics such as automatic musical instruments, a salute to 25 years of Mattel's Hot Wheels, and 100 years of toy trains. There's a turn-of-the-century office, a '30s kitchen, and a '20s grocery store that once "lived" in Chicago. One young visitor saw a typewriter here for the first time. Another was astonished by the crystal radio set.

● Los Altos History Museum

51 South San Antonio Road, Los Altos. (650) 948-9427. Thurs.–Sun., 12–4, and by appt. Free. Archives by appt. Gift shop. **Ages 8 & up.** *W. www.losaltoshistory.org*

This 1905 farmhouse, located in one of the few surviving apricot orchards in Santa Clara Valley, depicts life on the small family-run orchards that dominated Los Altos before World War II. Both the house and surrounding grounds provide a quiet respite from today's bustle. The exhibit in the upper level of the house shows how the "Iron Horse" made the town, homesteads, a hands-on family tree, orchard life, the Ohlone, the natural landscape, and the silicon harvest. Changing collections and traveling exhibits as well as lectures and educational programs bring history alive.

● Perham Foundation Electronic Museum

Call for information, since this is scheduled to join the Keely Park group or Foothills College in San Jose, (408) 734-4453. www.perham.org

Based on a private collection started in 1893 by six-year-old Douglas Perham, this is the most extensive display of early electrical and electronic devices in the West. Young scientists will be intrigued by exhibits of the first radio broadcast station, the first Silicon Valley electronics firm, the first TV picture tube (invented by Philo Farnsworth in San Francisco), a 10-foot robot, and hands-on demonstrations of electricity and magnetism.

● Sunnyvale Historical Museum

235 East California Avenue, at Sunnyvale Avenue (Mail: P.O. Box 61301), Sunnyvale 94088. (408) 749-0220. Tues. and Thurs., 12–4:30; Sun., 1–4, and by appt. Free. **Ages 8 & up.** *www.sunnyvalesun.com*

This one-room regional museum, set in Martin Murphy Jr. Park, captures the past with artifacts and pictures of area pioneers, the first wagon train to cross the Sierra and the Martin Murphy family, who acquired their land grant from the Castro family. Sunnyvale's history is also presented, including the orchard industry and the beginnings of the city.

● California History Center

De Anza College, 21250 Stevens Creek Boulevard, Cupertino 95014. (408) 864-8712. Mon.–Thurs., 9–12 and 1–4:30; closed July and Aug. Free. Parking fee on campus. Group tours by appt. **Ages 8 & up.** *www.calhistory.org*

Changing exhibits—from "First Californians" to "The Chinese in the Monterey Bay Area" to "Hard Rock Gold Mining"—explore California's rich and varied history. This living-history museum is housed in the restored Le Petit Trianon, the original house on De Anza land. Visitors may tour this elegant Louis XVI mansion and surrounding garden area with a pavilion reminiscent of Versailles.

● Minolta Planetarium

De Anza College, 21250 Stevens Creek Boulevard at Highway 85, Cupertino 95014. (408) 864-8814. Call for times and prices, since they change with each class session. Birthday parties, field trips, events. Gift shop. **All ages.** *W. www.planetarium.deanza.fhda.edu/pltwww/ghome.html*

The Minolta Planetarium uses a variety of audiovisual equipment to transport visitors into space to see the planets, stars, galaxies, and other celestial wonders. The main projector spreads the night sky across the 50-foot dome, the largest on any college or university this side of the Rocky Mountains. With 6,500 projected stars, down to the naked-eye limit, the night sky is truly awesome. Special effects and video projectors add interest and excitement to the experience. More than a dozen different star shows are available for viewing for all age groups.

● Hakone Japanese Gardens

21000 Big Basin Way (Mail: P.O. Box 2324), Saratoga 95070. (408) 741-4994. Mon.–Fri., 10–5; weekends, 11–5. Closed Christmas and New Year's. Parking: $5; free on Tues. Donation. Events and classes. Gift Shop. Children under 10 must take an adult. Tours for children, 25¢ per child. **Ages 6 & up.** *www.hakone.com*

Walk along curving foliage-lined paths, pass through a wisteria-roofed arbor, and step on three stones to cross a stream next to three waterfalls. Climb a moon bridge to see the goldfish. Discover a moon-viewing house and gazebos hidden in the trees. Spy stone and wooden lanterns and statues of cranes and cats hidden in the flowers. This wonderful garden was designed by a former court gardener to the emperor of Japan as a hill and water garden. The strolling pond style is typical of Zen gardens in the 17th century. The teahouse is open by appointment. Picnic tables are available.

● Villa Montalvo

Saratoga–Los Gatos Road, Saratoga 95070. (408) 741-3421. The hours for the arboretum, galleries, and park vary from day to day, depending on the

performance schedule and season, so please call before planning an outing. Free.
All ages. *www.villamontalvo.com*

Nature trails traverse a redwood grove, hills and meadows, and flower-covered arbors in this arboretum. The villa's grounds are also a bird sanctuary for more than 60 species of birds. The villa takes its name from a 16th-century Spanish author, García Ordóñez de Montalvo, who wrote a novel describing a tribe of Amazons living in a fabulous island paradise named "California." The Amazons rode on gryphons, and the many stone gryphons on the grounds will entrance youngsters. Music, dance, and other performing arts events, many geared for children, such as storytelling, puppetry, and children's ballet performances, are scheduled throughout the year. The villa also hosts Environmental Volunteers classes in the spring and a performing arts camp each summer.

● **Billy Jones Wildcat Railroad and Carousel**
Oak Meadow Park, Los Gatos. For tours and special runs, write to P.O. Box 234, Los Gatos 95031. (408) 395-RIDE. Spring and fall: Sat. and Sun., 10:30–4:30; daily in summer. Under 2 with an adult, free; others, $1. **Ages 4 & up.** *www.BJWRR.org*

"Old No. 2," a full-steam 18-inch gauge prairie-type locomotive, toots along a mile-long track pulling four open cars. The water tank, a necessity when operating a steam railroad, was designed and built by volunteers, as were the turntable, station, and engine house. Painted in Southern Pacific's "Black Widow" color scheme of black, orange, red, and silver, the "2502" has an interesting history as the newest member of the Billy Jones motive power fleet.

Volunteers restored the William E. "Bill" Mason Carousel and created the building to house it. The carousel is an English 1910 Savage roundabout shipped around the Horn to San Francisco for the 1915 Panama-Pacific exhibition. Twenty-nine hand-carved wooden horses and two chariots ride clockwise, along with five C. W. Parker, two Dare, and two Armitage-Herschel horses installed to replace missing horses. The replicated Wurlitzer organ adds to the fun.

● **The Museums of Los Gatos**
4 Tait Avenue, at Main Street (Mail: P.O. Box 1904), Los Gatos 95031. (408) 354-2646. Wed.–Sun., 12–4. Free. **Ages 8 & up.** *W.*
www.los-gatos.org/main/museums.html

The Museums of Los Gatos share what was once the town firehouse. There are changing art shows (including at least one show of children's art each year) on the main floor. The basement offers a grand collection of insects, birds, rocks, and other natural history specimens, including a "touch table" of unusual natural objects. Check the baleen whale exhibit, an American bald eagle, and a display of cinnabar from California's first quicksilver mines, essential for mining gold.

Across the park, past the fountain, is the History Museum of Los Gatos, Forbes Mill, 75 Church Street. (408) 395-7375. Wed.–Sun., 12–4, and by appt. Free. **Ages 8 & up.** W.

The storage room for a flour mill built in 1854 and 1881 has been transformed into a small museum of Los Gatos history. Amid local school artifacts, desks, and books, the display of "Mountain Charlie," who battled grizzly bears, is a favorite.

● Hidden Villa

26870 Moody Road, Los Altos Hills 94022. (650) 949-8650. Daily except Mon., 9–dusk. Closed during summer camp. Environmental education program, farm and garden tours, performances, summer programs, and individualized tours by appt. Rustic hostel accommodations for those wishing to experience the charm of country living. Call for schedule and prices. $5 parking fee. **All ages.** *www.hiddenvilla.org*

Hidden Villa's 1,600-acre wilderness preserve is relatively unchanged since the days when Ohlone Indians gathered food from its hillsides and took fish from its creeks. A self-guiding tour of the farm area is available, as are four suggested wilderness treks. Visitors can picnic, visit a working organic garden, and see the farm animals. Deanna Fale, who told us about Hidden Villa, wrote, "The preschool tour we took at Hidden Villa was wonderful. The children smelled bay leaves, basil, etc. They held a newly hatched egg. Petted a ewe about to give birth. The guides are knowledgeable and gear their talks to the various age groups. The one-hour tour for 4-year-olds was just about right."

● Campbell Historical Museum

51 North Central Avenue, at Civic Center Drive, Campbell 95008. (408) 866-2119. Thurs.–Sun., 12–4. Adults, $4; seniors, $3; ages 7–17, $2.50. Gift store. **Ages 7 & up.** *W. www.cityofcampbell.com*

Explore the rich historical past of the Santa Clara Valley at the Campbell Historical Museum. Changing exhibits about home life, recreation, work, and community provide insights into the daily life of others who have traveled here before us. Experience unique hands-on features at each exhibit that will engage and intrigue. Examine treasured artifacts such as uniforms, clothing, photos, and a fire truck that help tell the story of who we are today. Videos of Campbell's history are available.

● Ainsley House

300 Grant Street, between the Campbell City Hall and Library, Campbell 95008. (408) 866-2119. Thurs.–Sun., 12–4, Mar.–Dec. **Ages 8 & up.** *W on first floor. www.cityofcampbell.com*

Docent-led tours of this exquisitely restored 1925 Tudor Revival historic house museum, the home of former canning industry pioneer J. C. Ainsley and his wife, Alcinda, feature life in the Santa Clara Valley in the 1920s and 1930s. (Tours every 30 minutes; adults, $6; seniors, $4; children 7–17, $2.50; members and children under 12, free.)

● Mission Santa Clara de Asis

Santa Clara University, 500 El Camino Real, Santa Clara 95053-3217. (408) 544-4000. Daily, 8–5. Free. **Ages 7 & up.** *W. www.scu.edu*

Founded in 1777 and now part of the university campus, the present mission is a replica of the third building raised on this site by the mission fathers. An adobe wall from the original cloister still stands in the peaceful garden. The original cross of the mission stands in front of the church, and the bell given by the king of Spain in 1778 still tolls.

The **De Saisset Museum** (Tues.–Sun., 11–4. 408-554-4528. www.scu.edu/deSaisset) is on campus and makes an interesting brief stop. There are changing art and cultural exhibits. In the basement is a display of artifacts from the Mission era and the early founding of Santa Clara University.

● Intel Museum

2200 Mission College Boulevard, Santa Clara 95052. (408) 765-0503. Mon.–Fri., 9–5; Sat., 10–5 except holidays. Guided tours by appt. Free. Gift store. **Ages 8 & up.** *W. www.intel.com/intel/intelis/museum*

What's a microprocessor? A semiconductor? A megabyte? Discover the answers at the home of the world's largest computer chip manufacturer. The hands-on exhibits teach how electronic chips are created from silicon, the primary component of sand. Get a look at how computers do what they do, see how chips are constructed, and learn how video and computer come together in changing exhibits that give a better understanding of the industry that gave Silicon Valley its name. Visitors may experience the latest generation of computers by playing games like "Chaos Island" and "I Spy." Closed-circuit TVs monitor workers in the Intel plant actually making chips in "clean rooms."

● Great America

4701 Great America Parkway, off Highway 101 (Mail: P.O. Box 1776), Santa Clara 95054. (408) 988-1776. Spring and fall weekends and daily in summer, 10–8; later on Saturdays and holiday weekends. Scream Factory Halloween October weekends, 6 to midnight. Ages 7–59, $45.99; ages 3–6 and under 48 inches tall, $33.99; seniors, $39.99. Concerts. Parking, $10. Season pass (regardless of age): $64.99 for individuals, $54.99 for each person in a "family 4-pack." Free parking. Group rates available. Paramount's Great America and through BASS/TM outlets. **Ages 5 & up.** *W. www.pgathrills.com*

Billed as Northern California's most thrilling theme park, Paramount's Great America is also the "screamingest!" There are more than 50 rides and attractions. Ride Delirium, spinning and twirling as it swings 65 feet in the air, or pilot your own vehicle through the sky on Flying Eagles. Two new Nickelodeon characters, Jimmy Neutron: Boy Genius and Nick Jr.'s Dora the Explorer are on hand. Events and concerts are free with park admission. There are also more than 20 family rides and attractions, from Rugrats and Blue from Blue's Clues, to Yogi Bear and Scooby Doo. Older kids will dare to ride Stealth, the world's first flying coaster, experiencing flight without floors, ceilings or walls. And the youngest will be happy to Slime it up with SpongeBob Squarepants. Be sure to bring a second set of clothing—the water rides are irresistible.

● Children's Discovery Museum
180 Woz Way, San Jose 95110. (408) 298-5437. Tues.–Sat., 10–5; Sun., 12–5. Open holiday Mondays. Ages 1–59, $7; seniors, $6; members, free. Theater specials, storytelling, and programs. Groups by appt. (408) 298-5437 ext. 259. Gift shop. Café. **Ages 1–12.** *W. www.cdm.org*

The purple-angled Children's Discovery Museum is fun inside and out. Spectacular hands-on exhibits and games capture the imagination of pre- and grade-schoolers instantly. Here they can don helmets and climb behind the wheel of a real fire truck or an old Ford. Or slide down a culvert and clamber through sewer pipes "under the city." In Waterworks, children pump pedals and spin big screws to transport water from one level to another. Alice in Wonderland leads kids down the Rabbit Hole and helps them create a Mad Tea Party and play Crazy Croquet. Youngsters can enter an Ohlone hut, make tortillas and adobe bricks, and do farm chores, while learning about the layers of history in their world. The Doodad Dump beckons inventors to glue together infinite varieties of thingamajigs. The museum specializes in creative physical and fantasy play. Our favorite is "Bubbalonga"—especially the bubble-stretcher.

● Tech Museum of Innovation
205 South Market Street, San Jose 95113. (408) 274-TECH. Nov.–Mar., Tues.–Sun., 10–5; Apr.–Oct., daily, 10–5. Adults, $9; ages 3–12, $7; seniors, $8. Gift shop. Café. Lectures, programs, classes. Groups and evening rentals: (408) 795-6101. **Ages 3 & up.** *W. www.thetech.org*

The Tech Museum is a hands-on science and technology museum engaging people of all ages and backgrounds to explore and experience technology and inspire the innovator in everyone. Enter the doors of the Tech and you'll be dazzled by a blaze of color, excitement, and energy. This is an inviting, mind-and-hands-on kind of place. Through 250 engaging interactive exhibits you can experiment with the latest in technology and achieve your own sudden flashes of insight and creativity. Can you be a bumblebee?

Design your own roller-coaster and then ride it, too. Try out the jet pack simulator. Create a multimedia video with yourself as a superhero, or test a modern racing wheelchair. Communication, exploration, innovation, and life tech are the four major themes. Exhibits change regularly. We were particularly taken with the one that examined the evolution of reading, from papyrus to pixels. And the virtual bobsled. The Imagination Playground encourages creative play in a high-tech world with machines, videos, and a ToyTech room.

One youngster wrote, "I have learned a lot about science thanks to the Tech Museum." Another said, "When people hear the word museum, they think of some boring place, but the Tech Museum is the exact opposite."

● San Jose Museum of Quilts and Textiles

110 Paseo de San Antonio, San Jose 95112. (408) 971-0323. Tues.–Sun., 10–5; Thurs. until 8 P.M. First Thurs. of the month, free. Adults, $4; seniors and students, $3; under 12, free. Store. **Ages 10 & up.** *W. www.sjquiltmuseum.org*

This is the first museum in the United States dedicated to the exhibition, preservation, and study of quilts. Changing shows include historical, traditional, and contemporary quilts and other fiber arts from around the world. Children's programs may be scheduled.

● San Jose Museum of Art

110 South Market Street, San Jose 95110. (408) 294-2787. Tues.–Sun., 11–5; Fri., 11–10. Closed holidays. Free. Tours daily at 12:30 and 2:30, plus 6:30 on Fridays. Café. Gift shop. **Ages 8 & up.** *www.sanjosemuseumofart.org*

The San Jose Museum of Art offers changing exhibits of 20th- and 21st-century art, including painting, sculpture, works on paper, photography, video, and mixed media. The last Sunday of every month is Kids ArtSunday, 11–3, free. Join families in a day of museum fun and learning. The museum's education department presents a stimulating range of hands-on art workshops, performances, gallery tours, and other activities designed to make the artwork on view accessible to young audiences. One adult must accompany the children.

● BamBoola

5401 Camden Avenue, San Jose 95124. (408) 448-4FUN. Tues., 10–5; Wed.–Sat., 10–9; Sun., 10–6. Adults, free; 3–12, $9.95; ages 2 and 3, $4.95. Parties by reservation. Pretend Village. Passes and discounts. Ice Cream Corner. Groups. **Ages 4–11.** *W. www.bamboola.com*

This "edutainment" center, an island of play, discovery, and fun, is geared toward hands-on learning. There's an interactive maze, a pretend village, sand and water play, a climbing rock, a dinosaur dig, arts-and-crafts classes, an outdoor jungle garden, interactive cooking, and face painting. Grandma's Attic features a treehouse, a reading nook, dress-up, and puppet play.

● **Peralta Adobe and Fallon House Historic Site**
175 West St. John Street, at San Pedro, San Jose 95110. (408) 993-8182. Weekends, 12–5. Guided tours, weekdays, by appt. Adults, $6; seniors, $5; ages 6–17; $4. **Ages 8 & up.** *www.historysanjox.com*
Built in 1797, the Peralta Adobe is San Jose's oldest structure. It is furnished with period pieces and artifacts that help to interpret the early pueblo lifestyle. The *recamara,* or bedroom, is furnished as it might have been in 1800; the *sala,* or living room, looks as it might have in 1860.

The Fallon House next door, built in 1855, was the opulent home of one of San Jose's most charismatic mayors, Thomas Fallon. The house's 15 rooms are fully furnished in the Victorian style of the 1860s. Together, the site offers a unique look into San Jose's historic past.

● **Rosicrucian Egyptian Museum**
Rosicrucian Park, 1342 Naglee Avenue, at Park, San Jose 95191. (408) 947-3636. Tues.–Fri., 10–5; weekends, 11–6. Adults, $9; seniors and students, $7; ages 5–10, $5; under 5, free. $5 extra for guided tour. Guided Tomb Tour for an additional $2. Call to schedule during the week: (408) 947-3665. Groups and rentals: (408) 947-3632. Closed Thanksgiving, Christmas, and New Year's Day. Gift shop. **Ages 6 & up.**
www.rosicrucian.org
The wonderful, faraway world of ancient Egypt awaits to mystify and enchant you in an amazingly large and varied collection. Egyptian mummies, sculpture, paintings, jewelry, cosmetics, scarabs, scrolls, and amulets are here in abundance. The ornate coffins, mummified cats and falcons, and descriptions of the embalming process are totally absorbing—especially to youngsters, who want to know how old everything is. You can see boats that take the dead to the next world, makeup, and hairpins. Sumerian clay tablets, a model of the Tower of Babel, and a walk-through replica of an Egyptian noble's tomb vie for your attention.

Videos tell of the discovery of King Tut's tomb, the Pyramids, and other subjects. This is the only museum in America that is of authentic Egyptian design, and it houses the largest public collection of Egyptian artifacts west of the Mississippi. One fourth-grader wrote, "I loved your museum. My favorite display case was the open mummy and the coffin with scribbles instead of hieroglyphs. I liked the model tomb, the sarcophagus was really neat. I liked the fake Rosetta Stone and the movie. The cartouches were neat, too. I got one."

● **Winchester Mystery House**

525 South Winchester Boulevard, between Stevens Creek Boulevard and Interstate 280, San Jose 95128. (408) 247-2101. One-hour tours daily except Christmas: 9–5 in winter; 9–7 in summer. Adults, $16.95; seniors, $13.95; ages 6–12, $10.95. Reduced group tour and catering rates by reservation: (408) 247-2000. Flashlight tours on Friday the 13th and Halloween Evening tours. Birthday packages available. Café. Gift shop.
Ages 7 & up. *www.winchestermysteryhouse.com*

Sarah Winchester, widow of the Winchester Rifle heir, was told that as long as she kept building something, she'd never die. So for 38 years, carpenters worked 24 hours a day to build this 160-room mansion filled with mysteries. Doorways open to blank walls, secret passageways twist around, and the number 13 appears everywhere—13-stepped stairways, 13 bathrooms, ceilings with 13 panels, rooms with 13 windows—all in the finest woods and crystals money could buy. The Tiffany window with spiders and 13 stars is gorgeous. Thirteen stately palms line the main driveway.

A self-guided tour of the Victorian Gardens, the Winchester Historical Firearms Museum, and the Antique Products Museum is included in the tour price. In tribute to Mrs. Winchester's fascination with the number 13, celebrity "bell ringers" sound the old tower bell 13 times at 13:00 hours every Friday the 13th and July 4th.

● **History San Jose**

1650 Senter Road, San Jose 95112. Kelley Park at Senter Road. (408) 287-2290. Tues.–Sun., 12–5. Free Tues.–Fri., when most buildings are closed. Adults, $6; ages 6–17, $4; seniors, $5. Group rates, by appt. Party and picnic facilities. Gift shop. Cafés. **Ages 6 & up.** *W. www.historysanjose.org*

Reconstructed and restored landmarks bring to life the look and feel of late-19th-century San Jose in this 14-acre complex with 28 restored and replicated buildings. Walk around the plaza or ride the trolley and visit O'Brien's candy store, in 1878 the first place to serve ice cream sodas west of Detroit. Inspect the print shop, the 1880s Pacific Hotel, Dashaway stables, the 115-foot electric light tower, the Ng Shing Gung Temple, the Empire firehouse, a 1927 gas station, the Trolley Barn, Coyote post office, Steven's Ranch fruit barn, H. H. Warburton's doctor's office, and the 1909 Bank of Italy building. The many Victorian homes have been saved and moved to museum premises, including poet Edwin Markham's Greek Revival home. Our favorite is the little Umbarger House, a delicious orange and ochre 1870s "Painted Lady" gingerbread confection that has been completely furnished, right down to the clothes in the closets and the dishes in the sink. The Imperio is a replica of a 1915 chapel where Holy Ghost festivals were held by the Portuguese community. Letters, photographs, diaries, artwork, cookbooks, historical artifacts, and Holy Ghost costumes celebrate the Portuguese culture.

● Japanese Friendship Tea Garden

1300 Senter Road, Kelley Park, San Jose 95112. (408) 277-5254. Daily, 10–sunset. Free. Parking fee, $5. **Ages 5 & up.** *www.niwa.org*

This tranquil garden is patterned after the Korakuen garden in San Jose's sister city of Okayama. The three lakes are designed to symbolize the word *kokoro,* which means "heart-mind-and-soul." Picturesque bridges and waterfalls, shaped rocks and trees, and land and water flowers are wonderful to wander around. Naturally, the children will head over to watch the families of koi, fat gold, white, or black carp, which come when dinner is offered. Stop at Stop #13 to read the Haiku poem on the stone marker:

I've changed my dwelling
To bathe in Summer coolness
So tranquil, so calm.

● Happy Hollow Park and Zoo

1300 Senter Road, Kelley Park, San Jose 95112. (408) 277-3000. Open daily; call for hours and fees. Advance group reservations available. Parking fee, $5. Parties. **Ages 2–12.** *W. www.happyhollowparkandzoo.org*

Enjoy Danny the Dragon as he prowls through a bamboo forest, or listen as a chorus of sea animals invites you to enter Neptune's kingdom. Climb a stairway in the Crooked House and slide down a spiral slide. Visit the many play areas dotting the park, and view a puppet show at the puppet castle theater. The zoo offers youngsters a chance to see exotic animals from all over the world. They can cuddle a baby goat or pet a baby llama.

● Raging Waters

2333 South White Road, San Jose 95148. Capital Expressway and Tully in Lake Cunningham Regional Park. (408) 238-9900. Daily, June 14– August 27. Weekends, spring, and fall days; hours vary. Admission, $24.95; children under 48 inches tall, $19.99. Snack bars. Shops. **Ages 4 & up.** *www.rwsplash.com*

The San Francisco Bay Area's largest water park features 23 acres of slides and attractions for the whole family including a 350,000-gallon wave pool and an interactive water fort. Lather up with sunblock and get ready to ride the high-intensity water thrill rides such as the Great White Shark or the Barracuda Blaster—500 feet of splashy twists and high banking turns. Fly on a seven-story speed slide (there are 30 slides!) or zip down a Shotgun waterfall. Younger kids will love to splash around in the Wacky Water Works 350,000-gallon freshwater wave pool or climb on the structure at Pirate Island designed for super waterfights.

● Youth Science Institute—Vasona Nature Center

296 Garden Hill Drive, Los Gatos 95032. Vasona County Park, off Blossom Hill Road. (408) 356-4945. Mon.–Fri., 9–4:30; weekends, 12–4:30. Free. Parking fee, $4. Groups. Events. Picnic facilities. **All ages.** *www/ysi-ca.org/vasona/vshome.html*

The Vasona Nature Center is a junior museum focusing on aquatic life and water ecology. Live animals on display include fish, reptiles, and amphibians; other exhibits show fossils and dinosaurs. School and community children's science classes are taught at the center. The Viola Anderson Native Plant Trail winds past the center and overlooks Vasona Lake.

● Youth Science Institute—Nature Center in Sanborn Park

16055 Sanborn Road, Saratoga 95070. Sanborn-Skyline County Park, off Highway 9. (408) 867-6940. Tues.–Fri., 9–4:30; weekends, 12–4:30. Parking fee, $4. Classes. Picnic tables and hiking trails. **Ages 7 & up.** *www.ysi-ca.org/sanborn/sbhome.html*

Located in the beautiful Santa Cruz Mountains, YSI's Nature Center in Sanborn Park is a junior museum located in a redwood forest, so there are natural history displays on the redwood forest. Chaparral, oak woodland, and riparian habitats exist in the park and are explained in the center. Exhibits include live animals from the Santa Cruz Range, earthquake and geology displays, an insect zoo, and a garden of native plants and plants used by Native Americans. The famous San Andreas Fault runs directly through the park. Fourth-grader Christine wrote, "I liked the hike and the games the Indians played. I like making the cattail rope and grinding the acorns. I had fun on the field trip."

● Youth Science Institute—Alum Rock Park

16260 Alum Rock Avenue, San Jose 95127. Alum Rock Park, off Highway 680. (408) 258-4322. Tues.–Sat., 12–4:30; Sun., between Easter and Labor Day, 12–4:30. Adults, 50¢; children, 25¢. Parking fee, $4. **Ages 7 & up.** *www.ysi-ca.org/alumrock.arhome.html*

YSI's Nature Center has exhibits of the animals that populate the Mount Hamilton Range in which it is located. Birds of prey such as hawks and owls that have been injured and are nonreleasable have found a home here, and they work hard as part of YSI's school programs. The Holmes bird collection from the early part of the century contains some birds that are now extinct.

Information on a self-guided geology trail may be obtained at YSI, and a hands-on activity table is always available, with an ever-changing number of activities. One visiting schoolchild wrote, "I learned about the cycle. I made some paper out of recycle paper. I saw some bats that are dead. I saw a gopher snake. I saw a bullfrog. I saw an alligator lizard. I saw a Western toad."

● New Almaden Quicksilver Mining Museum

21350 Almaden Road (Mail: P.O. Box 124), San Jose 95120. (408) 323-1107. Fri., 12–4; weekends, 10–4, and by appt. Guided hikes of the 4,000 surrounding acres dotted with historic buildings. Gift shop. Free. **Ages 7 & up.** *www.parkhere.org/historical/history_almaden.html*

Step into the world of a 19th-century boomtown in this little museum (once a hotel, then living quarters for the third mining manager) tracing the history of the area's quicksilver, or mercury, mines, once the most productive in the world. Photographs of miners from China, Europe, and Mexico and Central America share space with exhibits on how quicksilver was extracted from the ground to be used in thermometers. Also see the mining artifacts gathered by Constance Perham, who as a young girl accompanied her father on trips to the mines.

See how cinnabar, mercury's red ore, was carved into jewelry and mixed with the resin of the lack tree to make the lacquer so popular in the East. The Ohlones also used the red ore for festivals, fiestas, and barter, so there are exhibits from the earliest natives, drawing from the Ohlones and artifacts from the many people who've lived here over the centuries. Kids especially like seeing the Randall Room, a representation of a manager's office.

● Gilroy Historical Museum

195 5th Street, at Church Street, Gilroy 95020. (408) 848-0470. Mon., Tues., Thurs., Fri., 10–5; Sat., 10–2. Tours by appt.; closed holidays. Donation. **Ages 8 & up.** *www.ci.gilroy.ca.us*

Telephones, tools, and toys are just part of this collection of more than 22,000 donated memories from Gilroy's pioneer families. A cigar-store Indian, a school desk, and Ohlone clothing and artifacts are kids' favorites. Rotating exhibits emphasize the tobacco industry that was important in the building of the town, which once was home to the world's largest cigar factory, and to Henry Miller, the local cattle king. Today, it's garlic that's king in Gilroy.

● Bonfante Gardens Theme Park

3050 Hecker Pass Highway, Gilroy 95020. (408) 840-7100. Daily in summer: Mon.–Thurs., 10–8. Fri., Sat., and Sun., 10–9. Winter weekends, 11–8. Adults, $29.95; ages 3–12, $19.95; 65 plus, $23.95. Parking, $7. Cafés. Shops. **All ages.** *W. www.bonfantegardens.com*

This first horticulturally inspired theme park is more "ooh-aah" than shriek. A lovely lake with paddleboats centers 75 acres of rides, theme gardens, food concessions, an event plaza, and some very unusual trees. Twenty-five one-of-a-kind Circus Trees, some more than 50 years old, were rescued from a Tree Circus in Scotts Valley. The Monarch Garden is a greenhouse so large that a train, a monorail, and a river run through it. The rock maze changes every day. And Rainbow Garden is a boat ride through colorful plantings.

The 1927 Illions Supreme Carousel has been painstakingly restored to its original beauty. The "splash and squirt program" and "pitch and win" carnival games (everybody wins!) and theater programs are fun, but one of the things that sets this park apart are the four learning sheds with informational videos on the trees and world around us.

● Lick Observatory

Highway 130, 25 miles southeast of San Jose, Mt. Hamilton 95140. (408) 274-5061. Gallery, weekdays, 12:30–5; weekends, 10–5 except holidays. Fifteen-minute talks on the half hour start at 1 on weekdays and 10:30 on weekends. Gift store. Free. **Ages 8 & up.** *www.UCOlick.org*

A long, narrow, winding road takes you to the top of Mt. Hamilton and the awesome domes of Lick Observatory. It was here that four of the satellites of Jupiter were discovered—the first since the time of Galileo. Now star clusters and galaxies are studied with the most modern equipment. The visitors gallery looks up at one of the largest telescopes (120 inches) in the world, the Shane reflecting telescope. The tour of photos and astronomical instruments is intriguing and educational. The gallery is half a mile from the visitors center. Call (408) 274-5061 for travel conditions and public program information. Since it's 4,200 feet high, snow is possible. And remember, there are no food or gas facilities nearby.

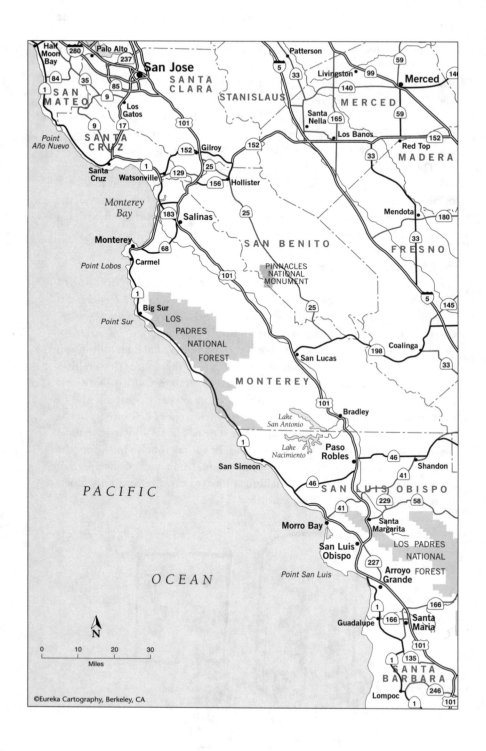

Heading South by the Sea

Driving down the coast from San Francisco, curving next to cliffs that head down to the sea, can be breathtaking. If you're driving from San Francisco to Monterey, we suggest you spend the night there before heading back. Getting to and from Santa Cruz is easier. And if you want to make a short stop or two on the way, Half Moon Bay is a sweet town for walking, and Capitola offers a trifecta of Capitola Wharf, one of best city beaches in the Bay Area (just east of the pier), and Gayle's Bakery and Rosticceria (504 Bay Avenue, 831-462-1200, www.gaylesbakery.com) for fabulous breakfasts, pastries, and Italian deli and the town's beachside pastel buildings and shops.

Twenty-seven miles south of Half Moon Bay on Highway 1 is Año Nuevo State Reserve, the home of a large colony of northern elephant seals. Call (650) 879-0227 or (650) 879-2025 for information and weather conditions.

● Capitola Historical Museum

410 Capitola Avenue, Capitola 95010. (831) 464-0322. Fri.–Sun., 12–4, and by appt. Donation. **Ages 8 & up.** *W. www.capitolamuseum.org*

Founded in 1966, the Capitola Historical Museum encompasses the history of the town from its founding as Camp Capitola through its transition to today's busy city-by-the-sea. Changing themed exhibits regularly include those mounted in cooperation with the Capitola Arts Commission and other local groups. Exhibits can range from historical clothing, the Capitola flower industry, to the history of the area through postcards.

■ The Santa Cruz Area

The Santa Cruz area is small, nestled on a bay southwest of San Jose and north of Monterey. Big Basin Redwoods, Natural Bridges (both have visitors centers with exhibits), and Loch Lomond parks are some of the natural sites of interest. Along with Castroville, home of the artichoke, they are perfect day trips from San Francisco. At Wilder Beach State Park, volunteers in period costume operate farm machinery and guide visitors through the Wilder home, furnished as it was at the turn of the century (weekends, 408-426-0505).

Here you can find bird-watching, butterfly watching, whale watching, herb and heritage walks, and walks that focus on sea and sky. In Santa Cruz, beaches are the main attraction. And the surf is dotted with wet-suited surfers. If you're coming from San Francisco, be sure to take along car games to while away the two-hour ride. Highway 1, along the coast, is more beautiful and easier to drive than the faster choice, Highways 101 and 17.

● Davenport Jail Museum

2 Davenport Avenue, Davenport 95017. (831) 425-8115.

At this writing the jail is closed for restoration in a joint effort of the Davenport Resource Center and Santa Cruz's Museum of Art and History, so call for times and prices.

● Roaring Camp Railroads

(Mail: P.O. Box G-1, Felton 95018) Take Highway 17 to the Mt. Hermon Road exit in Scotts Valley, then drive west 3.5 miles to the end of the road at Felton, and left onto Graham Hill Road. (831) 335-4484. Parking, $5. Roaring Camp steam train round-trip fares: ages 3–12, $10; over 12, $15.50. For beach trains, add $1.50. For Moonlight Steam Parties and groups, call for rates. Call for schedules. Shops. Café. Events throughout the year include model railroad exhibits, free, and rides in a 15-inch model train. **Ages 5 & up.** *www.roaringcamp.com*

Young and old-time train buffs now have two fabulous train rides to choose from, both originating at Roaring Camp. Great steam locomotives hiss and puff through the redwoods on the steepest narrow-gauge railroad grade in North America and around the tightest turns to the top of Big Mountain. The 1¼-hour trip transports riders back 100 years.

On the two-hour "Beach Train" between Roaring Camp and the Santa Cruz beaches, passengers ride in historic 1902 wooden and 1926 steel passenger cars and open vista cars pulled by early diesel locomotives, round trip or one way. Back in Roaring Camp, you can explore an 1880s logging town, wander along nature trails, rest beside an 1840s covered bridge, chow down at the Chuck Wagon Bar-B-Cue, participate in reenactments, gold panning, candle making, and on summer weekends, enjoy country-and-western music and melodramas.

● Santa Cruz Surfing Museum

Lighthouse Point, West Cliff Drive (Mail: 1305 East Cliff Drive), Santa Cruz 95062. (831) 420-6289. Wed.–Mon., 12–4. Donation. Gift store. **Ages 8 & up.** *W. www.cruzio.com*

The Santa Cruz Surfing Museum, the first surfing museum on the planet, is located in the Mark Abbott Memorial Lighthouse on Lighthouse Point, overlooking "Steamer Lane," the best surfboard inlet in the area. On display are photographs, surfboards, and other surfing memorabilia tracing more than 50 years of surfing in the Santa Cruz area. Kids over 10 love watching the continuous videos and delight in the board that's been nibbled on by a shark.

Santa Cruz Harbor Light, "Walton Lighthouse," perched at the end of a rock jetty at the entrance to Santa Cruz Harbor is brand new, created by the community. The 350,000-pound, 42-foot-tall tower is white with a red stripe beneath the railing, with a copper roof and finials. (Call the Santa Cruz County Conference and Visitors Center [CVC] for information at 800-833-3494/831-425-1234. www.santacruz.org)

● Seymour Marine Discovery Center

100 Shaffer Road, at the end of Delaware Avenue, near Natural Bridges State Park, Institute of Marine Sciences, UC Santa Cruz, Santa Cruz 95060. (831) 459-3800. Tues.–Sat., 10–5; Sun., 12–5. Adults, $5; students, 6–16, and seniors, $3; 5 and under, free. Group tours by appt. First Tues. of the month, free. Special programs, cruises, and discovery tours. Gift and book shop. **Ages 7 & up.** *W. www2.ucsc.edu/seymourcenter*

The Seymour Marine Discovery Center is Long Marine Lab's visitor education hub at UC Santa Cruz. Here kids can explore the marine life of Monterey Bay. Enjoy exhibit halls, aquaria, a seawater table, and unsurpassed vistas of the marine sanctuary. They can hold a sea star, marvel at an 87-foot blue whale skeleton, and learn to think like scientists. While educating people about the role scientific research plays in the understanding and conservation of the world's oceans, the center gives children an inside look at the workings of a world-class marine research laboratory.

● Mystery Spot

465 Mystery Spot Road (Mail: 74 River Street, Suite 209) Santa Cruz 95060. (831) 423-8897. Guided tours daily, 9–5 in winter; until 7 in

summer. Adults, $5; under 11, $3. Group rates available. **Ages 5 & up.** *W.*
www.mysteryspot.com

All the laws of gravity are challenged in this scary natural curiosity. Balls
roll uphill, the trees can't stand up straight, and you always seem to be
standing either backwards or sideways. One test here is to lay a carpenter's
level across two cement blocks, checking to see that their tops are on the same
level. Then stand on one and see your friend on the other suddenly shrink or
grow tall. You can also walk up the walls of a cabin that looks cockeyed, but
isn't. Alice in Wonderland's caterpillar would feel right at home.

● Santa Cruz Beach Boardwalk

400 Beach Street, at Riverside Avenue, Santa Cruz 95060. (831) 423-
5590. Weekends and holidays, 11–5 or 6; closed Christmas. From Memorial
Day to Labor Day, the park is open daily, 11–5, 7, or 10 P.M., depending on
the weather (hours: 831-426-7433). Package tickets for 60 individual rides,
$23.95; individual rides, $1.20–3.60. Group rates, by reservation. General
admission, free. Free off-site picnic tables. Free wheelchairs to borrow. Bike locks,
$5 a day. Birthday parties with Captain Ned and Seaweed the parrot by
appt. Free Friday night concerts in summer. **All ages.** *W.*
www.beachboardwalk.com

The 1924 Giant Dipper, one of the world's top 10 roller coasters, and the
classic 1911 Looff Carousel, with 72 hand-carved wooden horses, are both
magnets for kids at California's only remaining amusement park on the
beach. The last of the old-time West Coast boardwalks, Santa Cruz has
everything you hope to find on one: a Ferris wheel, bumper cars, skee ball, a
huge video arcade with laser tag, pinball and interactive games, cotton candy,
garlic fries, and sweet and scary rides—including the steel Hurricane roller
coaster and the Wave Jammer.

The **Neptune's Kingdom** entertainment complex (free admission, year
round; 831-426-7433) is a two-story treasure island of fun, with theme
miniature golf, family pool tables, air hockey, and "foos ball," as well as a
state-of-the-art video complex and a "historium" display of historical
photos. The **Casino Fun Center** (free admission, year-round; 831-426-
7433) beckons with a Sector 7 Laser Tag arena, a fantasyscope maze of black
light, Virtualink virtual reality play center, and the Daytona USA Special,
a fast interactive race. A Surf Bowl Bowling Center with 26 lanes is across
the street.

There are 19 restaurants and fast-food vendors on the well-maintained
boardwalk, and the best thing of all, a wonderful white beach, with
parasailing and kayaking facilities. On the pier nearby, you can fish and see
sea lions swimming around the pilings.

● Save Our Shores Interpretive Center

2222 East Cliff Drive, #5A, Santa Cruz 95062. (831) 462-5660. Mon.–Fri., 9:30–5. Free. **Ages 5 & up.** *www.evols.org*

This marine sanctuary center provides visitors with an overview of the Monterey Bay National Marine Sanctuary. To see the sanctuary up close, take an **adventure tour** from the Lower Yacht Harbor. You'll see otters, sea lions, pelicans, cormorants, and perhaps porpoises and whales on one of the 40-minute tours. Sunset tours highlight the glimmer of the boardwalk lights on the water.

● Santa Cruz Museum of Natural History

1305 East Cliff Drive, at Pilkington, Santa Cruz 95062. (831) 420-6115. Tues.–Sun., 10–5. Donation. Reserved parking on Pilkington in summer. Groups by appt. **Ages 6 & up.** *W. www.santacruzmuseums.org*

A "gray whale" welcomes you to natural history exhibits of animals, birds, and local plant groups. Learn how local Ohlone Indians live and grind acorns in a stone mortar. See a mastodon skull from a prehistoric denizen of the region and honeybees in action in an observation hive. Touch live tide-pool animals. You can picnic in the park that surrounds the museum or build a sand castle on the beach across the street.

● Museum of Art and History (MAH)

705 Front Street, Santa Cruz 95060. (831) 429-1964. Tues.–Sun., 11–5; Thurs. until 7 P.M. General, $4; students over 18 and seniors, $2; under 18, free. First Fri. of the month, free. Tours by appt. **Ages 6 & up.** *W. www.santacruzMAH.org*

MAH, the Museum of Art and History in the McPherson Center, is a cultural complex housing the Art Museum of Santa Cruz County, the History Museum of Santa Cruz County, the Museum Shop, and the historic Octagon Gallery. MAH integrates art and history to create a unique visitor experience. Changing exhibits throughout the year explore themes that range from traditional schools of painting to cutting-edge explorations in the digital world; from interpretations of historic artifacts to contemporary comparisons of culture. MAH also has a large history collection, part of which is on view in the Second-floor History Gallery. Docent-led tours, monthly children's workshops, film series, lectures, a history research library, and more are crowned by a third-floor sculpture garden.

● Santa Cruz Mission State Historic Park

School Street, Santa Cruz 95062. (831) 420-5849. Tues.–Sat., 10–4; Sun., 10–2. Fee, $2; seniors and under 12, $1; family, $5. Free Living History Programs. Gift Shop. Picnic facilities. **Ages 6 & up.** *www.parks.ca.gov*

This adobe building is the last remaining structure of Mission Santa Cruz, active from 1791 to 1834. The state's only authentically restored mission housing for Native Americans, it is a living testament to the interplay between California's rich Spanish and Native American heritages. On weekends, docents teach youngsters how to make candles, tortillas, adobe bricks, paper flowers, and tule reed dolls.

The **Mission Santa Cruz** itself is around the corner, at 126 High Street, Santa Cruz 95060. (813) 426-5686. Tues.–Sat., 10–4; Sun., 10–2. Groups by appt. Free. Shop. **Ages 7 & up.** www.geocities.com/missionbell

A half-size replica of the original mission and a portion of the cloister wing built on the approximate site, in a design conceived from a study of aged drawings and paintings, give visitors the feeling of the original. The walls are painted just as they were in Father Serra's day. On view are statues and paintings from the original mission, along with vestments, candelabra, and books. Outside, there's a small garden and a cemetery.

● William H. Volck Memorial Museum

332 East Beach Street (Mail: P.O. 623), Watsonville 95077. (831) 722-0305. Tues.–Thurs., 11–3, and by appt. Free. **Ages 8 & up.**
www.pajarovalleychamber.com

Local history is lovingly preserved in this community museum, a lovely 1868 Victorian with a garden, featuring items and artifacts from the Pajaro Valley. We like the fine collection of historic costumes and textiles, from gingham sunbonnets and aprons to opera hats and ball gowns.

The **Pajaro Valley Arts Council Gallery** (37 Sudden Street, Watsonville 95076. 831-722-3062. Wed.–Sat., 12:30–4:30, and by appt. Free. **Ages 7 & up.** W.) nearby houses contemporary and historical exhibitions that change five times a year. The recent "Hands and the Land," a study of the valley and its people, and "Mi Casa Es Su Casa," a show on the Day of the Dead and the "Angelitas," or dead children, fascinate youngsters.

● Elkhorn Slough National Estuarine Research Reserve

1700 Elkhorn Road, Watsonville 95076 (831) 728-2822. Wed.–Sun., 9–5. Over 16, $2.50; free for those with valid fishing/hunting license. Weekend guided walks at 10 and 1. Visitors center, free. Gift shop. **Ages 6 & up.** *W.*
www.elkhornslough.org

Videos are shown and special events are staged in the visitors center, run by the California Department of Fish and Game, which has displays of the natural history surrounding the area. The visitors center also offers hands-on exhibits and a relief model of the Elkhorn Slough watershed. Blooming plants are identified. There are five miles of guided nature trails through oak woodlands, grasslands, and freshwater and saltwater marshes.

In spring, the wildflowers are rampant and great blue herons and great egrets nest in the rookery by the trail. In summer, small leopard sharks and smooth hound sharks come in on the high tide to give birth and feed on crabs and clams. Migrating shorebirds attract visitors in the spring and fall. And in winter, ducks and shorebirds are plentiful.

● Elkhorn Slough Safari

(Mail: P.O. Box 570, Moss Landing 95039.) Take Highway 1 to Moss Landing, turn west opposite the PG&E stacks onto Moss Landing Road, turn at the first right onto Sandhold Road. Take another right into the Harbor District parking lot. Park against fence to your immediate right. (831) 633-5555. Two-hour 27-foot pontoon tours. Adults, $26; 65 and over, $19; ages 3–14, free. Charter rates. Group and senior discounts. Reservations only. Binoculars and identification guides available. Special activities for children. Refreshments. **Ages 6 & up.** *www.elkhornslough.com*

See hundreds of migratory birds—there are 270 species of birds annually—playful sea otters, curious harbor seals, and more in comfort. We always love spotting egrets and great blue herons as we learn about the slough's inhabitants, native plants, and history. Participants meet at Moss Landing.

● Public Relations Tours

Salz Tannery Tour (1040 River Street, Santa Cruz 95060. 408-423-1480. Free. Tours by appt. for groups of 8–25.) **Ages 8 & up.** The oldest tannery west of Chicago, Salz produces fine leather goods and accessories.

The Monterey Area

Since its discovery in 1542 by Spanish explorer Juan Cabrillo, the Monterey Peninsula has been a mecca for vagabonds and visionaries, pioneers in agriculture and art. It was here that California, after being under the flags of Spain and Mexico, was made part of the United States.

The Monterey area offers many sites worth investigating: the state's best-preserved tribute to its early history; a magnificent coastline in Big Sur; Salinas, proudly boasting its son, novelist John Steinbeck; a sweeping windswept valley now turning into fertile farmland; Pinnacles National Monument; and the Mission San Antonio de Padua.

Beaches along the coast are ideal for walks, tide pooling, and wildlife watching. Sand squirrels, deer, and geese rule in Pacific Grove, and you can see huge sea lions at Point Lobos State Reserve and whale-watch from the Big Sur cliffs or out on the ocean in tour boats. But the ocean averages 55 degrees Fahrenheit and the riptides make it too dangerous for swimming. Youngsters may enjoy splashing about in the few protected areas such as Lover's Point in Pacific Grove.

From San Francisco, allow three hours' driving time on Highway 101, taking the Monterey turnoff, or three and a half hours by the prettier coast route.

● San Juan Bautista State Historic Park

Highway 156 exit off Highway 101 (Mail: P.O. Box 787), San Juan Bautista 95045-0787. (831) 623-4881. Daily, 10–4:30. Over 12, $1. Separate donation for the mission. Check at ranger station at the Plaza Hotel for scheduled interpretive activities. Call for information on Living History Days, when volunteers don period costumes and reenact events from California's past. **Ages 6 & up.** *Partially W. www.parks.ca.gov*

A mission, a museum, an adobe house, an 1870s hotel and stables, a wash house, blacksmith shop, and cabin encircle the lovely plaza of San Juan Bautista, representing four periods in California history—California Indian, Spanish, Mexican, and early Californian.

Start your visit at the **Mission San Juan Bautista** (831-623-2127 for information. Daily, 9:45–4:45; adults, $2; under 12, $1 for mission, museum, and garden). Founded in 1797 and carefully preserved, the mission is still operated by the Catholic Church, and though it is not part of the State Historic Parks, it still anchors the square of history here. The old adobe rooms house many treasures, including a 1737 barrel organ, gaming sticks of the San Juan, or Mutsun, Indians, and artifacts from the original building. The *reredos* in the mission were painted by Thomas Doak, a carpenter from Boston who abandoned the ship *Albatross* and is considered to be the first American resident in California. The red tile floor, laid down in 1816, bears the footprints of the animals—coyotes, deer, even a mountain lion—who walked on the tiles while they were drying. The original bells still call parishioners to mass. In the mission gardens, today's youngsters can learn some of the same things the Indians were taught, and they can make baked goods in the outdoor ovens.

On the main street is the **Castro-Breen Adobe,** which also houses General Castro's secretary's office. This should serve as a model for other museums: Every room is completely labeled, with pictures to aid in the identification of the objects. The house is furnished as it was in the 1870s by the Breen family, who survived the Donner party disaster and eventually found a fortune in the gold fields. You'll see the candlesticks that came west with the Breens and the diary, wardrobe, gloves, fan, and card case of Isabella Breen. The kitchen is complete, right down to the boot pull.

The **Plaza Hotel,** next door, is noted for its barroom with billiard and poker tables standing ready. Built in 1813 as a barracks for the Spanish soldiers, it is now furnished as it might have been in the 1860s. A slide show brings "the early years" to life. Diagonally across the plaza is the **Zanetta House, Plaza Hall,** a completely furnished Victorian home, with dishes on the table and singing bird in the parlor, built on the foundation of the adobe that once housed the Indian maidens of the settlement. The **Livery Stable** is jammed with wonderful wagons, including a surrey with a fringe on top, a Wieland's beer wagon, a "tally ho wagon," phaetons, and buckboards. There's a blacksmith shop behind the stable.

The streets nearby have interesting shops and restaurants, making San Juan Bautista a perfect place to spend a relaxing morning or afternoon.

● Monterey

In *Two Years Before the Mast,* Richard Henry Dana called Monterey "decidedly the pleasantest and most civilized-looking place in California."

In this pleasant, bustling town, The Path of History, natural attractions, and busy shops lure visitors. Fisherman's Wharf is a mélange of restaurants, fish stores, and shops. Although seal watching is the favored pastime, you can go fishing (831-372-7440), whale watching (800-200-2203/831-375-4658. www.gowhales.com), or kayaking (831-373-5357). In Monterey, you can go hanggliding, ballooning, tide pooling, and on nature walks.

Today's Cannery Row is a far cry from the Cannery Row in John Steinbeck's books. Now it is a growing complex of restaurants, shops, and galleries offering entertainment for all. Its greatest attraction is the extraordinary **Monterey Bay Aquarium.**

The city of Monterey has made it easy for visitors to get around. The Waterfront Area Visitor Express, the WAVE, allows you to park in one spot and then bus everywhere, from the Del Monte Shopping Center, through downtown Monterey, to Fisherman's Wharf and along the water to the Aquarium, Lover's Point, Point Pinos, Asilomar, and back, all for just $1 a day, 50¢ for children, seniors, and disabled, Memorial Day through Labor Day.

And by following the yellow line painted on several streets, you follow **The Path of History.** Landmark plaques tell briefly who built historic houses, and why the buildings are landmarks.

● Maritime Museum of Monterey and Stanton Center

5 Custom House Plaza, Monterey 93940. (831) 373-2469. Daily, 10–5, except Thanksgiving and Christmas, later in summer. Adults, $5; ages 13–18, $3; ages 6–12, $2. Groups by appt. Workshops and children's activities. Research library open Tues.–Fri., 10–5. Gift shop. **Ages 5 & up.** *W.*

A spiffy modern building captures the maritime tradition of Monterey and celebrates a seafaring heritage linking Spanish explorers, mission settlement, trade, fishing, and the U.S. Navy. The First Order Fresnel Lens, standing nearly two stories tall and weighing almost 10,000 pounds, served as a warning to mariners off Point Sur. Today it lights up the museum's ship model exhibit, a sea captain's quarters, navigational instruments, and chronicles of a once-thriving whaling industry and Monterey's era as the sardine capital of the world. Fans will recognize the memorabilia from the Allen Knight collection, including the sardine boat and the sailor's ditty box. A personal favorite: the sampler created by nine-year-old Laura Green aboard the SS *Indove,* January 16, 1868, sailing to Abyssinia and the Suez. Old sailing accoutrements—octants, ships' bells, sailors' thimbles, arctic goggles, scrimshaw, and ships' logs—are fascinating.

Special sea chanty sessions, storytelling events, and other programs will bring kids back for more.

● Monterey State Historic Park
Stanton Center, State Park History Theater

Custom House Plaza, between Fishermans Wharf and Doubletree Hotel, Monterey (Mail for all buildings in MSHP: 20 Custom House Plaza, Monterey 93940). (831) 649-7118. Daily, 10–5. Tickets and information for MSHP Individual House Tours at Casa Soberanes, Larkin House, Cooper Molera Complex, and Stevenson House. Walking tour of Path of History from center at 10:30, daily. Special 2-day passes for all house tours and walking tour, $5. Groups for all buildings by appt. Tours depend on staff availability. All are closed Thanksgiving, Christmas, and New Year's. **Ages 5 & up.** *Please note that all MSHP buildings have the same website: www.mbay.net~mshp*

Monterey State Historic Park is California's most authentically presented remembrance. There are more original and restored buildings in one town (11) than there are anywhere else in America—including Colonial Willamsburg. Discover the birthplace of European history in Alta California with visits to restored adobes, homes, historic buildings, and gardens. You can drive along the yellow "Path of History" to see them all. Or you can start at the Stanton Center, see the free film illustrating Monterey's history through reenactments, which is presented every 20 minutes, and then walk to each home or building you wish to explore. There's also a brief introduction to the walking tour of Old Monterey's historic adobes. For group reservations, call (831) 647-6282.

● Custom House MSHP

1 Custom House Plaza (Mail: 20 Custom House Plaza), Monterey 93940. (831) 649-7118. Daily, 10–5 (until 4 in winter). Free.

The first United States flag that was officially raised in Mexican California was over this building, in 1846, at the beginning of the war between Mexico and the United States. It is here that each ship captain presented his cargo for the customs inspector. Today, you walk into a long room that holds the cargo Richard Henry Dana wrote about in his novel *Two Years Before the Mast.* There are casks of liquor, cases of dishes, bags of nails, coffee, flour, and wagon wheels. A screeching yellow and green parrot rules a roost of ribbons, ropes, cloth, shawls, soap, paper, tools, and trunks. In one area, piles of "California bank notes"—cowhides—wait to be used for trading. The Custom House guard's quarters upstairs features a carved bed and chest, a table, and a desk with an open ledger.

One young visitor wrote, "Thank you for letting us visit the Custom House. It was fun doing the scavenger hunt, my group found everything. The boat was neat. It was big too! I liked the play about the ship coming into the harbor. I liked Sebastiana too!"

● Pacific House Museum MSHP

10 Custom House Plaza, Monterey 93940. (831) 649-7118. Daily, 10–5.

The Pacific House, which has been a tavern, army storage, a courthouse, a newspaper, a hotel, and a ballroom, is now a newly redesigned interactive museum. The first floor is a hands-on museum of California history from 1500 to 1850. The second floor contains an extensive collection of Indian artifacts from the local Rumsien Indians and other California tribes. One fourth grader wrote, "Thanks for the amazing teaching tour. I liked the Native American parts. Thank you for the book marks. I liked the saddle that you let us get on-geddy up! But how did you make those eggs. Those are cool.

I liked when we got to touch the fur. It was soft. Thanks a lot for everything you did to show us all kinds of Indian stuff."

● Boston Store/Casa del Oro MSHP

Corner of Scott and Olivier Streets, Monterey. (831) 649-3364. Thurs.–Sat., 11–3, Sun., 12–4. Free.

Built by Thomas O. Larkin about 1845, this structure housed a general merchandise store operated by Joseph Boston and Company in the 1850s. The building was later called Casa del Oro because it served as a gold depository. The safe is still there. Today, the building is again a general merchandise store operated by Historic Gardens of Monterey with profits going to preserve the building. The herb garden outside is wheelchair accessible and the store has a booklet of Mr. Boston's herb recipes. The picket fence garden shop next door is in a building owned by MSHP.

● Monterey's First Theatre/Jack Swan's Tavern MSHP

Corner of Scott and Pacific Streets, Monterey. Building information: (831) 375-5100. Theater information: (831) 375-4916.

Jack Swan's lodging house gave its first performance of a stage play in 1847 to entertain bored soldiers. Self-guided tours and 19th-century melo-dramas will return when the adobe building is restored and renovated.

● Casa Soberanes MSHP

336 Pacific Street, at Del Monte, Monterey. (831) 649-7118. Tours daily at 11:30.

"The House with the Blue Gate" is an authentic, typical home of Mexican California. Built by Rafael Estrada in the 1830s, it was lived in by the Soberanes family from 1860 to 1922. With its thick walls, interconnected rooms, cantilevered balcony, and lovely garden, Casa Soberanes reflects life in Monterey, from its Mexican period beginnings to more recent times. The furnishings are a blend of early New England and China trade pieces with Mexican folk art. A collection of local art graces the house as well. The garden, which dates to the 1850s, is the oldest in the area.

● Larkin House MSHP

510 Calle Principal, at Jefferson Street, Monterey. (831) 649-7118. Guided tours daily, at 3.

Built in 1835–37 by Thomas Oliver Larkin, the first and only U.S. consul to Mexico stationed in Monterey, the house is an architectural and historical gem. It was the first home in Monterey in the New England style, with two stories. Some of the furnishings are original. The early-19th-century rooms hold antiques from many parts of the world, acquired by the builder's granddaughter, Alice Larkin Toulmin, who lived here from 1922 to 1957. Through the rose-covered garden is a small house, now a museum, used in 1847–49 by Civil War general William Tecumseh Sherman, then an army lieutenant.

● Cooper-Molera Adobe Complex and Store MSHP

Polk and Munras Streets, Monterey. (831) 649-7118. House tours daily except Fri. at 11, 1, and 3. Cooper Store and visitors center open daily. Check the website for Living History days and special events. Free.

This restored complex contains Captain John Cooper's town house (Cooper was Thomas Larkin's half-brother; his wife was Mariano Vallejo's sister, Encarnación). The site contains several adobe buildings, a carriage house display room, and period gardens complete with scratching chickens. It was occupied by three generations of Coopers from 1827 to 1968. The gift and book shop features handicrafts that hark back to the town's beginnings, including heirloom seeds from the property's garden.

● Stevenson House MSHP

525 Houston Street, Monterey. (831) 649-7118. Under restoration at this writing. Usually, Nov. 13 is an open house for Robert Louis Stevenson's "unbirthday" because he gave his original birthday away to a little girl born on Christmas Day.

In 1879 Robert Louis Stevenson spent a few months in a second-floor room of this boarding house. He had traveled from Scotland to visit Fanny Osbourne, who later became his wife. He wrote *The Old Pacific Capital* here. The house is restored to look as it did then, with several rooms dedicated to Stevenson memorabilia. Be sure to see the doll collection upstairs. There is a rumor of a ghost.

● Casa Gutierrez MSHP

590 Calle Principal, Monterey 93940. (831) 646-5640.

This adobe was built in 1841 by a young Mexican for his bride. He earned his living as a farmer and rancher and raised 15 children here. Notable for its historic value, the adobe now houses an art gallery.

● Colton Hall Museum of the City of Monterey MSHP

Pacific Street, between Jefferson and Madison Streets, Monterey 93940. (831) 649-7118. Daily, 10–12, 1–5. Free.

Colton Hall, the first town hall and the first public school of Monterey, was the site of the first Constitutional Convention of the State of California, in 1849. Here the California Constitution was written in Spanish and English and the Great Seal of the state was designed. The large meeting room is furnished as it was then, with displays depicting the scene in 1849 during the convention, as if the delegates had just stepped out for a break. The hall was built by navy chaplain Walter Colton, who served as the first American *alcalde* (mayor) in California from 1846 to 1849.

Behind Colton Hall is the **Old Monterey Jail,** open daily until 5. The walls are granite, two feet thick, the doors are iron, and the cells tell the stories of the jail and its inmates. Believe it or not, this was the city jail until 1959. The Old Monterey Jail was a second home for Danny, in John Steinbeck's *Tortilla Flat.*

● Cannery Row

Cannery Row Information Center, (831) 373-1902/649-6690. **All ages.** *www.canneryrow.com*

In his novel *Cannery Row,* John Steinbeck called the Row "a poem, a stink, a grating noise, a quality of light, a tone, a habit, a nostalgia and a dream." Today's visitor will find most of that here, along with restaurants, antique stores, and shops, many with water views.

Three workers' shacks have been restored for public viewing on the Irving Street walkway, between the Recreation Trail and Wave Street. Each looks as it would have when inhabited by a Spanish cannery worker in the 1920s, two Japanese fishermen in the 1930s, or a Filipino reduction plant worker in the 1940s. Just walk by and peek in the windows.

You could also rent a 1929 Mercedes, a 1929 Ford Model A, or a 1930 Phaeton to go sightseeing. Rent-A-Roadster is at 229 Cannery Row (831-647-1929).

There are 45 factory outlets and restaurants at the **American Tin Cannery** (125 Ocean View Boulevard, Pacific Grove, around the corner from the aquarium. 831-372-1442. Mon., Wed., and Sat., 10–6; Thurs. and Fri., 10–9; Sun., 11–5) and the **Edgewater Family Fun Center** (640 Wave Street. 831-649-1988; 10–6 daily, later on summer weekends. www.montereyfun.com), across from the aquarium, which boasts 100 interactive video, pinball, and redemption games for children of all ages as well as a super 34-horse, two-unicorn, and two-zebra 1905 carousel that is said to be the fastest in the West.

● Bubba Gump Shrimp Co.

720 Cannery Row, Monterey 93940. (831) 373-1884. Sun.–Thurs., 11–10 P.M.; Fri. and Sat., until 11; closing hours earlier in winter. **All ages.** *www.bubbagump.com*

Right behind the park bench with a suitcase, white sneaks you can stick your feet into, and a box of chocolates, the Bubba Gump Shrimp Co. celebrates *Forrest Gump* with Gump memorabilia and scrawled "Gumpisms" on every varnished wood tabletop. The movie plays continuously on video monitors and waiters challenge customers with Gump trivia questions. Shrimp is served 10 ways, from Mama Blue's Southern Charmed Fried to Jenny's Sweet Ginger and Garlic Shrimp Scampi, along with This Man's Army Bone-in Rib Eye Steak and Bubba's Far Out Dip, among other things. The water view is great.

The store next door sells *Gump* cookbooks, CD-ROM, videos, mugs, T-shirts, and chocolates. There is another Bubba Gump's in San Francisco on Pier 39.

● Spirit of Monterey Wax Museum

700 Cannery Row, Monterey 93940-1085. (831) 375-3770. Daily, 11–6, longer hours in summer. Adults, $4.95; ages 7–12, $2.95. Tours with special rates by appt. **Ages 6 & up.** *W. www.wax-museum.com*

Dozens of scenes tell the spellbinding story of Monterey and the people who lived it, from the Indians who were here before the Spanish galleons cast anchor to Steinbeck's rowdy crew. Visitors will meet Concepción, who fell in love with a Russian officer and waited in vain for his return; Robert Louis Stevenson; the Spanish dons who ruled Monterey; and Thomas Larkin, who was California's first "ambassador" to the United States. Kit Carson rides up and tells his story, Joaquín Murietta spouts poetry, and Steinbeck reminisces about his friends in the Lone Star Café.

● MY Museum

601 Wave Street, Suite 100, Monterey 93940. (831) 649-6444. Sun., 12–5, Mon., Tues., and Thurs.–Sat., 10–5. Ages 2 and up, $5.50. Group rates. **Ages 2–15.** *W. www.mymuseum.org*

This Fun Place for Kids! is a hands on, interactive version of Cannery Row, where youngsters can fish from a boat, buy food and supplies at the store, or cook food at MY grill. They can play a part at the puppet theater, where visitors tell stories and become puppeteers. Or dress up in a favorite costume and put on a show. The giant loom allows kids to take home a small weaving. They can imagine, build, examine, invent, discover, create, act, compute, explore, and touch everything.

● Monterey Bay Aquarium

886 Cannery Row, Monterey 93940-1085. (831) 648-4888. Advance tickets: (800) 756-3737 and www.montereybayaquarium.org. Daily, except Christmas, 10–6. Adults, $17.95; seniors and students, $14.95; ages 3–12

*and disabled, $7.95. Posted feeding schedules. Workshops and discovery labs
for members and school groups. Group rates and tours available. Gift shops.*
All ages. *W. www.montereybayaquarium.org*

"He's feeding fish to fish," one youngster exclaimed, while standing
entranced before the three-story kelp forest. All the wonders of a hidden world
come to light at the internationally acclaimed Monterey Bay Aquarium, one
of California's "top 11" attractions. In a startling undersea tour of Monterey
Bay, visitors will meet more than 250,000 living creatures in nearly 200
galleries and exhibits.

California sea otters frolic nose to nose with you in their own naturalistic
pool, visible on two different levels. You can investigate with telescopes and
microscopes, play with bat rays and starfish, or walk through a shorebird
aviary. Special exhibits change regularly.

Two favorites were the "Saving Seahorses" exhibit and "Jellies: Living
Art," a combination of fine art and living jellies including the spectacular
flower hat jelly and the blue jelly.

The Outer Bay wing is the first in the world to present the life of the open
ocean on a grand scale. After you go up an escalator, you discover you're
beneath a silvery school of anchovies flashing over you.

Wander through the permanent gallery of "Drifters," graceful, magical
jellyfish of all sizes. Banks of microscopes and live exhibits introduce visitors
to plankton, the foundation of the oceanic food chain. Some of the animals are
included in an aquarium exhibit for the first time ever. Then there's the
million-gallon indoor ocean showcasing the sunlit blue waters where
Monterey Bay meets the open sea. Sharks (including hammerheads and the
only oceanic white-tip shark at an aquarium), enormous ocean sunfish, sea
turtles, barracuda, and schools of tuna swoop by, as visitors watch from a
three-story, 54-foot-long window. Imagine that you're 50 miles offshore,
300 feet beneath the surface. It's dark, quiet, awesome.

Then head on out to "Flippers, Flukes and Fun," which is filled with super
hands-on exhibits to show younger children all about whales and other
marine mammals. They can even don flippers to pretend they're mermaids
and wander inside a whale's stomach, make a whale sing, a sea lion bark, and
a dolphin whistle. The Splash Zone family gallery beckons youngsters with
engaging animals and 30 hands-on exhibit experiences.

The new million-gallon Outer Bay exhibit at the Vanishing Wildlife
exhibit is awe-inspiring and shows the bay even farther out than the inner
ocean exhibit.

The Portola Café features a cafeteria, a full-service restaurant, and an
oyster bar, all with ocean views. There's also a snack bar. Films, slide shows,
special programs, flip charts, and hands-on interpretive exhibits challenge
and intrigue. Call for the next day when physically and developmentally

disabled youngsters can dive in the Great Tide Pool. And, in an outstanding example of community service, if you or someone else in your family has to have an MRI in Los Gatos or Santa Cruz, the aquarium now offers special goggles showing a live video from the aquarium's web cams.   Named one of the nation's top family-friendly vacation spots—and my choice as #1 in Northern California—the aquarium is outstanding, a beautifully designed treat for the whole family.

● Monterey Museum of Art

La Mirada, 720 Via Mirada Street, off Fremont, and Civic Center, 559 Pacific Street, Monterey 93940 (Mail: 559 Pacific Street). (831) 372-5477. Wed.–Sat., 11–5; Sun., 1–4. Tours by reservation. Adults, $5; students and ages 12–18, $2.50; under 12, free. Extended hours at Civic Center the third Thurs. of the month, 5–7, free. First Sun. of the month at La Mirada, free.
Ages 8 & up. *www.montereyart.org*

La Mirada adobe, built in the early 19th century, was the home of Mexican General José Castro. Here, visitors will explore early California history, experience a taste of life on the peninsula in the 1920s, and enjoy exhibitions of California regional art and art of the Pacific Rim. At the Civic Center Museum visitors will enjoy the work of California impressionists, photo exhibits, and more. Both museums rotate shows from their permanent collections with visiting shows.

● Dennis the Menace Playground

Pearl Street, El Estero City Park, off Del Monte Avenue, Camino del Estero and Fremont, Monterey 93941. (831) 646-3866. Daily, 10–dusk. Closed on nonholiday Mon., Sept.–May. Free. **Ages 2–12.** *W. www.monterey.org/rec*

Youngsters will want to head to this colorful playspace designed by cartoonist Hank Ketchum. Here, little potential "menaces" can let off steam in a steam switch engine, hang from the Umbrella Tree, sweep down the Giant Swing Ride, put their heads in the lion's mouth for a drink of water, and sail off in the boat. Families may want to rent a paddleboat.

● Pacific Grove Museum of Natural History

165 Forest Avenue at Central Avenue, Pacific Grove 93950. (831) 648-3116. Daily except Mon., 10–5. Closed Thanksgiving, Christmas Eve and Day, and New Year's Day. Groups by appt. Movies and special programs. Gift shop. Free. **Ages 6 & up.** *W. www.pgmuseum.org*

Each October, thousands of monarch butterflies arrive in Pacific Grove to winter in a grove of pine trees until March. The **Monarch Restoration Habitat** (on Ridge Road, off Lighthouse Avenue) is their home. Visitors who arrive in other months can see a marvelous exhibit of the monarch in this beautifully designed museum. There is also a large collection of tropical and other California butterflies as well as sea otters, fish, mammals, rodents, insects, and birds. The skeleton of a sea otter playing with a clamshell is touching. The life of the Costanoan Indians is revealed in an archaeological "dig."

Dioramas and the amazing relief map of Monterey Bay are also worth a look—if the youngsters can tear themselves away from climbing on Sandy the Gray Whale in front of the museum. There's a children's hands-on area and cold saltwater aquarium for families, as well as a nature garden with more than 100 species and varieties of California plants.

● Point Pinos Lighthouse

Off Asilomar Boulevard and Lighthouse Avenue, Pacific Grove 93950. Information at Pacific Grove Museum: (831) 648-5716. Thurs.–Mon. and holidays, 1–4. Free. **Ages 8 & up.** *www.pgmuseum.org*

Point Pinos (Point of Pines) was named by explorer Sebastian Viscaino in 1602. The lighthouse overlooks the meadows and sand dunes of a golf course on one side, and the whitecapped ocean on the other. Inside the Cape Cod–style building, which is the oldest working lighthouse on the West Coast (1855), newly refurbished and redecorated rooms bring back the homey look of the lighthouse when Emily Fish was the light keeper at the turn of the century. Volunteer docents in period dress tell lighthouse history. Upstairs in the tiny watch room, you can read Fish's logbooks of storms, the 1906 earthquake, and the 1906 Chinatown fire in Pacific Grove. The short distance to town along scenic Oceanview Boulevard offers many beautiful sights. Along the way you'll pass Lovers Point, with marine gardens, and tree-shaded picnic grounds.

At **Point Sur State Historic Park** (831-625-4419. Nineteen miles south of Rio Road on Highway 1, Big Sur. www.lighthouse-pointsur-ca.org), volunteers offer guided tours of this restored landmark, first lit in August 1889 and in continuous operation ever since.

● Carmel

A visit to the Monterey Peninsula is not complete without an hour or two of browsing in the picturesque "fairy-tale Tudor" village of Carmel. The Pine Inn Block, bounded by Ocean Avenue, Lincoln, Monte Verde, and 6th Avenue, is bustling with Victorian shops, galleries, gardens, and restaurants. The Carmel Heritage Society offers Saturday morning walks starting from their headquarters at First Murphy House (831-624-4447), and Gale Wrausman of Carmel Walks leads two-hour-long story-filled tours (831-642-2700. www.carmelwalks.com). Sunsets on the white-sand secluded beach at the foot of Ocean Avenue can be spectacular. www.carmelcalifornia.org

● Carmel Mission, Mission San Carlos Borromeo

Rio Road, off Highway 1, Carmel 93923. (831) 624-1271. Daily except holidays, 10–5. Adults, $4; children up to 17, $1. Gift shop, (831) 624-3600. **All ages.** *www.carmelmission.org*

The lovely mission church and cemetery, museums, and the adobe home of the pioneer Munras family combine to make this mission a "must stop." Father Junipero Serra rests in the church, and in the cemetery lies Old Gabriel, who lived 119 years and was baptized by Father Serra. The small Harry Downey museum in the garden houses pictures of the original mission and its restoration. There are Indian grinding pots, arrowheads, baskets, beads, toys, and other archaeological treasures. The long main museum offers fine art from the original mission and a replica of the stark cell Father Serra died in. You'll also find California's first library here—Father Serra's books, Bibles, travel commentaries, and technical works. Altar pieces, saddles, the furnished kitchen and dining room, a "clacker" used instead of bells, and a fabulous nativity crèche are also of interest, as are mementos of Pope John Paul's visit in 1987.

The **Munras Museum** is now a memorial to the Munras family. Visitors can see the keys from the original adobe, family pictures, music and provision boxes, a doctor's bag, jewelry, dresses, and a totally furnished living room.

● Robinson Jeffers Tor House

26304 Ocean View Avenue, Carmel 93923. (831) 624-1813. One-hour tours on Fri. and Sat. by reservation (831-624-1840). Adults, $7; college students, $4; high school students, $2. **Ages 12 & up.** *www.torhouse.org*

Budding poets will enjoy a visit to the home of California poet Robinson Jeffers on a high bluff overlooking the Pacific. Part English country cottage, part stone monument to the mystery of the human imagination, Tor House celebrates the nature around it. Jeffers himself built the low main cottage of "stone love stone," with memorabilia from his world travels embedded in the stone walls. The 40-foot Hawk Tower looks like a castle turret. He also built a wonderful "dungeon playroom" for his sons.

● Point Lobos State Reserve

Highway 1, south of Carmel (Mail: P.O. Box 62), Carmel 93923. (408) 624-4909. Daily, 9–5 in winter; later in summer. Cars: $3; seniors, $2. **All ages.** *http://pt-lobos.parks.state.ca.us*

Early Spanish explorers named this rocky, surf-swept point of land Punta de Los Lobos Marinos, or Point of the Sea Wolves. You can still hear the loud barking of the sea lions and see them on offshore rocks. Point Lobos is an outdoor museum: Each tree, plant, and shrub is protected by law, as are the cormorants, pelicans, otters, squirrels, and black-tailed mule deer that live here. One of the last natural stands of Monterey cypress is also found at the reserve. There are three picnic areas and 10 miles of hiking trails. Dogs are not permitted in the reserve. The sheltered cove, reached by a long, long staircase, is ideal for paddling with youngsters. An occasional seal will sunbathe nearby, while pelicans fly overhead.

● Steinbeck House

132 Central Avenue, Salinas 93901. Reservations: (831) 424-2735. Mon.–Sat., 11:30–2. Children's menu. Tours by appt. Gift shop. **Ages 10 & up.** *www.infopoint.com/mry/orgs/steinbeck*

John Steinbeck's childhood Victorian home, listed on the National Register of Historic Places, is now a luncheon restaurant offering fresh produce of the valley amid Steinbeck memorabilia. This is where the author of *The Red Pony* and *Tortilla Flat* grew up. The "Best Cellar" features Steinbeck's books. Every day, 15 volunteers from the membership of 200 Valley Guild members plan, help prepare, and serve luncheon. Profits go to Salinas Valley charities, and the house's restoration has been funded by the luncheon proceeds. As Steinbeck wrote, "It was an immaculate and friendly house, grand enough, but not pretentious."

The Steinbeck Library (350 Lincoln Avenue. 831-758-7311) displays a collection of John Steinbeck's memorabilia, including reviews and personal correspondence and a life-size bronze statue.

● National Steinbeck Center

One Main Street, Salinas 93901. (831) 775-4720. Daily, 10–5. Closed holidays. Adults, $9.95; seniors and students, $7.95; ages 13–17, $6.95; ages 6–12, $5.95. Group rates, by reservation. Library and archives. Special events. Café. Gift store. **Ages 5 & up.** *W. www.steinbeck.org*

The spectacular 37,000-square-foot National Steinbeck Center museum, dedicated to the life and works of author John Steinbeck, is the best thing that ever happened to an American author. Steinbeck won both a Pulitzer Prize and a Nobel Prize, but this phenomenal multimedia experience of literature, history, and art is an astonishing celebration of one author. Here visitors will hear books and letters, see plays and movies made, and experience Steinbeck's trials, tribulations, and triumphs.

It makes you want to read at least one Steinbeck novel immediately, no matter how old you are. Youngsters can actually ride the "red pony." Oldsters can peek into Steinbeck's camping truck, "Rosinante" and see Charley the poodle sitting in the front seat. In the re-creation of John's early bedroom, you can open a drawer and see his childhood books. You can get cold in front of the refrigerator boxcar full of "ice packed" lettuce and then see how the young hero of *East of Eden* failed his close-minded father (based on Steinbeck's grandfather). Lift up the coat on the rack in Lenny's bedroom and see the mouse from *Of Mice and Men*. "Doc" Ricketts's science lab, complete with the sounds and smells of the sea, evokes *Cannery Row*, as does Lee Chong's grocery. Migrant workers in tent cities bring *The Grapes of Wrath* to life.

Vintage photographs, oral histories, film clips, music, and excerpts from books and speeches bring everything to vivid life. The graphics and text panels provide multiple levels of information so all visitors will be able to enjoy something. The art gallery offers changing exhibits of art that portrays Steinbeck Country. And Valley of the World is the focus of a gallery that uses high-tech audiovisual exhibits, as well as sight, sound, touch, and taste, to show the human elements of farming. Interactive computer stations illustrate the science of agriculture. Memorabilia and films show farmworkers of various cultures bringing the land to life. Children of all ages will enjoy the Art of Writing Room, where they can read, view videos, write their own stories, or draw pictures in themed activity books.

Steinbeck wrote, "Literature is as old as speech. It grew out of human need for it and it has not changed except to become more needed." Katie, age 12, wrote, "This was a very interesting museum. I thought I was going to be bored but I guess I was wrong."

● Boronda Adobe

333 Boronda Road at West Laurel Drive, Salinas 93901. (831) 757-8085. Mon.–Fri., 10–2, and by appt. Free. Archival vault available to researchers by appt. **Ages 8 & up.** *W. www.dedot.com/mchs*

The Monterey County Historical Society has also restored Jose Eusebio Boronda's unaltered adobe, built in 1844, once part of the 6,700-acre Rancho San Jose. The oldest building in Salinas is now a little museum proudly showing many of its original furnishings.

Also on the site is the **Lagunita One Room School House,** built in 1897. This is the school Steinbeck wrote about in *The Red Pony*. A Queen Anne Victorian built by Salinan William Weeks is being turned into a house museum and a research center. A major archives and agriculture museum is in progress.

● The Farm

"Home of the Giant Farmers." Just west of Salinas on Highway 68, 15 miles east of Monterey at the Spreckels exit. (Mail: P.O. Box 247, Salinas 93902-0247) (831) 455-2575. Mon.–Sat., 9–6, Apr.–Nov. Adults, $5; ages 2–26, $3. Tours by appt. Special rates. Parking free. Snack bar. Produce stand. Picnic area. **All ages.** *www.thefarm-salinasvalley.com*

Oversized lifelike sculptures entice a visit to the "salad bowl of America." The demonstration market garden shows, on-site, the hands-on farming practices of the Salinas Valley. Youngsters will delight in the antics of the farm animals.

● Wild Things

Vision Quest Ranch, Animal Rentals Inc., 400 River Road, Salinas 93908. Four miles from Highway 68, right after Pine Canyon Road, halfway between Monterey and Salinas. (831) 455-3180. Tours at 1, daily, with an additional tour at 3, June–Aug. Adults. $10; 14 and under, $8. Reservations needed only for groups. **Ages 7 & up.** *www.wildthingsinc.com*

This exotic/wild animals facility is dedicated to providing professionally trained animals for film, television, live productions, education facilities, and more. See a collection of more than 100 birds, animals, and reptiles from around the world, some of which have become "animal stars" in the film industry. You learn how they are trained for film work and what they are really like to house and maintain. Up close.

● Mission Nuestra Señora de la Soledad

36641 Fort Romie Road, Soledad 93960. Highway 101 southwest of Soledad. Arroyo Seco off-ramp, then right on Fort Romie Road. (831) 678-2586. E-mail: missionolive@aol.com. Daily except holidays, 10–4. Closed holidays. Gift shop. Free. **Ages 8 & up.** *www.cuca.k12.ca.us/lessons/missions/soledad*

Founded in 1791 as the 13th in the chain of 21 California missions, this mission, dedicated to Holy Mary, Our Lady of the Solitude, was in desolate open plains and in ruins by 1859. Volunteers have restored it as a lovely oasis surrounded by gardens. Visitors may visit the museum and chapel and then spend time in the graveyard and picnic area.

● Mission San Antonio de Padua

(Mail: P.O. Box 803, Jolon 93928) On Fort Hunter Liggett, off Highway 101 from King City or Bradley. (831) 385-4478. Museum-Church, daily in winter 8–5; until 6 in summer. Gift shop, Mon.–Sat., 10–4; Sun 11:15–4. Sun. mass at 10 A.M. Donation. Information for fourth-graders may be obtained by a request accompanied by a self-addressed, stamped envelope. **Ages 7 & up.** *W. www.missionsanantoniopadua.com*

San Antonio de Padua is one of the finest of the missions. It was the third mission founded by Fra Junipero Serra, in 1771. A military base around it has preserved its natural setting. To visit is to feel that you're discovering the days of the padres and Salinan Indians of 200 years ago. The mission has been totally restored to look as it did in 1813. Inside the mission museum, on a self-guided tour, you'll see artifacts from mission days, tools for candle making and carpentry, the old wine press, and other old-time implements needed to run a working mission. The grist mill, the aqueduct system, waterwheel, and wine vat stand as the Indians saw them when San Antonio was at its height. The wildflower season in late April and early May is gorgeous. The annual Fiesta Bar-B-Q is held on the second Sunday of June, close to the Feast of Saint Anthony. Steinbeck described the mission in a state of abandonment in his novel *To a God Unknown*. Today, it is a working parish and contemplative center and retreat, served by the Franciscan Friars of California.

● Public Relations Tours

Roses of Yesterday and Today (803 Browns Valley Road, Watsonville 95076. 831-728-1901. **Ages 9 & up.** Info. and directions: www.rosesofyesterday.com). The big rose garden that specializes in old, hard-to-find roses is, in season, a sight to behold. Groups and school visits are encouraged and there are tables and benches for picnics.

Stone Container Corporation (1078 Merrill Street, Salinas 93901. 831-424-1831. Nov.–Apr., by appt. for children over 10. Free). Today's kids sometimes like the boxes toys come in more than the toys. Here's where they can see the manufacture of corrugated boxes and paper laminations.

Monterey Bay Chocolate Factory (1291 Fremont Boulevard, Seaside 93955. 831-899-7963. Tours: Mon.–Fri., 10–3:30. Store: Mon., 9:30–5:30; Tues.–Sat., 9:30–8:30; Sun., 12:30–5:30. Groups by appt. Free truffle. **Ages 8 & up.** www.montereybaychocolates.com). See chocolate made, meet the makers, and taste the chocolate.

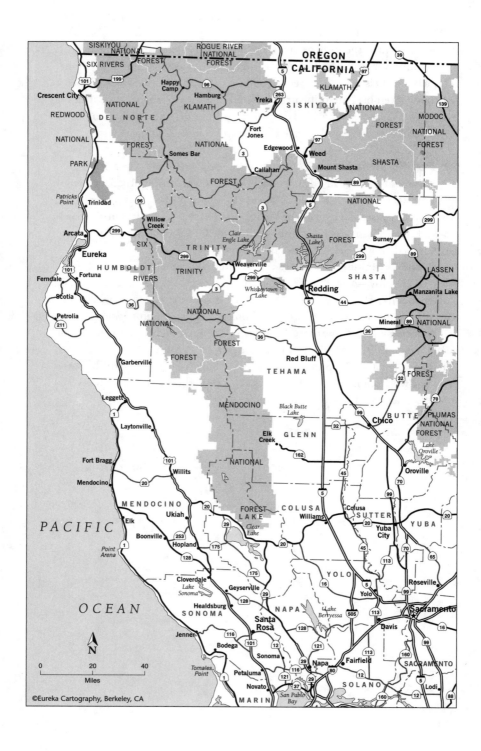

©Eureka Cartography, Berkeley, CA

Heading North

■ Napa, Sonoma, and Lake Counties

The Napa-Sonoma area is best known for the vineyards that grow on rolling hills and in the Valley of the Moon. But the country itself is welcoming and is seen to advantage from the hot-air balloons, gliders, planes, and parachutes now available for the brave of heart. Napa's first American settler, George Yount, was given a land grant by General Mariano Vallejo in 1836. He planted the first grapes so he could have wine for his table.

Wineries can be fun for youngsters to visit, not only because the winemaking process is fascinating, but because the wine industry is part of California's history and culture. In most wineries, your tour will follow the direction the grape takes, from vineyard delivery to the crushing and the aging vat, and on to the bottles in the tasting rooms. Many wineries also offer local food products such as jam or olive oil. Tasting rooms, which may charge, may also offer grape juice or nonalcoholic wine. Many wineries have picnic areas, free of charge.

Kid-friendly wineries include **Robert Mondavi** (Highway 29, 7801 St. Helena Highway [Mail: P.O. Box 106], Oakville 94562. 800-MONDAVI. 9–5. Free. Events. W. www.robertmondavi.com), which offers free concerts on the lawn; **Sterling Vineyards** (1111 Dunaweal Lane, off Highway 29, Calistoga 94515. 707-942-3344. Daily except holidays, 10:30–4:30. Adults, $10; under 21, $5; package includes guided tour at 11, 12, 1 and 2. www.sterlingvineyards.com) with its aerial Skytram ride; **Buena Vista Winery** (18000 Old Winery Road, off East Napa Road, 1 mile from Sonoma, Sonoma 95476. 800-926-1266. Daily, 10–5. www.buenavistawinery.com), with its atmospheric limestone caves, gallery, and great history; and **Viansa Winery and Italian Marketplace** (25200 Arnold Drive, Highway 121, Sonoma 95476. 800-995-4740. Daily, 10–5. Free. www.viansa.com), where Il Porcino, the huge Tuscan Boar whose twin is in the Mercato in Florence, rules over the picnic grounds.

If you have only one winery to go to, first choice would be the **Niebaum-Coppola Winery** (1991 St. Helena Highway, Rutherford 94573. 707-968-1100. Daily, 10–5. Free. www.niebaum-coppola.com), which has a café, an extensive well-stocked grocery-gift shop, and an astonishing museum.

The history of the land is combined with a history of the Coppola family. It turns out that Gustave Niebaum was a ship captain and winemaker in the late 1800s. A photo of the tasting room on Niebaum's ship is right by the door, near mementos of the Centennial Exposition in Paris. There are old cameras, stereographs, stereoscopes, and zoetropes from 1834 and 1835. Photos, journals, winemaking notebooks, timelines, and awards showcase the Coppola family. Carmine's flute and music from *The Godfather,* costumes from *Dracula,* and family-won Oscars fascinate. Don Corleone's desk and a

1937 Tucker "war car"—and the clay model used to design the car, which could go 117 mph—are headliners upstairs.

For up-to-date information on tours, balloon rides, resorts, sightseeing, hotels, visit www.napavalley.com

● Air Play

The rolling hills and soft wind currents of the area have made the skies here especially accessible. For those who are adventurous, and can afford it, try the following—and check the local Yellow Pages for others. Since companies open and fade with the wind, call for schedules and prices.

Above the West Ballooning. *(Mail: P.O. Box 2290, Yountville 94599)* *(707) 944-8638.* **Ages 6 & up.**

Aerostat Adventures *(Mail: P.O. Box 3882, Healdsburg 95448)* *(707) 433-3777.* **Ages 6 & up.**

Adventures Aloft, *6525 Washington, Yountville 94599.* *(707) 944-4408.* **Ages 6 & up.**

Balloons Above the Valley, *5090 Solano Avenue, Napa 94558.* *(800) 464-6824.* **Ages 6 & up.**

Crazy Creek Gliders, *18896 Grange Road, Middletown 95461.* *(707) 942-5000. Glider rides, instruction, and rental.* **Ages 6 & up.** *www.crazycreekgliders.com*

Napa Valley Balloons, *6795 Washington Street (Mail: P.O. Box 2860, Yountville 94599) (800) 253-2224/(707) 253-2224.* **Ages 6 & up.** *www.napavalleyballoons.com*

Sonoma Valley Balloons *(Mail: P.O. Box 385, Sonoma 95476)* *(707) 939-7858.* **Ages 6 & up.**

Up and Away Ballooning *(Mail: P.O. Box 68, Windsor 95492)* *(800) 711-2998.* **Ages 6 & up.** *www.up-away.com*

● Whale Watching: *New Sea Angler* and *Jaws*

(Mail: P.O. Box 1148, Bodega Bay 94923) (707) 875-3495. **Ages 8 & up.**

Those seeking more down-to-the-sea pleasures may choose to whale-watch on the ocean. *New Sea Angler* and *Jaws* head out twice a day on weekends and holidays, December 28 through April, from Bodega Bay. Both vessels also provide year-round, daily salmon and rock cod fishing trips. Special cruises are also offered, on request.

● Bodega Marine Laboratory

Between Bodega Head and Salmon Creek. (707) 875-2211. One-hour tours, Fri., 2–4. Free. **Ages 8 & up.**

The University of California at Davis conducts research here on marine and coastal habitats. In 1775, Francisco Bodega y Cuadra, a Spanish mariner, became the first European to anchor in the harbor. Today, Bodega Bay is the second largest salmon fishing port in California. Just walking along the beaches and dunes around the bay can make you feel like you're the first person to set foot here.

● Petaluma Historical Library-Museum

20 4th Street, Petaluma 94952. (707) 778-4398. Wed.–Sat., 10–4; Sun., 12–3. Free. Groups by appt. Costumed docents also lead walking tours of Historic Downtown Petaluma on weekends, at 10:30, May–Oct. **Ages 7 & up.** *W. www.petalumamuseum.com*

Downtown in "The Egg Basket of the World," the Petaluma Historical Library-Museum shows rotating and permanent displays, such as one on the local poultry industry and another on local river history. The bust of Chief Solano, photos of General Vallejo, and the Knickerbocker No. 5 fire engine are popular. Kids enjoy ringing the Korbel Lumber Mill Bell. A third-grader from the Meadow School wrote, "I like the stained glass window, the kitchen and where they did the laundry because it was really fun."

● Petaluma Collective Military Antiques and Museum

300 Petaluma Boulevard North, Petaluma 94952. (707) 763-2220. Daily, 10–5:30. Free. Guided tours by appt. **Ages 7 & up.** *W. www.militaryantiquesmuseum.com*

This large, fascinating military museum specializes in World War II mementos and memorabilia. There are eight large dioramas, including one on a World War I trench and another on the German Afrika Corps. Original artwork of and by the soldiers and comic depictions of the enemy, "American Home Front Art," wartime posters, "trench art," and a 1941 Ford jeep are popular in this mind-boggling collection of military mementos dating back to the Civil War. The retail area offers uniforms, medals, headgear, nonfunctioning weapons, books, ephemera, and personal mementos.

● Petaluma Wildlife and Natural Science Museum

201 Fair Street. Back of the parking lot next to the Petaluma High School. Individual and group tours by appt. (707) 778-4787. $2. **Ages 7 & up.** *W.*

Animals, minerals, and fossils are on exhibit along with small live animals, reptiles, and amphibians. Hands-on exhibits teach while they entertain. The tours are given by high school docents.

● Mrs. Grossman's Paper Company

3810 Cypress Drive (Mail: MGPC Consumer Relations, P.O. Box 4467), Petaluma 94955. Take exit 116 off Highway 101 and turn left at traffic light on Lakeville Highway, for 1 mile. Right at South McDowell Boulevard

Extension, follow for .5 mile. (800) 429-4549. Tours by appt. Free. Parties and picnic areas. Sticker store, Mon.–Fri., 9–5:30. (707) 765-8554. Art classes. **Ages 2 & up.** *W. www.mrsgrossmans.com*

Sticker heaven! One-hour-long tours include a video showing how stickers are made, a walk on the production floor where you'll see printing presses, packaging machines, and a laserweb that creates Paper Whispers. Then it's on to sticker art class where guests make their own personal sticker postcard. Then you get your own bag of stickers. You can also visit the museum to see every single sticker Mrs. Grossman, the sticker queen, has ever made. On special Friday afternoons, some of the employees bring their dogs in to help welcome you. One seven-year-old exclaimed "I like stickers because I can stick them on me."

● Sonoma County Farm Trails

(Mail: P.O. Box 6032, Santa Rosa, 95406) For a free copy of the map, call (707) 571-8288. **All ages.** *www.farmtrails.org*

Drive from a cactus nursery and smoked poultry specialist in Petaluma to apple ranches and Christmas tree farms in Sebastopol. The Farm Trails map lists farms that are open to the public and has a handy alphabetical product listing. Remember that all listed are working farms, and although they may post hours, it's best to call first, to be sure your visit is convenient.

In summer the most popular Farm Trails visits are the berry, apple, herb, fruit, and vegetable farms; animal ranches; and bee and butterfly habitats. Year-round visits feature cheese factories, wineries, pumpkin patches, holiday tree farms, and acres of flowers in springtime.

● Petaluma Adobe

3325 Manor Lane, east of Highway 101, Petaluma 94954. (707) 726-4871. Daily, 10–5. Tickets usable at all state parks that day. Adults, $1. Tickets usable on the same day at the Vallejo Home, Mission Sonoma, and Sonoma Barracks in Sonoma. Picnic areas. Tours, groups, and Living History Programs. **Ages 4 & up.** *www.parks.sonoma.net\adobe.html*

General Mariano G. Vallejo's ranch house, Rancho Petaluma, was built in 1836 as the centerpiece of a Mexican land grant of 66,000 acres. Here we learned that in Spanish, adobe means to mix, and that the thick, naturally insulating bricks were made from clay mixed with water and straw and then dried in the sun. A self-guided tour takes you into the workshop, weaving room, servants quarters, and the Vallejos' upstairs living quarters—graciously furnished with authentic pieces.

Outside, there are huge iron cauldrons, clay ovens, and the racks on which cowhides, the currency of the period, were stretched out to dry. Farm animals add authentic background sounds. At one time, General Vallejo had one thousand workers on the ranch, and it's not hard, standing on the second-floor porch of Rancho Petaluma, to imagine the bustle of yesteryear.

● Sonoma State Historical Park

20 East Spain Street, Sonoma 95476. (707) 938-1519. Daily, 10–5. Tickets usable at all state parks that day. Adults, $1. **Ages 5 & up.** *W. www.parks.ca.gov*

The flags of seven countries have flown over Sonoma: Spain, England, Imperial Russia, Mexico, the Bear Flag, and the United States. The stories behind them can be found in the plaza at the center of the town.

The **Vallejo Home,** off 3rd Street West, named Lachryma Montis, after its clear spring, "Tears of the Mountain," was General Vallejo's city house. Furnished as it might have been when he lived there with his family, the house feels as if Vallejo just stepped out for a moment. One daughter's painting is on a wall, along with family photos. Behind the house is the kitchen building and the Chinese cook's quarters. The Chalet in front was once the storehouse and is now a Vallejo museum containing his books, pictures, saddles, coach, and cattle brand, various remembrances of his family, and biographies of 10 of his 16 children.

On the plaza in town, three-fourths of a mile east, you'll walk by the site of Vallejo's first home in Sonoma. Since a fire in 1867, only the Indian servants quarters remain. In the reconstructed **Soldiers Barracks** (built in 1836), there are exhibits representative of Sonoma history, an audiovisual show, and other activities on weekends. Vallejo was imprisoned by American settlers in 1846 during the "Bear Flag Revolt." The settlers proclaimed the "Republic of California" and created their own emblem, the Bear Flag. A few weeks later, the United States took over. Also on the plaza, the **Toscano Hotel** (built in 1858) is a carefully restored mining hotel with cards and whiskey glasses still on the tables waiting for the card players to return. (Docents give tours on weekends.)

At the far corner of the plaza is **Mission San Francisco de Solano** (707-938-9560), the northernmost and last of the 21 Franciscan missions in California and the only one established under Mexican, rather than Spanish, rule, in 1823. Russians donated the bells and other helpful items. The padres' quarters is the oldest structure in Sonoma. Visitors can walk through the building, looking at interesting exhibits, a restored chapel, watercolors of the missions, furnished rooms of the padres, spurs and leggings of the *vaqueros*, and other interesting artifacts of mission life, including the primitively painted chapel. A *ramada* has been constructed in the garden for blacksmithing, weaving, bread baking, and other period crafts demonstrations.

During your wanderings you may want to stop in at the **Sonoma Cheese Factory** (on the plaza at 2 Spain Street, 95476. 707-996-1931. Daily, 8:30–6.

www.sonomajack.com) to see a slide presentation and watch Sonoma Jack cheese being handcrafted. While there, pick up food for a picnic, which you can enjoy in the park across the street.

● Traintown

20264 Broadway, Sonoma 95476. On Highway 12, the main road into town from San Francisco. (707) 938-3912. Daily in summer and on winter weekends, and holidays, 10–5. Adults, $3.75; children, $3.25. **Ages 2–9.** *W. www.traintown.com*

A 20-minute trip on the Sonoma Steam Railroad, a quarter-size reproduction of a mountain division steam railroad of the 1890s, takes you over trestles, past trees, lakes, tunnels, and bridges, and into Traintown. While the train takes on water in Lakeview, you can look through the quarter-size miniature mining town and listen to its recorded history. The ducks are normal size, but you still feel like Gulliver in the land of Lilliputians. You can also ride on a carousel or ferris wheel.

● Jack London State Historic Park

2400 London Ranch Road, Glen Ellen 95442. (707) 938-5216. Museum open daily, 10–5. For the museum and the enlarged park, $3 per car; seniors, $2. Park hours open later in summer. On weekends, there's a golf cart run for seniors and disabled to get to Wolf House and Beauty Ranch. The cottage where Jack and Charmian lived is open weekends, 12–4. Nature hikes on weekends. The first floor of the museum and the cottage are accessible. **All ages.** *www.parks.ca.gov*

"I liked those hills up there above the ranch house. They were beautiful, as you see, and I wanted beauty. So I extended the boundary up to the top of that ridge and all along it. . . . I bought beauty, and I was content with beauty for a while. . . . Do you realize that I devote two hours a day to writing and ten to farming?" So wrote Jack London, in 1915.

Charmian London built the House of Happy Walls, one of the finest tributes to a writer in California, as a memorial to her husband. Furnished with the furniture and art gathered for Wolf House, which burned before the Londons could move into it, this museum covers the life of the adventurous young novelist. Once a sailor, prospector, and roustabout, London struggled to gain acceptance as a writer—and you can see a collection of his rejection slips. Photos of the *Snark,* in which the Londons sailed the South Pacific, and treasures collected on their voyages line the walls. The rangers sell London's books "signed" with the stamp London used to save time. A fascinating film taken a few days before his death shows London frolicking with his animals.

London was also an experimental farmer. The 803 acres of his Beauty Ranch have been purchased by the state. Here you'll see the cottage where he and Charmian lived and wrote, concrete silos, the distillery, stallion barn, "pig palace," log bathhouse, and blacksmith's shop. A trail leads to the still-extant Wolf House ruins and to London's grave. Picnic areas.

● Napa Firefighters Museum

1201 Main Street, Napa 94559. (707) 259-0609. Wed.–Sun., 11–4. Groups and tours by appt. Free. **Ages 4 & up.**
www.cityofnapa.org/IndexSamp/Samples/Search/query.htm

Here's a chance to ride a firetruck and have your picture taken. School groups also get free fire chief's badges. The museum is a treasure trove of firefighting equipment, from an 1850 hand-drawn hand-pumper to a 1904 horse-drawn steamer, a 1913 horseless carriage Model T to a 1931 ladder truck. Uniforms, scrapbooks, photographs, hose carts, firefighting toys, and other machinery fill the room. People from the community share their collections for rotating shows of, for example, cameras or tools. There are pictures of firehouses from all over the world, from Ponce, Puerto Rico's black-and-red striped Victorian, to the one in St. Petersburg, Russia.

● Copia

The American Center for Wine, Food and the Arts, 500 First Street, Napa 94559. (707) 265-5900 or (888-51COPIA). Thurs.–Mon., 10–5, Oct.–Apr.; Mon., Wed., and Thurs., 10–5, Fri.–Sun., 10–9, May–Sept. Groups by appt. (707) 265-5948. Adults, $12.50; seniors and students, $10; children, $7.50. Rentals. Julia's Kitchen Café (265-5700). Stores. **Ages 10 & up.** *W. www.copia.org*

Foodies of all ages will find changing art and foods exhibits mini-tasting stations, walkable gardens, and free cooking demonstrations and programs throughout the day. The core exhibit, "Forks in the Road" offers a light-hearted look at the role of food and wine in American life. The changing exhibits of art, photography, decorative arts, and artifacts touch on themes related to food and wine. Tickets are available for classes, performances, and films at the center.

● Napa Valley Wine Train

1275 McKinstry Street, near Soscol and First Streets, Napa 94559. (800) 427-4124/(707) 253-2111. By reservation, with deposit only. A Deli Car ride, or Open Air Car Train ride, without a meal, is $35. Brunch, lunch, dinner, and special meals range in price from $60 to $110. Group rates. Gift shop. Gift certificates. **Ages 12 & up.** *www.winetrain.com*

Older youngsters may find this 36-mile, three-hour adventure a real treat. Brunch, lunch, or dinner is served in a meticulously restored 1917 Pullman dining car replete with etched glass, polished brass, and rich mahogany. You will be pampered as you roll through the vineyards and mustard fields of the Napa Valley. There are special kids ride free events, murder mystery dinners, and concerts while dining.

● Yountville-Vintage 1870

Highway 29, 6525 Washington Street (Mail: P.O. Box 2500), Yountville 94599. (707) 944-2451. Daily, 10–5:30. **Ages 10 & up.** *W.*
www.vintage1870.com

This lovely historic winery complex is part of the original land grant made to Salvador Vallejo in 1838 and was bought in 1870 for $250 in U.S. gold coin. The brick exterior of the building hasn't changed much, but the interior is now a charming complex of 36 stores, including a deli, toy cellar, and candy store. Restaurants, garden cafés, and picnic areas surround the property.

● Napa Valley Museum

55 Presidents Circle (Mail: P.O. Box 3567), Yountville 94599. (707) 944-0500. Wed.–Mon., 10–5; until 8 first Thurs. of the month. Adults, $4.50; seniors and students, $3.50; under 10, $2.50. **Ages 8 & up.** *W.*
www.napavalleymuseum.org

This gloriously modern museum celebrates the land, the people, and the industries of the Napa Valley with changing exhibitions of art, history, and natural history. The interactive wine exhibit takes you through a year in the winemaking process, its trials and its joys. The architect, Richard Fernau, says, "The whole purpose is to introduce people to the whole valley. I like to think of it as a gateway to the Wine Country."

● Silverado Museum

1490 Library Lane, two blocks east of Main Street (Highway 29), off Adams, St. Helena 94572. (707) 963-3757. Daily except Mon. and holidays, 12–4. Groups by appt. Book shop. Free. **Ages 5 & up.** *W.*
www.caohwy.com/s/silvemus.htm

Robert Louis Stevenson has been associated with the Napa Valley ever since he honeymooned in an abandoned bunkhouse of the Silverado Mine on Mount St. Helena. Today, anyone who grew up on *A Child's Garden of Verses* or *Treasure Island* will appreciate this tribute to the man who wrote them. Portraits of Stevenson abound, including one showing him as a four-year-old with long flowing curls. Original manuscripts, illustrations, the author's toy lead soldiers, tea set, doll, chess set, his baby silver, a postage stamp with scenes of *Dr. Jekyll and Mr. Hyde,* his desk with carved faces, memorabilia from his plantation in Samoa, and Henry James's gloves, are neatly displayed in this modern, cheerful museum. The "good-bye" note from his friends in Samoa—they called him "Tusitala," teller of tales—is surprisingly touching. The place makes you want to read a Stevenson book right away.

● Bale Grist Mill State Historic Park

3369 St. Helena Highway North (Highway 29), 3 miles north of St. Helena (Mail: c/o Napa Valley State Park, 3801 St. Helena Highway North, Calistoga 94515). (707) 963-2236/942-4575. Demonstrations occasionally on weekends and by appt. $1. Walk to the mill from Bothe Park, along the History Trail. **Ages 5 & up.** *www.parks.ca.gov*

This restored water-powered grist mill was built in 1846 and has been milling flour ever since. The 36-foot waterwheel is equipped with French buhrs, quartzite stones used to grind the finest flour. Exhibits provide an orientation to the area as well as descriptions of its natural history. You can buy flour to take home.

● Sharpsteen Museum and Sam Brannan Cottage

1311 Washington Street, Calistoga 94514. Take Highway 29 to Calistoga; right on Lincoln to Washington. (707) 942-5911. Daily except Thanksgiving and Christmas, 11–4, and by appt. Free. Gift shop. Lectures. **Ages 7 & up.** *W. www.sharpsteen-museum.org*

This museum, given to the city of Calistoga by Ben Sharpsteen, an Oscar-winning Disney Studios artist (the Oscar is on exhibit!), is dedicated to the preservation and presentation of the history of Calistoga. Calistoga's pioneer history comes alive in the scale model dioramas and shadow boxes. The diorama-mural "Saratoga of the West" covers one wall. Other dioramas depict Robert Louis Stevenson, the railroad depot, the Chinese settlement, life at Brannan's Hot Springs Resort, and more. There's also a stagecoach.

Sam Brannan, the founder of Calistoga and the first California millionaire, is present in spirit. One of his cottages has been moved to the site, restored, and furnished authentically, a delight for children and adults.

● Old Faithful Geyser of California

1299 Tubbs Lane, 2 miles north of Calistoga, Calistoga 94515. (707) 942-6463. Daily, 9–6 in summer, until 5 in winter. Adults, $6; seniors, $5; ages 6–12, $2. Exhibit hall. Fainting goats. Video room. Gift shop and snack bar. Picnic tables available. **All ages.** *www.oldfaithfulgeyser.com*

One of the more surprising results of the 1989 earthquake is that it made Old Faithful "old erratic." Once one of the few faithful geysers in the world, erupting every 40 minutes almost like clockwork, Old Faithful now shoots forth its plume of boiling water and steam, sometimes 60 feet high, every hour or so, with lapses of up to 20 or 30 minutes. A recent visitor found it "going off" every 14 minutes, up 60 feet high. But the effect is the same. As one little girl exclaimed, when she viewed the geyser after dark: "Look, Mommy, the geyser is washing the stars."

● **Petrified Forest**

4100 Petrified Forest Road, Calistoga 94515. (707) 942-6667. Daily, 10–5; until 6 in summer. Adults, $5; seniors and ages 12–17, $4; ages 6–12, $2. Gift shop. **All ages.** *W. www.petrifiedforest.org*

Volcanic eruptions near Mount St. Helena 4.3 million years ago formed this forest of petrified redwoods, "discovered" in 1870 by Charles Evans and written about by Robert Louis Stevenson in "Silverado Squatters." A lovely forest trail passes a 150-foot-long "Monarch" tunnel tree and "the Queen," which was already 3,000 years old when it was buried. On the way out, you'll walk through a nature store and museum.

● **West County Museum**

261 South Main Street, Sebastopol 95472. (707) 829-6711. Thurs.–Sun., 1–4 or by appt. **Ages 8 & up.** *www.wschs-grf.pon.net*

The restored depot of the Petaluma and Santa Rosa Railroad, originally built in 1917 for the electric railroad that served the area, now houses rotating exhibits that reflect the history of Western Sonoma County, from the early Native Americans to the present. There have been exhibits on the apple and on locals' experiences during World War II. The museum also houses the Triggs Reference Room, which contains research materials pertaining to Western Sonoma County history.

● **Safari West**

3115 Porter Creek Road, Santa Rosa 95404. (800) 616-2695/(707) 579-2551. Adults, $58; children under 12, $28. By reservation only. Group discounts and specialized tours. Café. Trading post. **All ages.** *W. www.safariwest.com*

Now you can experience the wildlife of Africa without a passport and come nose-to-nose with many of the 400 exotic birds, reptiles, and mammals. The 2½-hour trek starts with a guided ramble in the hills in safari vehicles to see the animals living in nature. There are herds of antelope, gazelle, zebra (both brown-striped and black-striped!), oryx, eland, aoudad, and ibex, and flocks of sacred ibis, kookaburras, African spoonbills, cattle egrets and lilac-breasted rollers. There are wart hogs, moombas, and dangerous Cape buffalo. After a snack break, you're introduced to birds and animals on a walking tour. The highlight of the trip for nine-year-old Natalie was when she got to feed a giraffe, pet its nose, and see a camel drink water from a bottle.

Since this is as close to Africa as you may ever get, don't forget to bring sunscreen, a hat, and a jacket. You might also want to spend the night in Safari West's Tent Camp Adventure, in relatively luxurious authentic stilted tents or cottages.

● Pacific Coast Air Museum

2440 Airport Boulevard, Charles M. Schulz Sonoma Airport, Santa Rosa. (707) 575-7900. Tues. and Thurs., 10–2, weekends, 10–4. **Ages 8 & up.** *www.pacificcoastairmuseum.org*

This small museum shares the love of flying with all comers. Each month it allows you to actually climb on board a plane and even sit in the cockpit. One time it could be an F-86 Saber; another visit could offer a F-16N Navy Viper. More than 50 years of aviation is represented by aircraft and artifacts.

● Redwood Empire Ice Arena—Snoopy's Home Ice.

1667 West Steele Lane, Santa Rosa 95403. (707) 546-7147. Hours are complicated by shows and events, so call for information. Ages 12 and over, $5.50. Under 12, $4.50; skate rental, $2. Lessons and events. Groups by appt. Snoopy's Gallery and Gift Shop: (707) 546-3385. Daily, 10–6. "The Warm Puppy" coffee shop. **Ages 3 & up.** *www.flyingace.net*

Everyone will enjoy skating in this Alpine wonderland, which Charles Schulz (the creator of Snoopy) built for his family and the community. Hours are complicated because there are frequent shows, so call before setting out. Be sure to make reservations for one of the special events. The gift store boasts the largest collection of Snoopy merchandise in the world. You can even find Snoopy dolls sized from four inches to five feet, as well as a collection of Charlie Schulz's favorite drawings and awards.

● Charles M. Schulz Museum

One Snoopy Place, Santa Rosa 95403. (707) 579-4452. Adults, $8; seniors and ages 4–18, $5. Weekdays except Tues., 12–5:30; weekends, 10–5:30. **All ages.** *W. www.flyingace.net*

This 27,000-square-foot, colorful, playful museum and research center is dedicated to that ol' blockhead, Charlie Brown, and his regal beagle. There will be 7,000 original sketches culled from "Sparky's" half-decade of funny-paper history, in constantly changing exhibits, along with an 8-by-12-foot wall decorated by Schulz in 1951, before he moved to Santa Rosa. Tours, programs, classes, and special events will make you think, make you laugh, and make you remember why you love *Peanuts*. Said Schulz, "Obviously I did not know that Snoopy was going to go to the moon, and I did not know that the phrase "Happiness Is a Warm Puppy" would prompt hundreds of other such definitions, and I did not know that the term "security blanket" would become part of the American language. But I did have the hope that I would be able to contribute something to a profession that I can say now I have loved all my life." Kids will enjoy the labyrinth in the shape of Snoopy's head on the grounds near the museum entrance.

● Sonoma County Museum

425 7th Street, Santa Rosa 95401. Just off Highway 101, downtown. (707) 579-1500. Wed.–Sun., 11–4. Adults, $2; seniors and students, $1; under 12, free. Groups and tours by appt. Gift shop. **Ages 6 & up.** *W. www.sonomacountymuseum.com*

The Sonoma County Museum, located in a beautifully restored 1910 Post Office and Federal Building, is dedicated to the county of Sonoma and to the theme "Where Land Meets Art." Changing exhibitions feature the cultural history of Sonoma County and art from the Native American epoch to today. Cultural vignettes, special exhibits for children, and the Hart Collection of California landscape art also make the museum worth a visit. Favorite artworks include paintings by Thomas Hill and the collection of work by Christo. One young visitor wrote, "I really liked looking at the pictures of the animals and seeing the carriage."

The nearby **Codding Museum of Natural History** (557 Summerfield Road, Santa Rosa 95405. 707-539-0556. Wed.–Sun., 11–4. Free) focuses on local, regional, and worldwide natural history.

● Luther Burbank Home and Gardens

Santa Rosa and Sonoma Avenues (Mail: P.O. Box 1678), Santa Rosa 95402. (707) 524-5445. Gardens free, daily, 8–7. Guided tours of house and greenhouse. Tues.–Sun., 10–3:30 in summer, weekends in winter. Ages 12 and over, $3. Carriage house and shop, Tues.–Sun., 10–4. Groups by appt. Gift shop. Events. **Ages 8 & up.** *www.lutherburbank.org*

Luther Burbank, "the father of horticulture," made his charmingly comfortable home here for 50 years. He developed the Santa Rosa plum, the Burbank russet potato, the Shasta daisy, and a spineless edible cactus in these gardens. A walk through the garden will tell you all about his experiments and successes. Try to find the plumcot tree, or the cherry tree with four kinds of cherries growing on it. Burbank furnishings may be seen on tours of the house spring to fall.

● Jesse Peter Museum

Santa Rosa Junior College, 1501 Mendocino Avenue, Santa Rosa 95401. (707) 527-4479. Mon.–Fri., 9–5, and by appt. Closed holidays, school vacations, and summer. Free. Call for events schedule. **Ages 7 & up.** *W. www.santarosa.edu/museum*

Native American arts are found in this busy multicultural museum. Southwest pottery, California basketry, and Plains beadwork are part of the permanent exhibits. Temporary exhibits include Mesoamerican, Asian, African, and South American art. Northwest Coast art, photographs, and sculpture and replicas of building sites are some of the other changing temporary exhibits.

● **Windsor Waterworks and Slides**
8225 Conde Lane, Windsor 95492. Next to Highway 101, 6 miles north of Santa Rosa. (707) 838-7360. Weekends in May; daily, mid-June through Labor Day. All Day Plan, $14.95. Pool and grounds only, $8.95. Group discounts and events. Call for operating schedule. Gift shop. Parking, $2 per car. **All ages.** *www.caohwy.com/w/winwatsl.htm*

Imagine sitting down on an inner tube, taking off down a 42-foot drop, speeding 400 feet through tunnels, around spirals, and up walls—and finally landing in a pool. This wet adventure in a water park offers four separate water slides, picnic grounds, a large swimming pool, splash fountain, wading pool, Ping-Pong tables, volleyball, horseshoe pits, and a video arcade.

● **Healdsburg Museum**
221 Matheson Street, Healdsburg 95448. (707) 431-3325. Tues.–Sun., 11–4. Free. **Ages 7 & up.** *W. www.healdsburg.org*

Local history themes such as Native American, rancho, agriculture, the Russian River, and the founding of Healdsburg appear in the newly designed second floor of this interesting museum. Fine examples of Pomo Indian basketry and crafts, antique firearms, and 19th-century costumes and tools combine with collections of the town newspapers dating back to 1878 and with more than 5,000 original historic photographs.

● **Union Hotel Restaurant**
Main Street (Mail: P.O. Box 1), Occidental 95465. (707) 874-3555. Daily, 11:30–9. Closed Christmas. Prices range from $8.95 for soup and salad to $19.95 for steak. www.unionhotel.com

Mangia! Dining at the Union Hotel, which has been in business since 1879, is more than just a meal, it's an experience: Italian food—more than you can possibly eat—is served family style on a plastic red-checked tablecloth. Regardless of the main course ordered (chicken, duck, or steak), the meal includes salami and cheese, bean vinaigrette, salad, lentil soup, zucchini fritters, ravioli, vegetables, good sourdough bread and butter, potatoes, and side dishes. No matter what, you'll have a bag of leftovers for tomorrow's lunch. A half-price child's dinner is available. Dessert is extra. The frequent waits are made bearable by the game room or a walk through the main street of the town.

● Canoe Trips on the Russian River

The picturesque, winding Russian River is perfect for family canoe trips. It's safe and lovely but can also be fast enough to be exciting. One- and two-hour, half-day trips, full-day trips, and two-day trips are available. Swimmers only. **Ages 10 & up.**

W. C. "Bob" Trowbridge (20 Healdsburg Avenue, Healdsburg 95448. 800-640-1386. Canoes, half-day, $45; full-day, $55 and $3 per person for the shuttle. Two-day trips. Reservations suggested. Call or write for information). www.trowbridgecanoe.com

Burke's Canoe Trips 8600 River Road, 1 mile north of Forestville on the banks of the Russian River (Mail: P.O. Box 602, Forestville, CA 95436). 707-887-1222; $40 a day. Each canoe can accommodate two adults and two children. www.burkescanoetrips.com. A 10-mile, self-guided canoe trip through the Redwoods with wildlife galore. Return shuttle complimentary.

Whitewater Adventures (Mail: P.O. Box 2472, Napa 94558). 800-977-4837/707-257-4444. Two-day overnight trip, meals included, on the Upper Cache River, $99 per person May to the first weekend of June; $129 per person June–Sept. One-day rafting trips, $49. Group discounts. Upper Cache is a whitewater run through the wild country where tule elk roam the volcanic canyons and bald eagles soar. www.whitewater-adv.com

● Fort Ross State Historic Park

Highway 1, 12 curving miles north of Jenner (Mail: 30 East Spain Street, Sonoma 95476). (707) 847-3286/865-2391. Daily, 10–4:30. Adults, $1. Cars, $5; seniors' cars, $4. Living History Day programs. Picnic areas. Hiking trails. **All ages.** *W. www.parks.ca.gov*

California history seems especially romantic in this scenic spot. The Russian Orthodox Chapel, with a bell you can ring in front, is as spare and quiet as it was when the fort was sold by czarist Russia to John Sutter for $30,000 in 1841. Nine of the wooden buildings have been restored, including the Kuskov house, which was the residence of Fort Ross's founder, Ivan Alexandrovich Kuskov. Visitors can climb up into the eight-sided blockade tower and seven-sided blockhouse to look out over the little beach and inlet where Russian fur merchants used to trade with the Indians. The visitors center contains displays and artifacts from the Native American, Russian, and ranch eras. Don't forget to toss a penny into the wishing well!

● Calpine Geothermal Visitors Center

1500 Central Park Road, Middletown 95461, off Highway 29. (707) 987-4270/(866) GEYSERS. Visitors center: Thurs.–Mon., 9–4. Closed holidays. Bus tours by reservation at 10, 12, and 2. Groups by appt. Free. Gift shop. Snack bar. Picnic grounds. **Ages 8 & up.** *www.calpine.com or www.geysers.com*

A trip to the Calpine Geothermal Center is a lesson in geothermal power. Hands-on exhibits include displays exploring geothermal geology, well-drilling technology, and a topographical model of the geysers showing the location of each of the power plants now in operation there. Other exhibits reveal the history of the geysers and explain the wastewater to electricity project in Lake County and the Santa Rosa Geysers Recharge Project in Sonoma County.

● Anderson Valley Historical Museum

Highway 128, Boonville 95415. (707) 895-3207. Weekends, 1–4. Closed in winter. Free. **Ages 8 & up.** *www.museumsusa.org*

The 1891 one-room Con Creek Schoolhouse is the center of this small museum complex that celebrates Anderson Valley's home life and its lumbering and agricultural history. "Boontling," the valley's unique folk language, kin to the folk language of the Amish, is popular here.

● Lake County Museum

Old Courthouse, 255 North Main Street (Mail: 255 North Forbes Street), Lakeport 95453. (707) 263-4555. Tues.–Sat., 10–4; Sun., 12–4. Memorial Day to Labor Day. Adults, $2; children, $1. Donation. Gift shop. **Ages 7 & up.** *W. www.museum.lake.K12.ca.us*

Beautifully woven Pomo baskets and hunting traps are nicely displayed in this country museum, along with arrowheads, spears, and small tools. Firearms used to tame the West, such as the Kentucky long rifle and the Slotterbeck—made in Lakeport in the late 1800s—are also intriguing. Lillie Langtry, the celebrated English actress who retired to her winery here (it's still in business), is honored. Other displays include turn-of-the-century clothing and household items and samples of the semiprecious gems and minerals found in Lake County. Did you know that the "Lake County diamond," a natural or faceted quartz crystal, could be pink or lavender? The museum is also the home of the Lake County Genealogical Society, which boasts hundreds of books to help you find your roots.

● Lower Lake Historical Schoolhouse Museum

16435 Main Street, Lower Lake 95457. (707) 995-3565. Wed.–Sat., 11–4. Free. **Ages 7 & up.** *www.lakecounty.com*

This old-fashioned schoolroom has been reconstructed to look as it did a hundred years ago. It features pioneer artifacts and a replica of a schoolroom. The auditorium serves as a community center with special displays and performances.

● Anderson Marsh State Historic Park

8825 Highway 53 (Mail: P.O. Box 672), Lower Lake 95457. Either take Route 20 to Route 53 or take Highway 29 to Lower Lake, then continue straight on Route 53. (707) 994-0688/279-4293. Farmhouse: Sat.–Sun., 10–4; in summer, 8–5. Parking fee, $2. Park: Tues.–Sun., 10–5, except holidays. Hiking trails. Picnic areas. Cultural History Days and Living History Programs. Groups by appt. **Ages 5 & up.** *www.parks.ca.gov*

The community has worked together to restore the 1855 Anderson farmhouse with authentic antiques augmenting the original cozy furnishings. Here, costumed docents wander, lost in their roles of yesteryear. The ranch house and outbuildings are reminders of California's rich cattle ranching heritage.

From an oak-covered ridge above the marsh, you can see a sweeping expanse of grassy lowland. The ridge is also the site of archaeological digs where archaeologists have uncovered evidence of human activity dating back 10,000 years. The Cultural Heritage Council conducts a field school for anyone, from junior high to adult, who wants to learn how to excavate, map, and catalog artifacts and how to make stone tools and shell beads. An Indian Village is under construction.

The tule marsh, shoreline, meadows, and woods harbor gray foxes, river otters, opossums, deer, and hares as well as ducks and other waterfowl.

Redwood Country: Mendocino, Humboldt, and Del Norte Counties

Redwood country is one of the most beautiful areas in America. Stately redwoods line the roads "as far as the fog flows," and the Pacific Ocean crashes into the shoreline. Some of the beaches are craggy and surrounded by dangerous currents. Others are calm and protected, with long empty stretches just made for solitary walks.

You can dash up from San Francisco on Highway 101 or you can spend hours winding along the coastline on Highway 1. You can enjoy the Victoriana of Ferndale and Eureka or you can lose yourself in the tiny fishing villages of Rockport and Noyo. Whale watching is a popular pastime from December to April. The waters may be too cold to swim in, but the fish thrive and are there for the catching.

You can get away from it all in the sylvan glens along the Avenue of the Giants, marveling at your smallness next to a 300-foot tree. Demonstration forests show the aims, methods, and benefits of industrial forest management within the redwood region. Tours are self-guided, and there are rest rooms and picnic areas available. You'll learn that only 1 percent of the tree is living—only the tips of its roots, the leaves, buds, flowers, seed, and a single thin layer of cells sheathing the tree. You'll see Douglas firs, white firs, and redwood residuals—the redwood trees that have sprung up from seeds and sprouts. You'll find the forests along Highway 128, on new and old Highways 101, and on Highway 299.

The Pygmy Forest at Little River makes an intriguing juxtaposition with the enormous sequoias and giant redwoods along your route. Ten Mile Beach in MacKerricher State Park and the secluded sandy beaches at the foot of Main Street in Mendocino and Glass Beach at the end of Main Street in Fort Bragg are great places to find driftwood treasures.

Redwood country lets you set your own pace—there are many places to see and things to do close to each other, and there are enough parks and beaches for you to relax or picnic in, whenever the mood strikes. It's a great getaway for a weekend or a week.

● Point Arena Lighthouse and Museum

(Mail: P.O. Box 11, Point Arena 95468.) (707) 882-2777. Daily, 11–2:30; summer weekends and holidays, 10–4:30. Closed Thanksgiving and Christmas. Adults, $4; children, $1. **Ages 7 & up.** *W.*
www.pointarenalighthouse.com

If you've ever dreamed about living in history, this is a good way to do it. The lighthouse keepers have restored the lighthouse, museum, and three of the large homes on the lighthouse station to rent to vacationers. Rental fees and fees from whale watching and guided tours help maintain the site.

The first Point Arena lighthouse had to be destroyed after the 1906 earthquake; a new 115-foot tower with a Fresnel lens began flashing its guiding beacon in 1908. An automatic rotating beacon was installed in 1977. The museum is housed in the 1869 Fog Signal Building, next to the lighthouse.

● **Mendocino Headlands State Park and Ford House Visitors Center**

Main Street (Mail: P.O. Box 1387), Mendocino 95460. (707) 937-5397/ 937-5804. Daily, 11–4. Videos and headlands walks. Groups by appt. Donation. **Ages 8 & up.** *www.parks.ca.gov*

The Ford House, the second house to be built in the town of Mendocino, was a wedding gift from J. B. Ford to his bride, Martha Hayes Ford, of Connecticut, in 1854. Today, it is the visitors center, interpreting the natural environment of the area, telling the history of Mendocino and the surrounding areas. It is also a gallery exhibiting work by local artists. The star of the place is a recently constructed a four-by-eight-foot scale model of Mendocino village as it was on December 14, 1890, with its 358 buildings including sheds, outhouses, and 34 water towers, built on a scale of ³⁄₆₄ inches to the foot. Buildings were carved in balsa wood by artist Len Peterson and secured to a foam-core terrain that replicates the surface contours of the village. There are tramway tracks for the lumber vehicles, a 3⅛-inch-tall Presbyterian church, eight hotels, four boarding houses, a bank, two dressmakers, and a cobbler's store.

Once an old lumber port, Mendocino is now a mecca for driftwood collectors, artists, and tourists. The town has appeared in many movies. (Today, it stars in the *Murder She Wrote* reruns. Jessica Fletcher's home is now the Blair House Inn.) The town has interesting little streets to browse along when it gets too foggy for beachcombing.

Among the highlights are the **Mendocino Art Center** (45200 Little Lake Street, 95460. 707-937-5819. Daily, 10–5), and the **Village Toy Store** (10450 Lansing. 707-937-4633. Daily, 11–5).

The old **Masonic Lodge Hall** (Lansing and Ukiah), with its massive redwood sculpture of Father Time and the Maiden, carved from one piece of redwood, is a landmark.

The **Kelley House Historical Museum** (45007 Albion Street [Mail: P.O. Box 922, 95460]. 707-937-5791. Daily, 1–4 except Wed. Donation) is a pleasant step back in time. The nearby **Temple of Kwan Ti,** one of the first buildings in Mendocino, may be seen by appointment (707-937-1381).

● **Mendocino Coast Botanical Gardens**

18220 North Highway 1, Fort Bragg 95437. Six miles north of Mendocino, (707) 964-4352. Mar.–Oct., daily, 9–5; Nov.–Feb., 9–4. Retail nursery

and garden store. Adults, $5; seniors, $4; juniors 13–17, $3; children 6–12,
$1; student groups and those under 6, free. Group discounts and tours.
Complimentary electric cars. **All ages.** *W. www.gardenbythesea.org*

Forty-seven acres of gardens with a formal perennial garden, coastal pine forest, fern canyons, and ocean bluffs explode with multicolored flowers and teem with protected wildlife, including 60 species of birds. Rhododendrons bloom in April and May; perennials, from May to October. The heather blooms all winter, and then, too, you can see gray whale migration. Picnickers are welcome.

One youngster wrote, "That was the most fun place I have ever been. I liked all the flowers that were there. I liked all the trails; I liked all the places, especially the ocean. I liked when we got to eat and played games. We did work and we almost got lost too in The Botanical Gardens."

● Guest House Museum

Main Street, c/o City Hall, 416 North Franklin Street, Fort Bragg 95437.
(707) 961-2840. E-mail: donrnel@inreach.com Tues.–Sun., 10–4.
Donation. **Ages 7 & up.** *Partial W.*

This gift to the city from the Georgia Pacific Company houses historical pictures of the logging industry, a huge bellows, mementos of the loggers, and models of ships. Films and talks contrast the difference between logging's industrial present and its rugged past. Be sure to walk down to the foot of Redwood Avenue to see the huge slice of redwood that was 1,753 years old in 1843.

At this writing, the George Pacific Mill was closing, so the fate of the nursery at the foot of Walnut Street and all the mill tools has not been decided.

● Skunk Railroad

Skunk Depot, Main and Laurel, Fort Bragg. (800) 77-SKUNK/(707) 964-
6371. Call to reserve or write to California Western Railroad, P.O. Box
907, Fort Bragg 95437. Full- and half-day round-trips available daily to
Northspur and Willits with prices ranging from $18 for children, $29 for
adults on the half-day, to $25 for kids and $45 for adults on the 8 ½-hour
full-day. Kids under 5, free. Family packages. **Ages 5 & up.**
www.skunktrain.com

The Skunk Railroad, named for the smell the first gas engines used to cast over the countryside, has been making passenger trips from Fort Bragg to Willits since 1911. During the 40-mile trip, which takes all day, the train crosses 30 trestles and bridges, goes through two tunnels, twists and turns over spectacularly curved track, and travels from the quiet Noyo riverbed to high mountain passes through redwood forests. The half-day jaunt takes you through the redwoods, crossing the meandering Noyo dozens of times, to the midway point for a 30-minute rest stop with picnic tables and snacks available. The bouncy diesel Skunk is well worth the price and time. If it's summer, try the open observation car for unforgettable pictures.

● Mendocino County Museum

400 East Commercial Street, Willits 95490. (707) 459-2736. Wed.–Sun., 10–4:30. Free. **Ages 7 & up.** *W. www.co.mendocino.ca.us*

The Mendocino County Museum is a storehouse of memories, dreams, and hard-won lessons of survival amid the rugged beauty of California's North Coast. Exhibits use local artifacts to celebrate and explain the life and times of Mendocino County. Oral-history interviews capture living memories on tape. Collections of Pomo and Yuki baskets represent the vanished ancestors and today's descendants of the region's Native Americans. Treasures from the wreck of the *Frolic* reveal a strong sea trade from China. A fanciful hippie van delights the imagination as "counterculture on wheels." A new wing is under construction and will house exhibits of early steam engines and logging artifacts.

● Drive-Through Tree

Old Highway 101 (Mail: P.O. Box 10), Leggett 95585. (707) 925-6363. Daily, 8:30–8:30 in summer, earlier in winter. Each car, $3. Gift shop. **All ages.** *W.*

This large, chandelier-shaped, 315-foot redwood was tunneled in 1934. A standard-size contemporary car just fits through. It's 21 feet in diameter and, in spite of the tunnel, is still alive. The winding dirt road leading to the tree takes you right to a gift shop and to the highway. There are 200 acres of nature trails and picnic areas by the side of a lake that is home to geese. There are also logging relics on the grounds. Kids like the log with a hole you can crawl into. One year, everyone in Leggett Valley School had their pictures taken on horseback, in the tree, for the yearbook.

● Confusion Hill and Mountain Train Ride

75001 North Highway 101, 15 miles south of Garberville, Piercy 95467. (707) 925-6456. Daily, 11–4; in summer, 8–7. Confusion Hill: adults, $3; ages 4–12, $2. Mountain Train Ride: Apr.–Sept. Adults, $3; ages 4–12, $2. Gift shop and snack bar, daily, 10–5. **Ages 4 & up.** *E-mail: confusion@asis.com*

When you see six huge bears clowning around, juggling balls—it's the world's largest redwood chainsaw sculpture—you'll know you're in the right place. The miniature Mountain Train follows many switchbacks to take you 1.25 miles up to the summit of a redwood mountain, through a tunnel tree, and back down. Try the other experience at Confusion Hill, a spot where gravity is defied. Facing front, you seem to be standing sideways; water runs uphill; your friends shrink or grow taller in front of you. Is seeing really believing?

● Avenue of the Giants

Humboldt Redwoods State Park (Mail: P.O. Box 100), Weott 95571. (707) 946-2409. Day use, $2; camping, $12 per night. Reduced senior rates. Visitors center, on Highway 101 north, next to Burlington Campground, 2 miles south of Weott, has maps of self-guided walks. (707) 946-2263. Daily, 9–5. Special programs. **All ages..** *www.humboldtredwoods.org*

Standing tall as a nominee for the most spectacular 33 miles anywhere is this bypass road winding leisurely beneath 300-foot trees. One of the few species to have survived from the time of the dinosaurs, the redwoods are majestic, awesome trees to behold. You'll drive through a protected wilderness of soaring trees and moss- and fern-carpeted landscape occasionally spotted with deer. Founder's Grove, Rockefeller Forest, and Children's Forest are some of the best of the special groves. The Chimney Tree near Phillipsville, the Immortal Tree near Redcrest, and the Drive-Thru Tree in Myers Flat are more commercial stopping places. The visitors center interprets the redwood environment, displays the flora, fauna and history of the area and presents an interesting slide show on request.

● Pacific Lumber Company

(Mail: P.O. Box 37, Scotia 95565) South of Eureka 27 miles. (707) 764-2222. Lumber manufacturing tours: Mon.–Fri., 7:30–11 and 11:30–3:30. Historic logging museum: Mon.–Fri. in summer, 8–4, free. Demonstration forest open daily in summer, 4.5 miles south of Scotia, just off Highway 101. Free. **Ages 8 & up.** *www.palco.com*

Scotia is one of the last company-owned towns in the country. The Pacific Lumber Company was established in 1869, and the present town of Scotia, originally known as Forestville, was established in 1888. During the summer, obtain a pass for the lumber manufacturing tour at the Scotia museum. Logging equipment is on display outside, and inside there are historic photographs. You can watch a video about the lumber company.

The sawmill is no longer operating, but visitors can see how finished lumber products are handled in the manufacturing division. Signs along the catwalk explain the various steps of processing.

Don't miss the Scotia fisheries exhibit near the parking lot that shows the company's efforts to enhance the salmon and steelhead populations on the north coast.

● **Fortuna Depot**
4 Park Street, Fortuna 95540. (707) 725-7645. Wed.–Sun., 12–4:30. Donation. **Ages 8 & up.** *W. www.caohwy.com/f/fordepmu.htm*

The 1893 train depot is now a small museum housing Fortuna memories of loggers, farmers, Indians, home life, and the railroad. The newly restored first room tells a story about the railroad and trains; George, the teletyper, is at the ready; fancy dresses and shoes wait for the next dance; fishing poles and tackle stand waiting for the next fishing trip; and pictures, school books, railroad memorabilia, and farmers' barbed wire round out the collection. The three old marriage certificates are lovely. The museum is located in Rohnert Park, a lovely family park with picnic tables and playground equipment.

Visitors in autumn may want to stop by **Clendenen's Cider Works** (12th Street and Newburg Road. 707-725-2123, most Mon. and Thurs.) to see the mill in action and buy fresh cider. A bakery has also been added, for pies, scones, and cookies, and you can watch the baker work, too.

● **Ferndale Museum**
Shaw and 3rd Streets (Mail: P.O. Box 431), Ferndale 95536. (707) 786-4466. Tues.–Sat., 11–4, and Sun., 1–4 in summer. Closed Mon. and Tues. in winter and all Jan. Adults, $1; ages 7–16 and under, 50¢; ages 6 and under, free, when accompanying an adult. **Ages 8 & up.** *W. www.caohwy.com/f/ferndmus.htm*

A blacksmith shop with a working forge, antique farming and logging equipment, and a working seismograph are permanent exhibits, along with rotating collections that show the lifestyles, work habits, and activities of Ferndale's ancestors. Since most of the successful businessmen made their money with farms, their Victorian homes were called "Butterfat Palaces" and the town was called "Cream City." Ferndale, a restored and repainted Victorian town, is a wonderful place to spend time.

● **Kinetic Sculpture Race Museum**
580 Main Street (Mail: P.O. Box 916), Ferndale 95536. (707) 786-9259. Daily, 10–5. Free. **Ages 8 & up.**

Ferndale's Kinetic Sculpture Race takes place over Memorial Day weekend from Arcata to Ferndale, when 50 or more entrants power their wildly decorated motorless vehicles over choppy water, slippery mud flats, sand dunes, and city streets. This gallery/warehouse museum is crammed with dozens of racing chariots. These past winners show the artistry and occasional foolhardiness of their creators. Videos of past races are run regularly.

● **Fort Humboldt State Historic Park**
3431 Fort Avenue, off Highway 101, Eureka 95501. (707) 445-6567. Daily, 9–5. Free. **Ages 7 & up.** *W. www.parks.ca.gov*

High on a windy hill, Fort Humboldt is primarily an outdoor museum of the logging industry. Old machinery is accompanied by large display boards telling what it was like to be a logger in the 19th century. A logger's cabin is furnished with a stove, a bed, a shelf of cans of beans, and a "pin-up" calendar. You learn how to "fall" a tree (the falling branches are called widow makers) and then see how it is dragged out of the forest and cut up. One logger notes that it's "a shame to wash clothes while they can still bend." An 1884 Falk locomotive and an 1892 Andersonia locomotive are on view. They're steamed up for rides the last weekend in April and the third Saturday, May to September.

Old Fort Humboldt, where Ulysses S. Grant served as a staff officer in the 1850s, is nearby. Fort Humboldt was retired as a military post in August 1870. The land and the one remaining building, the hospital, completed in 1863, were sold to W. S. Cooper in 1893 for $6,500. Today the hospital has been restored and is used as a museum.

A short drive away are the only two covered bridges in the area. Take Highway 101 south to Elk River Road and follow it along to either Zane or Berta Road. The bridges are covered not to protect them from snow but to protect the wood from rain. Boarding up the bridges preserves the wood longer and is less expensive than constant repainting.

● Clarke Historical Museum

240 E Street, at 3rd Street, Eureka 95501. (707) 443-1947. Tues.–Sat., 11–4. Free. **Ages 6 & up.** *W. www.clarkehistory.org*

This large regional history museum is housed in a palatial 1912 bank. A recent addition is devoted to the Native American Indian culture of northwestern California. The world's largest and most complete collections of Hoopa, Yurok, and Karuk regalia and basketry are at the Clarke, with more than 1,200 artifacts displayed. There are also extensive collections on the development of Humboldt County: shipbuilding, logging, milling, firearms, furniture, textiles, and Victorian decorative arts.

Alyssa and Courtney of Scotia noted,"We had a blast looking at all the things in the museum. Some of the baskets were really rad. We loved the children's corner. We especially liked the 3-D thing. It was cool. Altogether it was fun."

The Clarke Museum is located in Eureka's Old Town, the original, restored, commercial district on the shore of Humboldt Bay. This district of Victorian commercial and residential buildings, crowned by the remarkable Carson Mansion (on 2nd and M Streets, not open to the public), the greatest Victorian in California, includes many bookstores and boutiques. Be sure to visit the crafts shop of the Northern California Indian Development Council on F Street, next to the ice cream parlor. There's a self-guided tour of the town's "Painted Ladies."

● Discovery Museum

3rd and F Streets (Mail: P.O. Box 3456), Eureka 95502. (707) 443-9694. Tues.–Sat., 10–5; Sun., 12–5; over 2, $4. Events; parties. **Ages 4 & up.** *W. www.northcoast.com/~discover*

Rotating hands-on exhibits focus on science, culture, art, and technology for adventure and family fun. Planetarium shows, a puppet theater, dentist's "stuff," a boat, roller coaster-physics, and other things allow kids to touch, create, imagine, and explore.

● Blue Ox Millworks Historical Park

#1 "X" Street, Eureka 95501. (800) 248-4259/(707) 444-3437. Winter: daily, 9–5. Adults, $7.50; seniors and teens, $6.50; ages 6–12, $3.50. Group discounts. **Ages 6 & up.** *www.blueoxmill.com*

Real-live Blue oxen are part of the family in this working museum of Victorian-era machinery manufacturers of "gingerbread," ornamental wood, plaster, and wrought-iron trim. They also create hand-tooled leather, glass, brick, and tiles. A wood-fired kiln shows how pottery is fired. Guided and self-guided tours are available. Call for the schedule of workshops on traditional arts such as candle making, basket weaving, blacksmithing, and pottery. Kids will enjoy the skids camp, the 1800s farm with some petting animals, and seeing the *Ms. Corrina Bella,* a 40-foot sailing scow being built with traditional techniques.

The Blue Ox Millworks is more than a business, it's a school of traditional arts where kids can learn how to master an old craft as well as how to manage a workshop and turn junk (a collapsed building, for example) into good, usable wood—and profit. The students also help out at the half-day work-shops for tourists. The Hollenbecks believe that to thrive, kids need to reestablish that quintesssential feeling of belonging, as well as having a chance to do some-thing worthwhile. At the Blue Ox, such opportunities abound.

Blue Ox Millworks will soon be an 18-acre historical park, which will include 20 restored Victorian homes featuring crafts, studios, shops, a restaurant, hotel, and functioning farm—all providing opportunities for students to work, learn, and earn a salary during nonschool hours.

● Humboldt Bay Maritime Museum

423 1st Street, Eureka 95501. (707) 444-9440. Tues.–Sat., 12–4. Donation. **Ages 7 & up.** *W. www.caohwy.com/h/humbbmme.htm*

Nautical displays are housed in a replica of the McFarlan House, built in 1852, the oldest home in Eureka. A Fresnel lighthouse lens, a hand-operated bilge pump, a salmon gear pulley, old navigation instruments, a fathometer, an early radar unit, cork and glass floats, and a porthole from the cruiser USS

Milwaukee, which was wrecked on the Samoa peninsula in 1917, are shown. There have been hundreds of wrecks off the entrance to Humboldt Bay. The museum's dedicated volunteers continuously dive for and salvage remains of these relics for display.

● Humboldt Bay Harbor Cruise, *M/V Madaket* Bay Tour

Foot of L Street (Mail: 423 1st Street), Eureka 95501. (707) 445-1910 for times and prices. Reserve for Saturday night dinner cruise, Sunday brunch cruise, or special holiday cruises. **Ages 5 & up.**

The 75-minute cruise aboard this venerable vessel, a 1910 ferry, takes in the oyster beds, pelican roosts, saw mills, egret rookery, and a former Indian village, and includes history of the area. There are daily trips, depending on the weather.

● Sequoia Park Zoo

3414 W Street, at Glatt, Eureka 95501. (707) 442-6552. Tues.–Sun., 10–5; until 7 in summer. Children's Petting Zoo (only in summer): Tues.– Sun., 11:30–3:30. Free/donation. **All ages.** *W. www.eurekawebs.com*

Located in the heart of the redwoods, the Sequoia Park Zoo houses an excellent variety of both local and exotic animals including the gibbon, otter, emu, prairie dog, reticulated python, black bear, and Pacific giant salamander. The zoo is part of Sequoia Park, which encompasses picnic areas, a playground, flower gardens, a duck pond, and 54 acres of North Coast redwoods.

● Samoa Cookhouse

Take Cookhouse Road, in the Samoa section of Eureka, across Samoa Bridge on Highway 255 to Samoa Road and 2841 E Street (Mail: 445 West Washington Street, 95501). (707) 442-1659. Breakfast, lunch, and dinner are served every day except Christmas, with top prices for adults: breakfast, $7.95; lunch, $8.95; and dinner, $11.95. Kids are lots cheaper. **All ages.** *W. http://humboldtdining.com/cookhouse*

Delicious, large, hearty, affordable family-style meals are served in this old lumber-camp cookhouse that once served as relief quarters for shipwreck victims. Today, it's the last surviving cookhouse in the West. The long tables are set as they were in 1885, with red-and-white-checked cloths and large bottles of catsup. Our breakfast consisted of huge amounts of orange juice, coffee, delicious French toast, and sausage. Dinner the night before included thick cuts of ham and sole with all the fixings, and peach pie. Before or after the meal, wander through the adjoining rooms to see an assemblage of loggers' boots, photographs of shipwrecks, dinner bells, kitchen utensils, and a steam coffeemaker that once served 500 men three times a day.

● Humboldt State University Natural History Museum

1315 G Street, at 13th Street, Arcata 95521. (707) 826-4479. Tues.–Sat., 10–5. Donation. Groups by appt. Workshops, programs, field trips. Gift shop. **Ages 2 & up.** *W. www.humboldt.edu/~natmus*

Insects fossilized in amber, trilobites and ammonites, and an extensive international fossil collection are headliners in this grand collection of more than 2,000 fossil specimens from around the world, spanning 1.3 million years. Other exhibits highlight local natural history including crustaceans, butterflies, birds of the redwood forest, mollusks, sponges, corals, minerals, as well as earthquakes and tsunamis. There is a living observation beehive and a display of live native animals. In addition, there's a 50-gallon saltwater local tidepool life tank. Three interactive computer terminals offer an earthquake/volcano map, a variety of nature CD-ROM and in-depth information on the fossils. Nine hands-on discovery boxes and an eight-foot prehistoric life puzzlebench challenge visitors to learn about the difference between dinosaurs and other prehistoric animals.

Ashley wrote, "The allosaurus skull was my favorite exhibit. I think the saber tooth tiger skull was cool. The tortoise shell was huge and cool looking."

The nearby **Arcata Museum** (Phillips House, 7th and Union Streets. 707-822-4722. Sun., 12–4. Donation) offers guided tours of one of Arcata's earliest houses. Its rooms recall the late 1800s and early 1900s.

● Humboldt State University's Marine Laboratory

570 Ewing Street (Mail: P.O. Box 690), Trinidad 95570. Off Highway 101. (707) 826-3671. Mon.–Fri., 9–5, and Sat., 10–5. Free. School programs. **Ages 8 & up.** *W. www.humboldt.edu\~marinelb*

Located near Land's End, in the picturesque fishing village of **Trinidad,** this working laboratory is open to the public for self-guided tours. Hallway aquariums hold rare and common mollusks and crustaceans, and saltwater fish. Varicolored anemones, sea cucumbers, Siamese tigerfish, and shovel-nose catfish were there for our visit, along with a tame wolf eel and a giant red Pacific octopus. Exhibits change regularly, but a permanent favorite is the tidepool touch tank.

Stop at the Trinidad Lighthouse on your way to the lab. This is the spot where the Spaniards landed on Trinity Sunday in 1775. The original gear system of descending weights still works to turn the light, but the original two-ton bell is for display only.

● Sumeg Indian Village

Patricks Point State Park, Patricks Point Drive, Trinidad 95570. (707) 677-3570. Daily, 8–10:30, $2 per car. **Ages 6 & up.** *www.parks.ca.gov*

A reconstructed Yurok Indian Village featuring houses, a dance pit, and sweat lodges. The village is used for ceremonial dances, events, and interpretive programs. In the park, you can whale-watch from the high bluffs, wander miles of beach, search for agates, and explore tide pools.

● Mad River State Fish Hatchery

1660 Hatchery Road, Blue Lake. Two miles south of Blue Lake (Mail: 1660 Hatchery Road, Arcata 95521). (707) 822-0592. Daylight hours. Groups by appt. only. Free. Picnic areas. Feed the fish for 10¢. **All ages.** *W. www.californiafishandgame.com or www.redwoodvisitor.org*

Baby salmon and steelhead can be seen and fed here. There is fishing (also wheelchair accessible) adjacent to the hatchery. By the way, the river is not ferocious. It was named for a fight between Joe Greek and L. K. Wood, two explorers of the region, in 1849. One Headstarter named Nathan wrote,"It was nice feeding the fish. I liked when the fish jumped. It was nice letting the fish free."

● Blue Lake Museum

330 Railroad Avenue, Blue Lake 95525. (707) 668-4188. Sun., Tues., and Wed., 1–4; Free. **Ages 8 & up.** *W.*

This diminutive museum presents historical displays of the Mad River Railroad and logging operations, along with a collection of local Native American basketry. Tour local historic homes.

● China Flat Museum

Highway 299, at Highway 96 (Mail: P.O. Box 102), Willow Creek 95573. (530) 629-2653. Fri.–Sun., 10–4. May–Oct. Closed in winter. Donation. Gift shop. **Ages 7 & up.** *W. www.bfro.net/news/wcmuseum.htm*

Find "Bigfoot" here! Footprint casts and location maps, plus mining, logging, and Native American artifacts. Items from local ranching families are on display as well, along with Gold Rush tools, housewares, jewelry, and newspapers.

● Hoopa Tribal Museum

Hoopa Valley Indian Reservation (Mail: P.O. Box 1328), Hoopa 95546. Highway 96, off Highway 299 west. In the Hoopa Shopping Center across Trinity River Bridge. (530) 625-4110. Weekdays, 8–12, and 1–5; also Sat., 10–4, in summer. Free. Group tours and rates by appt. **Ages 7 & up.** *W. www.bss.sfsu.edu*

California's largest Native American Reservation is nested in the mountains of northern Humboldt. Stone implements, dishes, tools, baskets, and dance regalia of the Hoopa Indians—"the people who live up the river," as named by Jedediah Smith's Yurok guide—are shown here, along with items from other tribes, such as the Yurok and Karuk, the Dakotas, and Alaskan tribes. Many of the Hoopa items are on loan from local residents, for this is a living museum, run by members of the Hoopa tribe. The artifacts are still used regularly in traditional tribal ceremonies in the "Land of the Natinixwe."

Where the Trails Return, a documentary video explaining the Hoopa culture, tradition, and government, can be viewed at the museum, which will also arrange tours of the reservation to visit ceremonial grounds and villages. The ruins of Fort Gaston, built in 1851, include a dwelling once occupied by Ulysses S. Grant.

● **Orleans Mining Company Museum**
Highway 96 (Mail: P.O. Box 127), Orleans 95556. (530) 627-3213. Daily, 7 A.M.–8 P.M. The gas station is open until 10 P.M. Free. **Ages 8 & up.**. *W.*

An old ghost town, once the county seat, is coming to life again in Orleans, with dining hall, motel, bunkhouse for river rafters, a gas station, and a tackle shop. The walk-through museum, with old relics of miners, is constantly being remodeled. Visitors will see an old doctor's office, an old kitchen, a bar scene with mannequins in place, and a working generator with logging tools and equipment dating back to the first days of logging. The owner is most proud of his cast-iron frying pans—he's going for the *Guinness Book of World Records.*

● **Prairie Creek Redwoods State Park**
Highway 101 North, 127011 Newton Drury Parkway, Orick 95555. North of Orick 6 miles. (707) 464-6101 ext. 5300/5301. Parking, $2 per car. Camping, Junior ranger programs for children 7–12. Call for times and topics. Bookstore. **Ages 7 & up.** *W. www.parks.ca.com*

Roosevelt elk roam this state park and can be seen grazing on the meadow outside the visitors center. Inside the center you'll see an interesting exhibit on the elk and the trees, ferns, flowers, and animals in the area. Fine nature trails lead from the center. On one is a redwood hollowed out by fire that is still living. One hundred twelve school children have been inside it at one time.

● **Trees of Mystery and Skytrail**
15500 Highway 101 South (Mail: P.O. Box 96), Klamath 95548. South of Crescent City 16 miles. (800) 638-3389/(707) 482-2251. Open daylight hours year-round except Thanksgiving and Christmas. Adults, $15; seniors, $10; ages 6–11, $8. Group, family, and AAA discounts. Gift shop. Motel. Restaurant. **All ages.** *W. www.treesofmystery.net*

A talking 49-foot-tall Paul Bunyan greets you at the entrance, and then you walk through a hollowed redwood log into a forest of unusual tree formations, where recorded music and explanations take you past trees such as the "Fallen Giant" and the "Elephant Tree," and the immense and moving "Cathedral Tree." Back down the hill is our favorite section—Paul Bunyan's "Trail of Tall Tales"—where you hear how Babe the Blue Ox was found, how the Grand Canyon was dug, and how Sourdough Sam makes his pancakes. (His recipe includes the lard from one summer-fatted bear.)

The "Sky Trail" aerial gondola ride starts just above the Brotherhood Tree and takes you up, silently gliding through the redwood forest canopy at heights of up to 150 feet, to a peak of nearly 750 feet, where you'll see an unparalleled panorama of rugged coastal mountains and sweeping ocean vistas. The enclosed six-person gondolas are spaced along the cable and take 7 to 10 minutes to complete the one-third-mile journey. Then you can stay awhile at the multilevel observation deck and hop back on another gondola or hike down to the Brotherhood Tree.

Indians called this "a place of spirits," and the End of the Trail Museum in the gift shop offers an extensive array of clothes and an excellent museum of artifacts of tribes ranging from the Mississippi to the Pacific and north to the Aleutians. The "End of the Trail" sculpture, carved from a single block of wood, is right in front of the museum.

The **Drive-Through Tree** five miles south, on Highway 101 at the north end of the Klamath River Bridge (known for its decorative golden bears), is worth a short visit. Take the Terwer Valley off-ramp to State Route 16, then east for 200 yards. (Mail: P.O. Box 35, Klamath 95548.) 707-482-5971. $2 per car. The opening is 7'4" wide by 9'6" high, but the steep grade and sharp curve prohibits trailers to park beyond the toll station. Gift shop, rest rooms, picnic tables, and wandering emus!

● Klamath River Jet Boat Tours

17635 Highway 101 South (Mail: P.O. Box 947), Klamath 95548. Five miles south of the Trees of Mystery, 1 mile north of the Klamath River Bridge. (800) 887-JETS/(707) 482-7775. Groups and charters. May 1–Sept. 30, 55-mile trip from 9–12:30 or 3–7 and 30-mile trip from 1–2:30.
Ages 10 & up. *www.jetboattours.com*

Daily fun-for-all tours up the famous Klamath River will teach boaters the river's rich history, local Native American culture, and wildlife in a wonderful and exciting experience for all. You begin the journey at "Rekwoi," the Indian name for where the freshwater meets the Pacific Ocean. Along the trip you'll see ospreys, seals, California sea lions, California black bear, deer, elk, mink, otters, and eagles and hawks.

● Ocean World

Highway 101 South, Crescent City 95531. South of the Oregon border 20 miles. (707) 464-3522. Daily, 8–9 in summer; 9–5 in winter, depending on the weather. Adults, $7.95; ages 3–10, $4.95. Group rates. Gift shop. **Ages 3 & up.** *www.oceanworldonline.com*

Thousands of marine specimens live in this interactive sea environment. At the touchable tide pool you can pick up a starfish, tickle sea anemones, and touch many types of sea critters. You can look a shark in the eye, see bat rays flying through the water, pet a shark octopus, and see sea lions perform.

● Del Norte Historical Society Museum

577 H Street, Crescent City 95531. (707) 464-3922. Mon.–Sat., 10–4. Adults, $2; children under 12, 50¢. **Ages 7 & up.** *www.delnorte.org*

The 1935 version of *The Last of the Mohicans* was filmed in Crescent City, and this two-story museum, once a county jail, has a photo of the Indian who appeared in it. A replica Yurok bark house and stick games, headdresses, beads, dolls, and baskets of the Tolowa, Pomo, Hoopa, and Yurok tribes are shown, as are photos of Crescent City since its beginnings, with lots of "before and after" shots of the 1964 tidal wave. Unicycles, jail cells, a moonshine still, pioneer clothing, the Fresnel lens from the St. George Reef Lighthouse, and other collections by local residents bring new life to local history. Artifacts from the shipwreck *Brother Jonathan*—gold coins, china, pottery, bottles, hardware, etc.—draw visitors.

● Northcoast Marine Mammal Center

424 Howe Drive, near Beachfront Park, Crescent City 95531. (707) 465-6265. Daily, 12–5. Free. **Ages 6 & up.** *www.northcoastmarinemammal.org*

To learn about the effects of illness and predators on seals, visit these animals, caged out-of-doors, so they can be seen anytime during daylight hours. There are also seal pups "rescued" by people who thought they were abandoned. Since their mothers won't come near them if they smell of humans, they have to be raised here until they are old enough to be released back into the ocean. A brief description of each animal is posted by its cage.

● Battery Point Lighthouse

Foot of A Street, 577 H Street, Crescent City 95531. (707) 464-3089. Apr.–Sept., Wed.–Sun., 10–4, tide permitting. Adults, $2; under 12, 50¢. **Ages 7 & up.** *www.delnorte.org*

Battery Point Lighthouse, built in 1856, is located offshore from Crescent City on a little island accessible only at low tide. Lighthouse keepers and volunteers wearing period costumes offer guided tours that cover most of the lighthouse and its history. The beacon on display is the fourth one used in this lighthouse. The fifth beacon is in use now, as the lighthouse is active as a private aid to navigation. Visitors can see an old log book, the original 1856 banjo clock, shipwreck photos, and nautical mementos. The lighthouse is being restored to its first days in the 1850s.

Although many have hopes of being stranded by the tide, along with the resident ghost, the wealth of native plants and view of the ocean from the tower will make up for their disappointment in finding themselves safely back on the mainland.

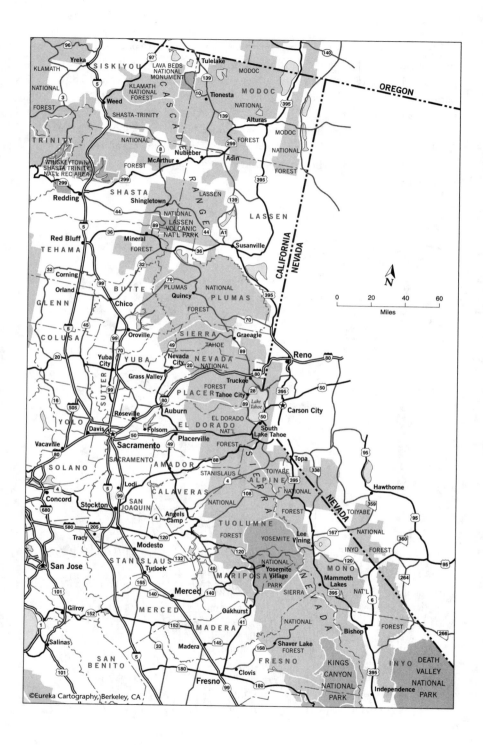

©Eureka Cartography, Berkeley, CA

The Big Valley

■ Solano, Sacramento, San Joaquin, and Stanislaus Counties

Today, the Sacramento area is the political heartland of the state of California. Two hours away from San Francisco, the city of Sacramento is worth a visit to get a feeling for how the world's eighth-largest economy functions.

At different times, the capital of California has been Benicia, Vallejo, and San Jose. The state capitol is now firmly ensconced under the beautifully restored dome in Sacramento. The rich farmland surrounding the city is reflected in the 40-acre Capital Park in the city. You will appreciate the mix of urban, suburban, and rural settings, which symbolize the variety of California's lifestyles.

Stockton, south of Sacramento, in rolling hills and farmland dotted by small towns, is one entrance to the Gold Country. Stockton is named in honor of Commodore Robert Stockton, who led the forces that took over California for the United States in 1847. The lakes and peaceful atmosphere of the San Joaquin Valley add to the ambience of the area, and water-sports lovers will find ample opportunities for houseboating, skiing, fishing, and every kind of boating.

● SixFlags Marine World

Marine World Parkway, Vallejo 94589. Located at the intersection of Highways 80 and 37. (707) 643-6722/644-4000. Open daily Memorial Day to Labor Day, weekends and school holidays Mar.–Nov., 10–6, and later, depending on weather. Call for up-to-date times and prices. Adults, $42.99; seniors and disabled, $32.99; children 48 inches tall and under, $24.99; under 2, free. Gift shops. Dolphin strollers and wheelchairs for rent. Picnic areas. Blue and Gold Ferry from San Francisco's Pier 39: (415) 705-5444/(707) 64-FERRY. BARTLINK: (707) 648-4666. Yearly memberships, group discounts available. **All ages.** *www.sixflags.com*

Dancing dolphins, killer whales, waterskiing extravaganzas, birds and butterflies, an Australian "walkabout," and a "Gentle Jungle" petting area are just some of the many attractions in this remarkable thrill-ride wildlife park and "oceanarium." For a real experience, come eye to eye with 15 different species of sharks as you move down a crystal-clear tunnel swirling with other fish in coral caves. Let a walrus wink at you. Meet lion clubs and snarly alligators. When the kids tire of looking at the aquarium and other exhibits, they can sit and watch one of the exciting shows or let off steam at the Whale-of-a-Time Playground. There are rides that make you spin, splash, smile, scream, loop, and laugh. Vertical Velocity is the tallest, fastest coaster in Northern California. Elephant rides, giraffe feedings, and animal encounters are among the dozens of ways to have a wonderful day.

● Vallejo Naval and Historical Museum

734 Marin Street, Vallejo 94590. (707) 643-0077. Tues.–Sat., 10–4:30. Adults, $2; seniors and students, $1. Kids under 12, free. Gift shop. Research library. Tours, special events. **Ages 7 & up.** *www.vallejomuseum.org*

Located in the former City Hall, this 25,000-square-foot museum proudly exhibits ship models, murals, naval memorabilia, and the periscope from the USS *Baya*. Revolving exhibits focus on community and naval history. A working periscope installed through the roof gives an excellent view of San Francisco and Mare Island. David G. Farragut, known for his Civil War battle cry, "Damn the torpedoes—full speed ahead," was the Navy Yard's first commandant and is remembered here.

● Mare Island State Historic Park

Exit Tennessee Street West off Interstate 80 or meet guide at prearranged place. Ferry: (707) 643-3779. (Mail: 328 Seawind Dr., Vallejo 94590) Tours by reservation only: (707) 644-4746. $10–14; with lunch, $20–24. Chapel rental: (707) 557-1538. Ages 6–12, $5. Admiral's Mansion, $4 additional. **Ages 6 & up.** *www.mareislandhpf.org*

View the Officers' Mansion Row and its beautiful gardens, the shipyards, historic cemetery and St. Peter's Chapel with the largest collection of Tiffany stained-glass windows west of the Mississippi. Even the cherubim and archangels are militant: Saint George slays his dragon; Sir Galahad tests a blade on his knee; and the Archangel Gabriel strides through the mist, horn at the ready, while the angel Zophiel stands guard.

● Benicia Capitol State Historic Park

First and G Streets, Benicia 94510. (707) 745-3385. Wed.–Sun., 10–5. Closed major holidays. Adults, $1; under 17, free. **Ages 8 & up.** *www.parks.ca.gov*

Benicia was named for General Mariano Vallejo's wife. Today the town is a mecca for artists and antique collectors. Benicia was, briefly, the third capital of California, and the Capitol building still looks much as it did in 1853. The exhibit rooms capture a bit of California history—right down to the whale-oil lamps, quill pens, shiny brass cuspidors, and varied headgear on all the desks. The Senate is on the first floor, the Assembly on the second. Interactive displays also bring the past to life. The first floor is wheelchair accessible. There is a TV documentary of the Capitol and Fischer-Hanlon House for those who can't climb stairs.

The **Fischer-Hanlon House** (open as guides are available) next door is also part of the state historic park complex. This fine old Federal-style house has been lovingly restored by volunteers. Included are the creamery and the carriage house with buggy and cart. This is a proper, upper-class merchant's home of the 1880s, and the Hanlon sisters enjoyed it until they gave it to the state in 1969.

Don't forget to go across town to visit the Benicia Historical Museum at the **Camel Barn** (2024 Camel Road. [Mail: 2060 Camel Road], Benicia 94510; 707-745-5435. Wed.–Sun., 1–4. Adults, $2; seniors and ages 6–12, $1. Tours by appt. *W.* www.beniciahistoricalmuseum.org), in the Arsenal on Camel Road off Park.

These large sandstone warehouses now serve as nicely designed art galleries and a historical town museum, but they actually housed 35 army camels from 1856 to 1864. They were all sold to a camel herder in Nevada who set them free. One was actually spotted in the desert in 1922. Building #7 contains the remains of the Galilee, one of the last wooden seagoing ships built in the Matthew Turner Shipyards in Benicia. Building #8, the Powder Magazine, is one of the few remaining examples of the stonemasons' art in California, from the vaulted ceilings to the carvings over the capitals and on the lintels. Building #9 houses the museum with its memorabilia reflecting the past as it relates to the future. Other buildings in Benicia Industrial Park include a clocktower and the 1860 Commandant's Home, now being restored, where poet Stephen Vincent Benet lived while his father was commanding officer of the post.

The **Benicia Fire Museum** (900 East 2nd Street. 707-745-1688. First three Sun. of the month, 12–4, and by appt.) is one of five such museums west of the Mississippi. On display are antique fire extinguishers, a collection of water grenades up to 150 years old, two antique fire engines, and many more items appealing to firefighting buffs.

● Jelly Belly Candy Company

One Jelly Belly Lane, Fairfield 94533. (707) 428-2838. From Highway 80 West, take Chadbourne exit in Fairfield. At first stop, turn left onto Chadbourne Road and continue past first stoplight. Left one block past light into Courage Drive. Left on North Watney Way and left on Jelly Belly Lane. From Highway 80 East, exit at Highway 12/Rio Vista. Right at first light onto Beck Avenue, right on Courage Drive, right on North Watney Way and right on Jelly Belly Lane. Gift store. Visitors center. Java Jelly Café. Picnic Area. Tours daily, 9–5. Groups. Party rooms. Free. **All ages.** *W. www.jellybelly.com*

"The day I went to the Jelly Belly factory I fell in love. You could see how they make the candy and how they put the chocolate on the raisins. They put the raisins in a barrel and the barrel turned. You'll get samples of candy. You will enjoy it. I did. They have jelly beans in 40 flavors which are very good. The Jelly Belly is an interesting place to go and see how candy is made. You should go. You will have a blast." So gushed Tina Miranda, a fourth-grader at David A. Weir School, Fairfield.

The Jelly Belly visitors center is the launching area for factory tours and an educational activity center. There's a demonstration candy-making kitchen as well as a café, Java Bar, ice cream bar, and candy store where you can stock up on Belly Flops. The 35-minute tours are offered about every 15 minutes. Visitors stand on a catwalk above the factory floor and a guide narrates the production process while TV monitors provide close-ups of each machine. (The machines take weekends off, so tours are quiet then.) Jelly Belly's robots pull cases of different beans off the assembly line, stack them on the appropriate stacks. There are 50 flavors of Jelly Bellys, only four calories per jelly bean—and it takes 7 to 10 days to make one. Free samples!

● **Thompson Candy Company**

2445 South Watney Way, Fairfield 94533. (707) 435-1140. Mon.–Sat., 9–5. Sun., 12–5. Seasonally. **Ages 7 & up.** *www.thompsoncandy.com*

Founded in 1879, Thompson Candy Company has developed an extensive line of bar chocolates and molded novelties. The plant offers viewing windows into the factory operations as well as sales at its factory store.

● **Vacaville Museum**

213 Buck Avenue, Vacaville 95688. (707) 447-4513. Wed.–Sun., 1–4:30. Adults, $1; students, 50¢. Wed., free. Gift shop. Native plant interpretive garden. Tours by appt. Video theater and special programs. **Ages 8 & up.** *W. www.vacavillemuseum.org*

As a center for Solano County History the museum explores the county's colorful past. Exhibits in the main gallery change regularly. Past exhibits have told the story of the Nut Tree, looked at the fruit orchard industry, or chronicled the lifestyle of earlier times. One favorite was "Common Threads: Solano County Clothing from the Wardrobe Through the Wringer," with dress forms, sewing machines, and washing machines.

Third-grader Cassandra wrote, "I really liked everything there but I liked the walking the most. I liked the walking the most because I like to see mansions and other cool houses. I also liked the computers and the story about the Chinese girl. Thank you for taking us on a great tour!"

● **Jimmy Doolittle Air and Space Museum**

Travis Air Force Base, Building 80, Burgen Boulevard (Mail: 400 Brennan Circle, Travis Air Force Base 94535). (707) 424-5605. Mon.–Sat., 9–4. Free. Stop at the main gate or visitors center for a pass. Gift shop. Picnic area. **Ages 8 & up.** *W. www.travis.af.mil*

A B-29 Superfortress bomber is just one of the 32 vintage airplanes on display outside this cavernous museum. There are fighters and transports and helicopters from World War II, the Korean War, and Vietnam. Inside you'll find engines, flight uniforms, photographic exhibits, a space capsule, and a few planes from Desert Storm. Kids will love climbing into some of the cockpits. Airplane buffs will love it.

● Western Railway Museum

Rio Vista Junction, 10 miles east of Fairfield at 5848 State Highway 12 (Mail: 5848 State Highway 12), Suisun 94585-9641. (707) 374-2978. Wed.–Sun. in summer, weekends in winter, 11–5. Adults, $7; seniors, $6; children up to 14, $4. Charters and groups by appt. Events. Picnic areas. Gift shop. **Ages 4 & up.** *www.wrm.org*

The Western Railway Museum was put together by a nonprofit organization of people who love trains. A major museum is in the works. Meanwhile, visitors can ride on or walk through and around the more than 120 retired trolleys and steam locomotives or just watch the railroad buffs at work. Our favorite is the old-fashioned Salt Lake Utah observation car (remember Judy Garland in *The Harvey Girls*?). The Birney "dinkey" streetcars, the New York city "el," the Pullman ready for sleep, the Toonerville trolley from the Key System, and Oakland and San Francisco streetcars will spur youngsters' imaginations. The gift shop holds the largest collection of railroad books in the West, along with cards, old ads, tickets, and badges.

On weekends, mid-March to mid-May, the **Prairie Train Wildflower Express** makes special excursions through the Jepson Prairie at the height of the wildflower blooming season.

In December, the **Santa Claus Express** allows kids a chance to talk to Santa Claus. Both trains recall the best of the railroad travel era, with complimentary hors d'oeuvres and beverages and entertaining guides.

● Rio Vista Museum

16 North Front Street, Rio Vista 95471. (707) 374-5169. Weekends, 1:30–4:30, and by appt. (707) 374-2321. Adults, $1. **Ages 8 & up.** *www.riovista.org*

All of the treasures in this little museum have been donated by local residents. There are antique etchings and photos; newspapers and books; and farm implements such as tools, plows, a buggy, a wagon, a forge, and a foundry, typewriters, a wine press, Chinese hats, and local birds' eggs. The museum was created during the Bicentennial, "so we won't forget all about the past."

● Explorit Science Center

3141 5th Street (Mail: P.O. Box 1288), Davis 95617. (530) 756-0191. Tues.–Fri., 2–4:30; Sat., 11–4:30; Sun., 1–4:30. General admission, $3; under 3, free. Gift store. **Ages 2 & up.** *W. www.explorit.org*

This small, entertaining, hands-on science museum offers fun for even the youngest child. Three snake buddies, cockroaches from Madagascar, and other critters rule over a collection of changing exhibits such as an international sand sample collection and a take-apart center, where kids can look at the insides of things such as a probe microscope and solar energy panels. The big sand pool in the back is also fun.

● Yolo County Historical Museum

512 Gibson Road, Woodland 95695. Highway 80 to Highway 113. (530) 666-1045. Mon. and Tues., 10–4; weekends, 12–4, and by appt. Adults, $2; ages 12 and under, free. Picnic areas. **Ages 8 & up.** *W.*

Housed in the Greek Revival–style mansion built by William Gibson to remind himself of his Virginia home, this museum records area history as seen through the lives of one family. Each room represents a different era and furnishing style, from 1850 to 1940. There are eight other buildings in the museum complex including a dairy, a root cellar, a tiny building with a display of washing machines from the 1870s, a local blacksmith shop that worked until 1904 and a barn with an exhibit of local agriculture and horticulture. There's an herb garden too. Little Melissa wrote, "I really enjoyed Gibson House a lot. The sterioptiscope [sic] was neat! The commode must have been very handy. The hog oiler looked handy too. The hair pictures were very neat. The sad iron was pretty heavy. Those wringers were dangerous! Gibson House was fun!"

● Yolo Short Line Railroad

341 Industrial Way, Woodland 95776. (800) 942-6387. Weekends and holidays, May–Oct., 11:30. Adults, $13; seniors, $11; ages 4–14, $8. Family fares. Group discounts. Charters; Saturday Train Robbery Barbecue Express by reservation, $30–$38; $10–$20 without barbecue. **Ages 4 & up.** *www.ysrr.com*

The YSL is an old-fashioned excursion railroad that rolls along the original 1912 Sacramento Northern route, through farmland, along the Sacramento River, and over an 8,000-foot-long wooden trestle to West Sacramento. The round-trips take two hours and 20 minutes. You can buy snacks or take picnics and eat at one of the tables on the "open-air" baggage car. There are closed cars, too. Your five-car train will be pulled by a diesel engine or #1233, a World War I–vintage steam locomotive.

● Hays Antique Truck Museum

1962 Hays Lane at the Heidrick Ag History Center, Woodland 95776. (530) 666-1044. Between Main Street, Interstate 5, and Road 102. Mon.–Fri., 10–5; Sat., 10–6; Sun. 10–4. Closed holidays. Adults, $6; children 6–14, $4. Group discounts. One admission entitles the visitor to also view the Fred C. Heidrick Antique Ag Collection. Gift shop carries teacher information packet. **Ages 7 & up.** *W. www.truckmuseum.org*

Junior (and senior) mechanics will find this a must-stop. There are more than 100 vintage trucks, representing 100 different makes and models, from the turn-of-the-century truck with solid rubber tires to the gorgeous '50s vintage hauler. Special displays place trucks in period settings. The Hays Antique Truck Museum is one of the largest collections of antique trucks in the world. The Heidrick Antique Ag Collection of tractors and antique agricultural equipment is the world's biggest. Interactive displays in the courtyard and garden complement the enjoyment of your stay.

● Old Sacramento State Historic Park

Sacramento was the major transportation hub for north-central California, providing a convenient location where water and land transportation systems could meet. Today, along the Sacramento River where Captain John Sutter established his Embarcadero in 1839, an important part of Sacramento's history has been restored to its former glory. One hundred ten restored or reconstructed structures built during the Gold Rush and 1880s, including restaurants, stores, offices, and museums, stand as living memorials to their past. Visitors walk on wooden sidewalks and cobblestone streets, meet living-history players and ride horse-drawn carriages and covered wagons.

The **Visitors Center** (1104 Front Street at K Street. 916-442-7644. Daily, 9–5) offers maps for walking and audio tours along with tour tokens. Event hotline: (916) 558-3912. www.oldsacramento.com will tell all. Museums closed Thanksgiving, Christmas, and New Year's.

The Dash Trolley takes you from Old Sacramento up past the K Street Mall and the Convention Center downtown for free, 11–3 daily. (916) 321-BUSS.

The Spirit of Sacramento and *Matthew McKinley* are historic paddle-wheelers docked at the Old Sacramento Waterfront. Both offer champagne brunch, sightseeing tours, dinner-dances, happy hour, and murder mystery nights and can be chartered for private parties. Gift tickets and group rates are available. (800) 433-0263, (916) 552-2933, www. spiritofsacramento.com

The River Otter Water Taxi stops at the region's favorite tourist attractions, restaurants, and watering holes during their 50-minute tours along the river from April to October. The ticket booth at the L Street Landing is open 11:15 A.M. to 7:45 P.M. daily. Charters are available. Adults, $5; children, $3. (916) 446-7704. www.riverotter.com

The Pony Express statue commemorates the 1,966-mile mail run from Sacramento to St. Joseph, Missouri. It took less than ten days and 80 riders completed the relay run in 1860.

Other stops of interest on your walking tour include: the **Old Eagle Theater** (box office: 916-323-6343) at Front and J Streets, which first opened in 1949, presents old melodramas and plays. School tours, by appointment (866-240-4655). See "City of the Plain," a 13-minute audio/visual slide show of Sacramento's history.

The **Central Pacific Passenger Station** (daily, 10–5; free with Railroad Museum ticket) at Front and J Streets is a reconstruction of a station that was built in 1876. Waiting rooms, ticket offices, baggage rooms, and railroad cars tell their stories. This is where passengers board the hourly excursion trains on summer weekends. Lunch is offered in an authentic setting.

The **Old Sacramento Schoolhouse** at Front and L looks just as it did in the 1880s. In winter, you can go inside when there are docents; otherwise, just peek in the windows. (916) 483-8818. Open irregularly.

The **Big Four Building** (1111 I Street. Daily, 10–5. Free) was constructed as the result of the merger of Sacramento's early settlers, Collis Huntington and Mark Hopkins with Leland Stanford and Charles Crocker. They formed the Central Pacific Railroad, thus becoming the "Big Four" of California railroading. The Huntington-Hopkins Hardware Store inside, a reconstruction of one of the West's more historic hardware stores, shows off old tools and supplies in a surprisingly appealing display. Merchandise that could have been sold in the 1880s, such as spinning tops and enamel coffee pots, is for sale.

The **Wells Fargo Museum** in the B. F. Hastings Building at Second and J Streets (Daily, 1–5. Free. ATM available. 916-440-4263) was the first western terminus of the Pony Express and the Sacramento office of Wells Fargo. Hours can be limited because of state budget cutbacks, but when open, Wells Fargo and Pony Express exhibits beguile, as do the reconstructed Supreme Court rooms, the Grass Valley stage, and posters on the early post office system. You can tap out Morse code or write with a quill pen.

● **California Military Museum**

1119 2nd Street, Old Sacramento 95814. (916) 442-2883. Tues.–Sun., 10–5. Adults, $3; seniors, $1.50; 5–17 and military, $1. **Ages 7 & up.** *Gift shop. W. www.militarymuseum.org*

Located right next to the original California Militia Headquarters, this grand collection glorifies California's military history from Mexican skirmishes in the 1770s to Operation Desert Storm. Thirty thousand items on three floors include flags, pictures, medals, newspaper articles, documents, memorabilia, and lots of firearms.

● **Discovery Museum History Center**

101 I Street, Old Sacramento 95814. (916) 264-7057. Daily, 10–5, Memorial Day through Labor Day. Adults, $5; seniors and teens, $4; ages 5–13, $3. Gift shop. **Ages 2–12.** *W. www.thediscovery.org*

Located in a replica of the 1854 City Hall, the History Center houses one of the largest gold collections in the world from the 1849 Gold Rush. Visit the working 1860s Print Shop or explore the hands-on play stations and weekend craft activities for children 12 and under. School and group tours and outreach programs available, (916) 485-8836.

● **California State Railroad Museum**

2nd and I Streets, Old Sacramento 95814. (916) 445-6645. Daily except holidays, 10–5. Adults, $3. Groups by appt., (916) 445-4209. Gift store and research library. **Ages 5 & up.** *W. www.californiastaterailroadmuseum.org*

This state-of-the-art museum combines slide shows, theater presentations, panel exhibits, dioramas, interpretive exhibits, shiny locomotives, and historic railroad cars to walk in, around, and through so you can see how railroads have affected our history and culture. You start your self-guided tour with a movie—and then walk through the back wall of the theater into Gold Rush California. There, wander through Lucius Beebe's elegant private car; the Railway Post Office Car, where you can sort mail; and the St. Hyacinthe Sleeping Car, which really rocks; these three are highlights of the 21-car collection. The museum is justifiably proud of its shiningly restored "Cochiti," the 1940s dining car from the Santa Fe Super Chief, with its 37 place settings of rare silver, china, and glassware, sample menus, and full galley. Don't forget to see the toy and miniature train collection upstairs.

In summer, the California State Railroad Museum's Sacramento Southern Excursion Train offers special hourly steam train excursions along the Sacramento River from the Central Pacific Freight Depot at Front and K Streets. October's "Goosebumps Express" is also a great hit. (Call 916-552-5252 for schedule. Adults, $5; ages 6–12, $2.)

● **Crocker Art Museum**

216 O Street, between 2nd and 3rd Streets, Sacramento 95814. (916) 264-5423. Tues.–Sun., 10–5; Thurs. until 9. Closed major holidays. Adults, $6; seniors, $4; ages 7–17 and students, $3. Tours for hearing or visually impaired. **Ages 7 & up.** *W. www.crockerartmuseum.org*

This gracious home was built around 1873 to house the paintings and prints collected by Judge Edwin Bryant Crocker. The collection includes pottery from the fifth century B.C. through contemporary works of art. Rococo mirrors, frescoed ceilings, and curving staircases make the building itself a work of art. Touring exhibits, educational programs, tours, concerts, and events are scheduled throughout the year. Don't miss the Gold Rush–era paintings by Charles C. Nahl, *Fandango* and *Sunday Morning Life in the Mines*.

● Leland Stanford Mansion

802 N Street, Sacramento 95814. (916) 324-0575.

The century-old home of former California governor, senator, and railroad baron Leland Stanford is closed for restoration.

● California State Capitol Museum

10th and Capitol, Capitol Mall, Room B 27, Sacramento 95814. (916) 324-0333. Daily, 9–5. Free. Guided tours 9–4 on the hour. **Ages 7 & up.** *W. www.assembly.ca.gov/museum*

After 13 years of construction, the State Capitol building was completed in 1874 and is now restored to its historic 19th-century dignity and beauty, with a mural of Columbus expounding on the earth to Queen Isabella beneath the capitol dome. It's fun to wander the halls, to see the county window displays and the restored offices and to hear the rustle of politics in action. The museum chronicles the building's history and offers films, tours, and changing and permanent exhibits. The low-relief panels on the new east facade of the building depict California flora and fauna.

● Old Governor's Mansion SHP

1526 H Street, at 16th Street, Sacramento 95816. (916) 323-3047. Daily, 10–4, with tours on the hour. Adults, $1; ages 16 and under, free. **Ages 7 & up.** *www.parks.ca.gov*

The official residence of California's 13 governors from 1903 to 1967 is now a handsome Victorian house museum that captures the history of the state. The melange of furnishing styles, including 14-foot ceilings, Italian marble fireplaces, chandeliers, and French mirrors reflects the different inhabitants. The old carriage house has been converted to a museum where you may view photographs of the governors and their families.

● Golden State Museum

1020 O Street, Sacramento 95814. (916) 653-7524. Tues.–Sat., 10–5; Sun. 12–5. Adults, $5; seniors, $4; ages 6–13, $3.50. Closed major holidays. Family guides, educational materials, group rates. Events. Gift shop. **Ages 7 & up.** *W. www.goldenstatemuseum.org*

This splendid museum is an exciting exploration of California's present, past, and future, with innovative media presentations, educational displays, hands-on activities, and a monumental public art piece. Vibrant stories of people, places, promise, and politics span generations and capture the essence of California as never before. Twenty-five hundred historic documents and artifacts from the California State Archives blend with the newest technology to bring the state to life.

● Towe Auto Museum

2200 Front Street, Sacramento 95818. (916) 442-6802. Daily, 10–6 except major holidays. Adults, $6; high schoolers, $2.50; grade schoolers, $2. Group rates. Groups by appt. Guided tours. Special events. Gift shop. **Ages 6 & up.** *W. www.toweautomuseum.org*

America's automotive heritage is brought to life by the special "dream exhibits" including "The Dream of Cool," "Sunday in the Park," and "The Dream of Speed," which re-create the love affair we have with vehicles and momentum and at the same time provide historical information about the automotive industry. A guide will explain the story of the development of the automobile in America or the operation and technology of the nuts and bolts of these mechanical wonders. Special exhibits include a replica of Henry Ford's first vehicle, the Quadricycle, the Hall of Technology, mannequins in period attire and many unique vehicles such as a Muntz, a Shelby Cobra, and a Pierce Arrow.

One little girl wrote, "We liked your car that you saved and we like the limousine and the ambulance rescue and the police car and the starcruiser."

● Sutter's Fort State Historic Park

2701 L Street, at 28th Street, Sacramento 95816. (916) 445-4422. Daily except Thanksgiving, Christmas, and New Year's Day, 10–5. Summer fees: adults, $3; ages 6–16, $1. Winter fees: adults, $1. Self-guided audio tour included. Tours, groups, Environmental Living Programs, and demonstrations by appt. (916) 323-8112/(866) 240-4655). Living History Days or Pioneer Demonstrations Days monthly. **Ages 6 & up.** *W. www.parks.ca.gov*

Monica wrote, "Dear Sutter's Fort, Thank you for giving us the opportunity to participate in the ELP. It was fun looking at the rooms like the bakery, the kitchen, and the others. It was fun working there, too. I enjoyed it."

Sutter's Fort is one of the best places to relive California history. The fort and its buildings and stables have been well reconstructed, and the cooperage, doctor's office, candle-making room, kitchen, blacksmith shop, immigrant room, blanket factory, carpentry shop, guard room, bunk room, and Sutter's bedroom are as they once were.

The information provided through the audio system is clear, helpful, and entertaining. For example, while facing a model of James Marshall showing Sutter the gold he found at the mill, you hear their conversation and Sutter's German-Swiss accent. Knowing that the fort is the actual site where James Marshall's gold from Coloma was tested makes it more exciting.

An orientation room in the museum relates Sutter's biography and the life of the California pioneers. A doll that survived the Donner party tragedy is on display. ELP enables fourth- to sixth-graders to actually spend a night at the fort, spinning wool, weaving baskets, and preparing their evening meal over fireplaces and in the beehive ovens. Living History Programs also allow youngsters of all ages to step back into the Wild West.

● California State Indian Museum

2618 K Street, between 26th and 28th Streets, Sacramento 95816. (916) 324-0971. Daily except major holidays, 10–5. Adults, $1; under 16, free. Films. Groups by appt. (866) 240-4655. Teacher's Guide available. **Ages 6 & up.** *W. www.parks.ca.gov*

This mesmerizing museum is a treasure house of the California Native American world. Dioramas and well-labeled exhibits display Maidus grinding acorns, the healing child dance, headdresses, maps, minerals, musical instruments, games, jewelry, household goods, baskets, and featherwork. Ishi, last of his California tribe, is remembered here. Hands-on areas, such as a place to touch different pelts and a place to use a mortar and pestle, add spice to the exhibits. Many Native Americans volunteer for special events, especially in the outdoor demonstration area, which contains a tulle house, bark house, acorn leaching pit, acorn granary, and a hand-game house.

Nathan wrote, "My favorite thing was the very small baskets and the disguise of deer skin and other animal skin. I never knew about the sweat house and it was cool. It was very fun and interesting."

● Fairytale Town

William Land Park, 1501 Sutterville Road, off Interstate 5, Sacramento 95822. (916) 264-5233. Daily, 10–4:30, except rainy days and Christmas. Adults, $3.75; ages 3–12, $3.50; under 3, free. Combination tickets to Fairytale Town and the Sacramento Zoo are available at either gate. Parties. Snack bar. Events. **Ages 2–9.** *W. www.fairytaletown.org*

Nursery rhymes and favorite stories come to life as children crawl through the Holes in the Cheese, sit in Cinderella's Pumpkin Coach, and slide down the circular slide after visiting Owl's House. You can visit the Three Little Pigs and Farmer Brown's Barn.

Children's birthday parties can be held in King Arthur's Castle (916-264-7061) and in Sherwood Forest.

Fairytale Town's motto: "Answer the enchanting call from inside our Humpty's wall. Gladly leave the world behind for fairytales of every kind. Find Mother Goose, the Crooked Mile, a puppet show to make you smile, a pirate ship, a castle moat. Mary's lamb and a billy goat."

● Sacramento Zoo

William Land Park, 3930 West Land Park Drive at Sutterville Road, Sacramento 95822. (916) 264-5888. Daily except Christmas, 10–4; in *summer, 9–4. Adults, $4 weekdays, $4.50 weekends; ages 3–12, $2.50 and $3. Combination ticket with Fairytale town: adults, $5.25; children, $3.50. There are strollers to rent. Gift shop.* **All ages.** *W. www.saczoo.com*

Who would imagine that there would be a Lake Victoria in California? This 200,000-gallon freshwater lake is home for African and South American waterfowl including Argentine ruddy ducks and crested screamers.

More than 400 animals live in this tree-shaded garden and zoo. Discover exotic and endangered wildlife from around the world—snow leopards, red pandas, sungazers. The inhabitants of the reptile house are favorites; others are the wallaroos, flamingos, giraffes, and hippo. Orangutan, tiger, lion, and chimpanzee exhibits show these beautiful animals in natural settings. The Rare Feline Center houses a Geoffroy's cat, jaguar, and margay. Experience all of this amid hundred-year-old oaks, lush gardens, and picnic areas. Watch animal "actors" on stage; see them up close and personal.

Funderland, at the entrance to William Land Park, is a sweet little amusement park for youngsters with rides like Teacup, a train, a merry-go-round, "coasters," or Flying Dragon. (17th Avenue, Sacramento 95822. 916-456-0115. Admission, free. Rides are 1 ticket per person. Weekday tickets: $1.25 each. Ten for $10. Unlimited ride wristband, $11; weekends and holidays, $1.50 per ticket. Ten for $12. Winter: Fri., 12–5; weekends, 10–5. Summer: Mon.–Fri., 11–5; weekends, 10–5. Closed Dec. and Jan. Parties. Face painting, balloonist, snack bar. **Ages 2–12.** W.)

● Discovery Museum Science and Space Center

3615 Auburn Boulevard, Northeast (near Interstate 80 and Watt Avenue), Sacramento 95821. (916) 575-3941. Tues.–Sun. and Mon. holidays, 12–5. Sat. and Sun., 10–5. Summer hours: daily, 10–5. Adults, $5; seniors and teens, $4; ages 6–12, $3. Groups and outreach programs by appt., (916) 485-8836. Store. Picnic and party facilities. **Ages 3–12.** *W. www.thediscovery.org*

Located on 14 acres of nature trail, the Science and Space Center has Sacramento's only public planetarium, an animal nature discovery room, a wildlife pond, and hands-on science exhibits. Home to the Challenger Learning Center space simulation program, the Science and Space Center offers community missions and weekend craft activities for children 12 and under.

● Waterworld USA Sacramento Six Flags

1600 Exposition Boulevard, Cal Expo, Sacramento 95815. (916) 924-0556. Daily late spring to late fall, 10:30–6. Adults, $21.99; children under 48 inches tall, $16.99. Season passes, group, and party rates. **Ages 4 & up.** *www.sixflags.com*

There are 250 ways to get wet and wild at this Waterworld, including the Cannonball Falls, where you plummet over six feet. There's also the Cobra, an intertwined double flume that is twice as much fun to race with a friend.

The Hurricane and the Cliffhanger aren't for sissies, either. Parents can relax instead in the Calypso Cooler with its gentle current. Don't forget big towels, snacks, and sunscreen.

● Effie Yeaw Nature Center

6700 Tarshes Drive, back gate of Ancil Hoffman County Park (Mail: P.O. Box 579), Carmichael 95609. (916) 967-0777. Daily, 10–5. Closed Thanksgiving, Christmas, and New Year's Day. School programs, guided walks. Gift shop. **Ages 6–14.** *W. www.effieyeaw.org*

Sacramento teacher Effie Yeaw always dreamed of "A Place for Children to Discover Nature" and volunteers have made sure that such a place exists. The center is more "out" than "in," offering outreach programs about nature in schools and other centers. The Nature Center will give you three self-guided trails through the 77-acre nature study area along the American River. They'll even loan you the binoculars to see wild turkeys, deer, and other wildlife. There are Cultural Heritage programs such as Frontier Ranch Life, Pioneer Children, or "Maidu Indian Day," which makes use of the replica structures of a Maidu summer village on the property. Inside there's a mountain lion exhibit, live animal wild kingdom, and other exhibits that change regularly.

● McClellan Aviation Museum

McClellan Air Force Base, 3204 Palm Avenue (Mail: P.O. Box 553), North Highlands 95652. Enter at the Palm Gate. (916) 643-3192. Mon.–Sat., 9–4; Sun., 12–4. Closed major holidays. Adults, $3; seniors, $2; ages 12–18, $1.50; under 12, free. Group rates and tours by appt. Gift shop. **Ages 7 & up.**

The McClellan Aviation Museum aims to be one of the best collections of aircraft and aviation memorabilia in the West. Museum programs include guided tours, lectures, oral and visual history programs, and a large screen video theater presenting a wide selection of aviation subjects. The gallery takes the visitor from the genesis of the McClellan era, 1939, to the present-day high-tech "Revolution in Air Logistics." You can see a 1943 L-2M Grasshopper, a P-80B Shooting Star, an F-101B Voodoo, and 27 more, along with engines, an O-11A La France fire/crash rescue truck, and "Birth of the Blues," a look at the evolution of the air force uniform.

● Nimbus Fish Hatchery

2001 Nimbus Road, Rancho Cordova 95670. On the American River. (916) 358-2820. Daily, 8–2. Free. A nickel for fish food. **Ages 7 & up.** *W. www.recreation.gov*

After fighting their way from the Pacific Ocean, salmon and steelhead spawn here each fall and winter. The hatchery has a capacity of 20 million salmon eggs and accounts for 60 to 70 percent of the commercial catch off the

California coast. Visitors can see raceway ponds, the fish weir and ladder entrance, a holding pond, the sorting and spawning area, nursery ponds, and the hatchery building. October, November, and February are the best times to visit.

● JB Ranch Horseback Adventures

8444 El Modena (Mail: P.O. Box 130), Elverta 95626. Take Watt Avenue north to Elverta Road, left on Elverta, right on El Modena to JB Gibson Ranch. (916) 991-9500. Groups, tours, and individual visits by reservation. **All ages.** *www.jbranch.com*

This is really a working ranch. There are cows, hens, and horses to feed, and chickens and ducks. There are ponies and horses to ride, old buggies, a blacksmith shop to play in, and hayrides to enjoy.

● FourPaws

14440 Twin Cities Road, Rancho Seco Park in Herald (Mail: FourPaws 849, Galt, CA 95632). (866) FOUR PAWS. Sat., 10–3, Memorial Day to Labor Day. Picnic areas. **All ages.** *W. www.pawsweb.org*

Pat Derby and Ed Stuart have created the Performing Animal Welfare Society to give refuge to antelopes and deer, African foot stock, and other animals needing rescue or retirement from performing venues, circuses, and overcrowded zoos and petting zoos. The 25-acre refuge itself is open daily, year-round, but call before venturing forth. The **Amanda Blake Memorial Museum** next door is a suitable memory to the red-haired heroine of *Gunsmoke* and is filled with notes, photos, and reminiscences of the actress's movie life and love of animals.

● Folsom Powerhouse SHP and American River Water Education Center

7794 Folsom Dam Road, U.S. Bureau of Reclamation, Folsom 95630. Folsom Historic Powerhouse. (916) 985-4843. Wed.–Sun., 12–4, and by appt. Free. www.parks.ca.gov

American River Water Education Center. (916) 989-7100. Tues.–Sat. 9–4:30. Free. Reservations strongly suggested. **Ages 9 & up.** www.mp.usbr.gov/arwec

Tours of the Folsom Dam are not available now, but a video tour of the Folsom Dam can be viewed upon request. Take a one-hour tour through the historic powerhouse and learn about its history. See the original apparatus used to create hydroelectric energy and comparisons to the current Folsom power plant at Folsom Dam. The second half of the program may include a nature walk or an electricity-related lab activity.

The history and headwaters of the American River Watershed are shown through hands-on activities at the sand table and through exhibits focusing on this integral part of California's waterworks. The program may include a center tour, water-related video, a video tour of Folsom Dam's bike trails walk to overlook and see the dam, and a water-related hands-on activity.

● Folsom City Park and Zoo

50 Natoma Street, Folsom 95630. (916) 351-3527. Tues.–Sun., 10–4. Open on major holidays. Ages 13 and over, $3; ages 5–12, $2. Guided tours, classes, and outreach program. Gift shop. **All ages.** *www.folsom.ca.us*

This small zoo is a unique wildlife refuge for North American native animals. Many of the animals were raised as pets; some are disabled. None can live in the wild. The zoo is located in City Park, which offers shaded picnic and barbecue areas and an extensive area of new playground equipment for both preschool and older children. A one-third-scale steam train runs in summer and fall (916-985-7347).

● Folsom History Museum

823 Sutter Street, Folsom 95630. (916) 985-2707. Ages 13 and over, $1. Wed.–Sun., 11–4. Guided Tours by appt. Gift shop. **Ages 7 & up.** *W. www.folsomhistorymuseum.org*

The Historical Society has opened the Folsom History Museum in the 1860s Wells Fargo Assay Office. The museum offers exhibits on local Indian and Gold Rush history, early settlers and pioneers, and important local sites. The museum's antique quilt show each August and September is looked forward to each year, as is the Pony Express Re-Ride in June.

The **Interpretive Center** located next to Folsom's Chamber of Commerce visitors center gives visitors a historical look at Folsom's past through vehicles, museums, equipment and replicas of a miner's shack, blacksmith shop, carriage shed, and more. You can pan for gold here, too, 8:30–1, Fri., 11–4 on weekends. Free. Downtown, historic Sutter Street has been restored with old buildings and shops that remind visitors of early times.

The nearby **Folsom Prison Museum** (916-985-2561 ext. 3016. Daily, 10–4. $1) is at the visitors gate, where you can experience a little of the prison's "end of the world" atmosphere. Gatling guns, prisoners' made-up weapons, a video presentation, and an 1880 cell complete with "an 1880 inmate" tell the tale. Buy a postcard with Black Bart's rap sheet on it at the museum store. Tours by appt.

● Micke Grove Park and Zoo and San Joaquin County Historical Museum

11793 North Micke Grove Road, Lodi 95240. Off Highway 99 at Armstrong Road exit. 8 to dusk except Christmas. Vehicle entry fee, $2 weekdays, $4 weekends, $5 Easter and Mother's Day. Rental facility reservations: (209) 953-8800. **Ages 3 & up.** *W. www.co.san-joaquin.ca.us*

Zoo: *(209) 953-8840/331-7270. 10–5. Adults, $2; 6–17, $1. Museum: (209) 953-3460/331-2055/Wed.–Sun., 10–3, and by appt. Adults, $2; seniors and ages 6–12, $1.*

Japanese Garden: *Mon.–Fri., 9–2; weekends, 9–1:30. Free.*

Funderwoods: *(209) 469-9654/369-5437 for hours and prices.*

Micke Grove Park and Zoo has it all. The zoo features more than 180 birds, mammals, and reptiles. Visitors will enjoy native animals and exotic species from all over the world, including several endangered species, such as the popular Chinese alligator, snow leopard, and cotton top tamarin. The Tropical Forest Canopy with its Rodrigues fruit bats, Paseo Pantera—Path of the Mountain Lion—and the Island Lost in Time with lemurs, parrots, and radiated tortoises from Madagascar are special.

Funderwoods Amusement Park offers amusement rides such as the Tilt-a-Whirl and Scrambler, plus delicious treats and party packages.

At the remarkable multibuilding **San Joaquin Historical Museum,** "Man and Nature Hand in Hand" is the theme. In the main building, changing exhibits are always based on memories of the pioneer people, including a millinery shop and Victorian sitting room, both meticulously furnished. On the grounds, you can visit the Tree and Vine building, the Delta building, an 1800s Calaveras schoolhouse, a 1920s kitchen, a harness shop, a ranch blacksmith shop, a farm tools and tractor collection, a model of a dairy, and the Sunshine Trail Garden for the Blind. "Earth is so kind, that just tickle her with a hoe and she laughs up a harvest," is what one Delta farmer wrote, while another prophesied, "We will dig gold with a plow."

In addition to an authentic **Japanese Tea Garden,** the park features softball fields, horseshoe pits, picnic and playgrounds, and a rose garden.

● **Pixie Woods**
Louis Park (Mail: City Hall, 9 East Lindsay Street), Stockton 95202. (209) 937-7366. Fall and spring: weekends, 12–5. Summer: Wed.–Fri., 11–5; until 6 on weekends. Closed from November to mid-February. Ages 12 and over, $2.25; under 12, $1.75. Train, boat, and merry-go-round, 75¢. Parties by appt. **Ages 2–12.** *W. www.stocktongov.com*

Stockton's fairyland is for the "young in age and young in heart." You enter the Rainbow Gates to a magical forest and enchanted lagoons and begin a journey that will take you through some of your favorite fairytale settings. Ride the Pixie Express or take a trip on the Pixie Queen, a replica of the paddlewheel steamers that long ago graced the Delta waterways. And be sure to visit Pirates' Cove and the magical volcano. See a puppet show in the Toadstool Theater. Have an adventure in Frontier Town and pet the animals in McDonald's Farm.

● Haggin Museum

*Victory Park, 1201 North Pershing Avenue, Stockton 95203. Off Interstate
5. (209) 940-6300. Daily, except Mon. and holidays, 1:30–5. Adults, $5;
seniors, students, and ages 10–17, $2.50; children under 10, free. Free 1st
Tues. of the month and family days. Groups by appt. Gift shop.* **Ages 6 & up.**
W. www.hagginmuseum.org

Three floors of history and art fill this handsome brick building. The
"Pioneer Room" boasts of interactive video programs and other displays
dealing with the history of Stockton. Interpretive displays of California
include an arcade of 19th-century storefronts, arms, a firefighters gallery, and
an American Indian Gallery. The Holt Hall of Agriculture includes a fully
restored 1919 Holt 75 caterpillar tractor and a 1904 combine harvester. The
art galleries include work by American artists such as Albert Bierstadt and
William Keith. The letter by Daniel Boone, the 1927 Stephans Brothers
speedboat, and the display of 100-year-old dolls are of special interest to kids.
So are the Egyptian mummy and the historic fire engines.

● Children's Museum of Stockton

*402 West Weber Avenue, Stockton 95203. (209) 465-4FUN, Tues.–Sat.,
9–4; Sun., 12–5. Jun–Aug., Mon.–Sat., 9–4. Adults, $4; ages under 2, free.
Groups, school programs, parties, summer camp.* **Ages 2–10.** *www.stocktongov.com*

This wonderful, hands-on, interactive museum encourages kids to climb
on a fire engine, "work" in a grocery store, explore the arts and crafts station,
and check out the hospital, firehouse, TV station, and art center. In the Kids
World mini-city, kids can play at shopping for groceries, swinging by the
post office, stopping at the bank, or visiting the optometrist, just the way
their parents do. The park is a special place for children under four.

Youngsters will also enjoy a visit to the **Clever Planetarium** (209-954-
5110) at San Joaquin Delta College, 5151 Pacific Avenue, in Stockton.

● McHenry Museum

*1401 I Street, Modesto 95354. (209) 577-5366. Tues.–Sun., 12–4. Free.
Tours by appt. (209-577-5344). Gift shop.* **Ages 7 & up.** *W.
www.modesto.org/rnd*

"Not to know what happened before one was born is to remain a child,"
said Cicero. And that is the credo of this historical museum, which aims to
appreciate the past and the people who pioneered this area. A complete
doctor's office, a general store, a re-created blacksmith shop, gold-mining
paraphernalia, firefighting equipment, and a collection of guns and cattle
brands are permanent exhibits. Changing displays focus on families, ethnic
and religious groups, quilts, fans, dolls, and other areas of interest. Slide

shows, movies, and musical events are held in the auditorium. Also, there are traveling exhibits to schools and groups.

Down the block, history buffs will want to visit the **McHenry Mansion** (906 15th Street at I, Modesto. 209-577-5341. Sun.–Thurs., 1–4; Fri., 12–3; Free. Gift shop. Group and individual tours and party rentals available. www.modesto.gov.com). Built in 1883, the Italianate mansion is one of the few surviving reminders of Modesto's past. Today it has been completely restored and refurbished, right down to the William Morris–designed wallpaper, the rose brass gas chandelier in the front parlor, the 19th-century English wall-to-wall carpeting, and the milled redwood columns on the front veranda.

● Great Valley Museum of Natural History

1100 Stoddard Avenue, Stockton 95350 (209) 575-6196. Tues.–Sat., 9–4:30 in winter; 10–4 in summer. $1 per person; $3 per family. 6 and under, free. Classes. Groups. **Ages 5 & up.** *W. www.mjc.yosemite.cc.ca.us.greatvalley*

Learn about the animals and plants that live in California's unique Central Valley in two welcoming buildings. Visit the Great Animal Hall with its habitats of the great valley animals and Native American memorabilia, artifacts, and tools. The Discovery Room offers hands-on activities, a vivarium, and a collection of great animals of the world—South America, Asia, and Africa—in a dioramic setting. Although the museum offers changing exhibits dealing with the wonders and fragility of our natural world, its focus is the natural history and ecology of the Big Valley.

● Newman Museum

1209 Main Street, Newman 95360. Thirty miles southwest of Modesto on Highway 33. (209) 862-0239. Mon.–Fri. and summer Sat., 9–1. Free. **Ages 6 & up.**

The Newman Historical Society has banded together to help Barbara and Tom Powell restore and reopen their little museum. The changing exhibits are examples of community work-togethers, such as the one on wedding attire of the 20th century or the one on Hills Ferry, a town on the San Joaquin River that was passed by when the railroad founded Newman in the late 1880s. Farming tools, pioneer tools, firearms, Chinese artifacts, and a collection of 29 branding irons dating to 1864 are also on display.

● Castle Air Museum

5050 Santa Fe Drive, west of Buhach Road, former Castle Air Force Base (Mail: P.O. Box 488), Atwater 95301. Off Highway 99 near Merced. (209) 723-2178. Daily except holidays, May–Sept., 9–5; Oct.–Apr., 10–4. Adults, $7; seniors and ages 8–16, $5; under 7 and active military, free. Shop and restaurant. **Ages 7 & up.** *W. www.elite.net/castle-air*

When you enter the gates you are greeted by history with the supersonic SF-71 Blackbird on your right and the infamous B-24 Liberator on your left. Your journey through time has already begun. There are bombers and jets of all ages, starting with the B-17 Flying Fortress and ending with the only surviving RB-36 Peacemaker in the United States. Inside the museum, you'll find memorabilia commemorating pilots, crew, chiefs, women in aviation, and more. There are 45 aircraft in this airplane lover's dream.

● **Oakdale Cowboy Museum and Tourist Center**
355 East F Street (Mail: P.O. Box 1155), Oakdale 95361. (209) 847-5163. Mon.–Fri., 10–3. Groups by appt. Donation. **Ages 6–16.** *W.*
www.oakdalecowboymuseum.org

The sights, sounds, and smells of the Wild West are alive in this small but energetic museum. With its focus on the land and its people, the museum seeks to embody the past and embrace the future. It shows where real cowboys and cowgirls came from, and where they'll be in the future. It also shows the evolution of rodeo from a ranch pastime to a modern high-skill professional sport. Visitors will see Gene Autry's "Flying A" brand, National Champions of the World saddles, spurs, ropes, action photos of bull riding, barbed wire, a 9½-inch-wide Clydesdale horseshoe, cowboy gear, and more. A really fascinating place for all ages.

Oakdale has many good tastes in one small location. Although Hershey's has stopped giving tours, the **Hershey's Visitors Center and Gift Shoppe** still shows a video of chocolate making and offers special chocolate buys (120 South Sierra Avenue, Oakdale 95361. 209-848-8126. Mon.–Fri., 8:30–5. School tours by appt.).

The **Oakdale Cheese Factory** (10040 Highway 20, Oakdale 95361. 209-848-3139. Daily, 9–6. Free. Groups. Gift store with Dutch novelties and cheesecake. Picnic area, petting zoo, produce stand. www.oakdalecheese.com). Tours through viewing windows and by video show the Bulk family making their traditional Gouda cheese.

The **Sierra Railroad Company** offers passengers a unique combination of luxury dining while traveling through the scenic countryside of the Sierra Foothills. Dinners on the Golden Sunset Dinner Train every Saturday evening and brunch on the Sierra Daylight, Sunday, 10:30–2:30, can be most enjoyable. There are themed parties and special events regularly. For information and reservations, call (800) 866-1690/(209) 848-2100, or visit online at www.sierrarailroad.com.

■ The Gold Country

To drive along Highway 49 is to relive California's history and legends. This is the Gold Country—the land of writers such as Mark Twain, Bret Harte, and Joaquin Miller, the bandits Black Bart and Joaquin Murietta, and heroes such as Ulysses S. Grant and Horatio Alger.

Passing through little towns named Copperopolis and Jenny Lind, visitors who look carefully will see the traces of the hundreds of thousands of people—Cornish, Welsh, English, German, French, Italian, Mexican, Peruvian, Australian, Chinese, and African—who migrated to this place seeking fame and fortune from the "tears from the sun." The town of Volcano still has an old Chinese store and a Jewish cemetery. Meander through historic stone buildings with tall iron doors and capture the new gold rush of these still thriving towns full of shops, galleries, and restaurants.

In the Gold Country, you'll find the only town in the United States ever to name itself a nation: Rough and Ready seceded from the Union in April 1850, to become a republic with its own president, constitution, and flag; by the Fourth of July, it had slipped quietly back into the Union.

The many parks and campgrounds are mostly near quiet streams that once teemed with gold panners. Calaveras Big Trees State Park beckons with giant sequoias or towering Sierra redwoods, incense cedars, white fir, and Ponderosa and Sugar pines Although there are mining, river rafting, ballooning, and kayaking expeditions available, to me, the best thing to do in the Gold Country is just explore, get a little lost. You'll have memorable experiences you couldn't possibly find listed in a book and you'll hear about towns that exist now only in history books. On the other hand, you could pick up a pan and start sifting!

● Railtown 1897–State Historic Park

5th and Reservoir Streets (Mail: P.O. Box 1250), Jamestown 95327. Off Highways 49 and 108 (Mail: California State Railroad Museum, 111 I Street, Old Sacramento 95814-2265. E-mail: railtown@mlode.com). Depot store: (209) 984-3953. Information: (916) 445-6645. Guided tours of the Historic Sierra Railroad shops, daily, 10–4 except Thanksgiving, Christmas, and New Year's Day. Adults, $2; ages 6–12, $1. Steam Train rides weekends: Apr.–Oct., 11–3. Adults, $6; youngsters, $3. Group rates. Varying times and prices for special themed train rides. Railtown depot store and interpretive center; daily, 9:30–4:30. Picnic areas. **Ages 3 & up.** *W. www.railtown1897.org*

The Sierra Railway has been working since 1897. It has been starring in movies since the Marx Brothers went west. You can walk through working turn-of-the-century machine shops, the historic Sierra Railroad Shops. After a short film, you'll be guided through the roundhouse to see rolling stock that's starred in more than 200 movies and TV shows, from *High Noon,*

Petticoat Junction, and *Wild Wild West* to *Mother Lode, Cannonball, Butch Cassidy and the Sundance Kid,* and *Back to the Future Part III.* Train rides are 40 minutes long, round-trip.

● Gold Prospecting Adventures

Old Livery Stable, 18170 Main Street (Mail: P.O. Box 1040), Jamestown 95327-4653. (209) 984-GOLD. Reservations: (800) 596-0009. Call for details. **Ages 5 & up.** *www.goldprospecting.com*

Every day, a tape showing Jamestown's history and how to prospect for gold is presented free. It includes scenes about a couple who walked into Ralph Shock's store in January 1895 carrying a shopping bag with 11 pounds of gold nuggets valued at $140,000. There's a "slough" right on the main street of Jamestown for an instant panning experience. Families and groups can go on expeditions that take an hour or two days, by foot, river raft, train, or helicopter. Harlan of Modesto wrote, "Thank you so much for teaching me how to pan for gold. It could come in handy sometime. I enjoyed your explaining about gold and its uses. I also enjoyed panning for gold. . . ."

Gold-panning expert Ralph Shock has these suggestions for gold panning: "At a bend in a creek with a light flow of water, dig behind rocks, fallen limbs and uprooted trees. Use an 8- to 10-inch pan and dig a deep hole for material for your pan. Fill it three-quarters full, then stir lightly, underwater, so the lighter material floats out. Pick out the big rocks and shake the pan back and forth at least 20 times. Dip the pan's rim into the water, again sweeping so the lighter material floats out. Shake and sweep until you have a tablespoon of dirt left. Tip so sand and gravel is at the top and gently swirl water across the material to uncover the gold left in your pan. Using a dry fingertip, transfer your gold to a water-filled vial."

The **California Gold Country Visitors Association** (Mail: P.O. Box 596, Jackson 95642. 800-225-3764) can tell you where to pan for gold, raft the rivers, explore the redwood groves, dine, sleep, shop, and enjoy Yosemite and Tahoe.

Other gold panning tours can be arranged through Pine Acres Gold Panning on the Mokelumne River (Mail: P.O. Box 278), Pine Grove 95665. (209) 296-4100/296-4659. www.volcano.net/~pineacre. E-mail: parrc@volcano.net. For hands-on touring, you may also want to contact Gabby's Historic Gold Rush Tours (209) 296-3106. E-mail: gabbysgold@volcano.net. Or try the Gold Gulch Museum at Yosemite Gallery, 35463 Highway 41, Coarsegold 93614. (559) 683-8727. www.yosemitegallery.com. Family fun and adventure can be found on horseback at Wild West Trails, (209) 267-1166. www.wildwesttrails.com. And for something completely new, try Highland Llama Trekkers for pack trips and day hikes. 14223 Highland Drive, Grass Valley 95945 (530) 273-8105. www.llamatrekkers.com

● Tuolumne County Museum and History Center

158 West Bradford (Mail: P.O. Box 299), Sonora 95370. (209) 532-1317. Sun.–Fri., 10–4; Sat., 10–3:30. Group tours by appt. Picnic tables in the courtyard, once the former prisoners' exercise yard. Free. **Ages 7 & up.** *www.tchistory.org*

This thriving museum is proud of its Gold Exhibit, which features the Tuolumne County Gold Collection—44 specimens, including two solid gold nuggets. Information about the three gold rushes (in 1849, at the turn of the century, and modern open-pit mining) is found in photos, lithographs of early mining scenes, and a large map showing where all the gold camps were located. Mark Twain has a corner to himself. More than 160 pictures, vignettes, and historical items tell the exciting story of Tuolumne County and its six geographical regions. The museum is in the 1857 county jail. The cellblock in back has exhibits of pioneer crossings of the Sierra Nevada mountains between 1841 and 1860 and an extensive gun collection in a jail cell, with fascinating tales of the stalwart, independent men who used them. Visitors can walk into the cell to see the guns in their cases. Another cell has a display vignette of an old-time gun shop. Two blocks west on Bradford and Highway 49 (West Stockton Road) is **Prospector's Park,** with a five-stamp mill, an authentic *arrastra,* or gold-mining platform, and a waterwheel that works on an impulse method, along with information plaques.

● Sonora City Fire Department Museum

201 South Shepard Street, Sonora 95370. (209) 532-4541. Call for times and prices.

A brand-new museum is in the process of being built to celebrate Sonora's fire department. Speaking trumpets from the 1850s, handmade uniforms from the 1870s, and leather firemen's helmets will be displayed along with trophies and hand-operated firefighting equipment, including the Eureka No. 1 hand pumper, which was shipped around the Horn from New York in 1876.

Sonora, once called the Queen of the Southern Mines, is a well-preserved town. Visitors may be interested in stopping by the Archaeology and History Display in the **A. N. Francisco Building** (48 West Yaney Street. Weekdays, 9–4. Free) to see bottles, fragments, and objects found on the site of the building during construction. Another display case contains memorabilia from the 1854 *Union Democrat,* including old type, photos, headlines, and old editions.

● Tuolumne City Memorial Museum

18663 Carter Street (Mail: P.O. Box 1174), Tuolumne 95379. (209) 928-3516, Sat. and Sun., 1–4. Free. **Ages 7 & up.** *W. www.tuolumnemuseum.org*

Four main rooms encompassing 2,600 square feet celebrate Tuolumne's past. The star exhibit is the West Side Lumber Mill and Logging Railroad on a one-twentieth scale, covering nearly 100 square feet. A one-room school-

house, furnished bedroom, old town pictures, a doll collection, ladies bou-
tique, graduation photos, and store artifacts are in one wing, along with a
kitchen that tells the story of cooking and laundering in bygone days. Gold
mining, lumber, and foundry industries are in the north room, and the east
wing features U.S. armed forces memorabilia and Miwok Indian culture
displays.

On the outskirts of Sonora off Tuolumne Road is a large collection of
Tuolumne County farming, mining, and logging history, available to groups
by appointment. Al Hauschildt has been collecting more than 40 tractors,
100 gasoline engines, Model T Fords, heavy equipment, and more for many
years. He's in the process of building a life-size model of a small historic town
with a blacksmith shop, mercantile, gas station, and an old depot station. Call
(209) 928-3249 for information.

● Columbia State Historic Park

*(Mail: P.O. Box 1824) Columbia District 95310. Highway 49, north of
Sonora. (209) 532-0151. Museum, (209) 532-3184. Daily, 10–4 in
summer; variable in winter. Closed Thanksgiving and Christmas. Free.* **All
ages.** *W. www.sierra.parks.state.CA.US*

Columbia, "The Gem of the Southern Mines," is the best of the restored
gold-mining towns. The quiet streets and wooden sidewalks lead you to
buildings, stores, and eateries outfitted as they were in the town's heyday. The
Columbia Gazette Office still prints a small newspaper; the **Columbia
Candy Kitchen** still sells hand-dipped candy; the 1857 **Douglas's Saloon**
still dispenses an occasional draft beer along with sarsaparilla. Peek into the
carpenter's shop and the schoolhouse, which has a bell tower, pump organ,
desk, and potbellied stove. **Parrott's Blacksmith Shop** sells ornaments
made on their coal-fired forge. The Chinese herb shop, the town jail,
firehouse, blacksmith shop, and drugstore are other attractions. The gold
scales in the Wells Fargo Office weighed out more than $55 million in dust
and nuggets of the $87 million mined here. You can also ride a stagecoach and
pan for gold!

Fallon House, a Victorian-era hotel, houses an ice cream parlor and the
Sierra Repertory theater, which has given performances for more than 30
years. The City Hotel has been restored to Victorian glory and is also justly
proud of its dining room.

During a **Hidden Treasure Gold Mine Tour** (209-532-9693; $7) visitors
see the quartz vein that gold formed millions of years ago and discover what
"side drifts" and "glory holes" are all about. You can also have gold-panning
lessons in the Matelot Gulch Mine Store. The park museum offers slide shows
and exhibits on the Chinese (once one-sixth of Columbia's population), and
the gold miners. Your family could happily spend a day—or a weekend—in
this thriving town of yesteryear.

● **Moaning Cave**

5350 Moaning Cave Road, Vallecito 95251. Off Parrots Ferry Road, between Columbia and Highway 4. (866) 762-2837/(209) 736-2708. Daily, 9–6 in summer. Oct.–May, weekdays, 10–5; Sat. and Sun., 9–5. Adults, $10; ages 3–13, $5. **Ages 7 & up.** *www.caverntours.com*

Gold miners first explored Moaning Cave in 1851, but Native Americans had revered the site for centuries because of the haunting, moaning sounds coming from the cavern's entrance. Today you enter the main cavern by descending a metal spiral staircase or by settling into a harness and rappelling nearly 165 feet to the cavern floor. Visitors are invited to take a 45-minute walking tour of the main chamber or make reservations to don caving gear and join an exciting three-hour excursion deeper into the cave, which has been explored to a depth of 410 feet. The main chamber is tall enough to hold the Statue of Liberty. Aboveground activities include gemstone mining, gold panning, and a free nature trail.

● **California Caverns**

9565 Cave City Road, Mountain Ranch (Mail: P.O. Box 78), Vallecito 95251. Open May–Oct. depending on water levels; June–Oct., daily, 10–5. Other times: daily, 10–4. (866) 762-2837/(209) 736-2708. Adults, $10; ages 3–13, $5. **Ages 7 & up.** *www.caverntours.com*

"When we emerged into the bright landscapes of the sun everything looked brighter, and we felt our faith in Nature's beauty strengthened, and saw more clearly that beauty is universal and immortal, above, beneath, on land and sea, mountain and plains in heat and cold, light and darkness," wrote John Muir after wandering through the 200-foot-deep crystalline jungles. California Caverns offers an 80-minute "Trail of Light" tour and "Wild Cave" expedition tours for the adventurous. During the Gold Rush, the cave was used for social gatherings, town meetings, and weddings. The same company controls the Boyden Cavern in Kings River Canyon, Sequoia National Forest, east of Fresno.

● **Mercer Caverns**

(Mail: P.O. Box 509) Murphys 95247. Ebbetts Pass Highway, 1 mile from Murphys. (866) 762-2837/(209) 728-2101. Daily, 10–4:30 in winter; Sun.–Thurs, 9–5, and Fri. and Sat. 9–6 in summer. Adults, $10; ages 5–12, $6, subject to change. School tours by appt. **Ages 6 & up.** *www.mercercaverns.com*

This 45- to 50-minute tour of 440 steps, 208 down and 232 up, past stalactites and stalagmites, aragonites and helictites, takes you into a subterranean wonderland. (Stalactites hang tight from the ceiling; stalagmites are mighty mounds on the ground.) Eerie rock formations like the Organ Loft, Angel Wings, and the Chinese Meat Market are dazzling examples of the artistry of nature. Mercer Caverns was discovered in 1885 by a tired, thirsty prospector, Walter J. Mercer, who noticed bay bushes growing near a limestone bluff and thought he had found a well. Stacey loved the story about Mr. Mercer, but "my favorite part was the beautiful formations that you turned into very wild fairy tales. I especially liked the Rapunzel story. It was so fantastic the way the limestone shaped itself into the shape of a girl with long hair. The little frog prince that was so embarrassed it turned around all the time was cute too."

Mercer Caverns has an information center and store on Main Street in Murphys. While in Murphys, visit the Kautz Ironstone Vineyards Heritage Museum to see the 2½-foot-tall 44-pound crystalline gold specimen—a huge gold nugget.

● Black Chasm National Landmark

15701 Pioneer-Volcano Road, Volcano 95689. (866) 762-2837/(209) 736-2708. Daily, 9–5 holidays and in summer; 10–5, in winter. Adults, $10; ages 3–13, $5. **Ages 7 & up.** *www.caverntours.com*

California's newest show cave is a visual treat from start to finish. On the 50-minute walking tour, descend a series of steps and walkways that loop around the formation-covered cavern walls. Here, flowstones interspersed with stalactites, draperies, and helictites compete for space above the stairways. In the Colossal Room, a platform seemingly suspended in midair hangs above a 70-foot drop to small glimpses of the jewel-like lake below, made bright turquoise by naturally occurring calcium bicarbonate.

At the Landmark Portal, a large group of spectacular stalactites hangs over the entrance. Massive arrays of rare, sparkling white helictite crystals are in the Landmark Room. Above ground try the fun gemstone mining in which everyone is guaranteed to make some finds!

● Sutter Gold Mine

13660 Highway 49, Sutter Creek 95685. One mile north of Sutter Creek. (866) 762-2837/(209) 736-2708. Adults, $14.50; ages 3–13, $10. Daily, 9–5, June–Sept.; daily 10–4, Oct.–May. **Ages 7 & up.** *www.caverntours.com*

Sutter Gold Mine tours provides a chance to see the famous Mother Lode quartz vein structure from the inside. Ride the Boss Buggy Shuttle deep into the mine and see the inner workings of a modern gold mine. Learn about the history of the Gold Rush and the geology of the area. The "Family Tour" is suitable for the whole family. The "Deep Mine Experience" takes participants through smaller drifts where mining equipment is set up, providing a rare opportunity to experience the miner's work-a-day world, walking through water-logged tunnels and climbing ladders. Aboveground activities include gemstone mining, gold panning, mining movies in the Gold Theatre, and picnics on the grounds.

● Angels Camp Museum

753 Main Street, Angels Camp 95222. (209) 736-2963. Daily, 10–3. Adults, $2; children, 50¢. Groups by appt. **Ages 6 & up.** *W. www.cityofangels.org/museum.htm*

A sulky, phaeton, surrey, hearse, steam tractors, and a mail stage are part of this extensive collection of antiques, clocks, old wagons, and rolling stock. Old mining equipment and the working stamp mill are especially fascinating. Indian artifacts and memorabilia of the county's past are nicely presented. Homage is paid to Mark Twain and the annual Jumping Frog Contest.

North of Columbia on Highway 49, before you reach New Melones Reservoir, you'll come to a turnoff leading to the Mark Twain Cabin on Jackass Hill. This is a replica built around the chimney of the original cabin, which burned down many years ago. While living here in 1864 and 1865, Twain wrote his book *Roughing It* and gathered material that inspired later stories such as the famous "The Celebrated Jumping Frog of Calaveras County."

● Calaveras County Historical Museum

30 Main Street (Mail: P.O. Box 721), San Andreas 95249. (209) 754-1058. Daily, 10–4. Adults, 50¢; children, 25¢. Gift shop. **Ages 7 & up.** *W. www.calaverascounty.org*

The Hall of Records Building in the County Courthouse and Jail has been transformed into a beautifully designed treasure house. You can walk through the judge's chambers and then go downstairs to see the cell where Black Bart awaited trial. The museum focuses on the Miwok way of life and on the people living in San Andreas during the 1880s, with representative rooms and exhibits. There's a full-size bark teepee. The upper floor displays the geologic history of the gold country. I liked Jenny Lind's practice piano. One fourth-grader from Fairfield wrote, "I liked it a lot—and it helped me with my term paper." An Italian stone oven in the Jail Yard is used to bake bread for meetings and social events.

● Amador County Museum

225 Church Street (Mail: 500 Argonaut Lane), Jackson 95642. (209) 223-6386. Wed.–Sun., 10–4. Donation. **Ages 7 & up.**

A "Congress of Curiosities"—almost an old-fashioned Sears Roebuck catalog come to life—makes this cheerful museum a pleasant stop. Armstead C. Brown built this house for his wife and eleven children in 1859. The children's bedroom and the chair used by a woman while driving her own covered wagon west are personal favorites. A tape and live narration (one-half-hour long) shows how gold was mined.

At the **Kennedy Gold Mine,** you can view by guided tour working scale models of the Kennedy Mine Tailing Wheel No. 2, the Kennedy Mine head frame, and a stamp mill, along with a gold room tracing the history of the area from the discovery of gold to the advent of the hard-rock machinery (Sat. and Sun., 11–3 and by appt. 8 and over, $1).

Visit the real Kennedy Gold Mine (Mail: P.O. Box 684), Jackson 95642. (209) 223-9542. Fri., Sat., and Sun., mid-March–Nov., 10–3. Adults, $7; ages 6–12, $4. Guided or self-guided tours and by appt. E-mail: kmmine@volcano.net

One mile out of town on North Main Street at the intersections of Highways 49 and 88, there are two wheels on each side of the road, 58 feet in diameter. They were used to transport waste from the mine to a reservoir a half-mile away. Almost lost in history, the huge wheels are still impressive. Today you can see the richest gold mine in the richest part of the Mother Lode. The unique headframe is still the tallest mining structure in the Mother Lode, and you can still see the 90-year-old mine office and the dynamite storage shed, and learn the lore of the land.

● **Knight Foundry Historic Water-Powered Ironworks**
81 Eureka Street (Mail: P.O. Box 1776), Sutter Creek 95685. (209) 267-0201. Sat. and Sun., 10–4, and by appt. Groups by appt. Adults, $6; seniors and students, $4. **Ages 8 & up.** *W. www.suttercreek.org*

Called "the Jurassic Park of Metallurgy," this is America's only remaining water-powered iron works and machine shop. It looks and works just the way it did in 1872. Visitors with an interest in learning historic skills can take hands-on workshops at the foundry for one or more days, or can sign on for a full craft apprenticeship in pattern making, blacksmithing, machine tool work, or molding and casting in the foundry. A restoration-work-in-progress, the foundry plans to build a full-scale 1850s steam locomotive from scratch, and workshop participants can be engine builders for a day. The big and small wheels make such good use of the water that electric lights are lit by waterpower!

● **Chaw'se Indian Grinding Rock State Historic Park**
14881 Pine Grove-Volcano Road, Pine Grove 95665. East of Jackson nine miles. (209) 296-7488. Day use: $2 per car; $10–20 per bus. Museum open daily, Mon.–Fri., 11–3; Sat. and Sun., 10–4; longer in summer. Camping available. Picnic areas. Gift shop. **Ages 6 & up.** *W. E-mail: igr@goldrush.com www.parks.ca.gov*

This spiffy roundhouse-inspired museum boasts one of the finest collections of Native American artifacts in the state. Artifacts from 12 California tribes include games, ceremonial garb, trading shells, and hands-on exhibits. Orientation videos show bow-and-arrow making, dances, and other experiences. Rangers offer regular demonstrations of basket making, clam disc making, and more.

At first, the huge flat limestone bedrock, 173 feet long by 82 feet wide, looks empty. But then you look closer and discover the petroglyphs scratched in by the first people of California between 2000 and 3000 years ago to commemorate their hunting and fishing tales. You'll also see the 1,185 mortar cups where the Miwok women ground the seeds, bulbs, fungi, and acorns that served as the staples of their diet. Acorns are high in fat, protein, and carbohydrates and can make mush, soup, bread, and cakes. The acorn meal was sifted and washed many times to remove bitterness, then the meal was mixed with water in a basket and heated by hot rocks dropped into the mush. One family would consume 2,000 pounds of acorns a year. This is the largest bedrock mortar in North America. Visitors may also see restorations of a ceremonial roundhouse, a granary, eight bark dwelling houses, and a hand-game house. One of the self-guided trails shows you how plants were used by the North Sierra Miwoks.

● Chew Kee Store

Fiddletown 95629. Six miles east of Highway 49 and Plymouth on Fiddletown Road on the way to Volcano. Sat., Apr.–Oct., 12–4, and by appt. Free. **Ages 10 & up.**

Built in the mid-1850s, the Chew Kee Store is believed to be California's only surviving Chinese rammed-earth structure from the Gold Rush era. The herb doctor, Dr. Yee, left in the 1860s to provide care for the railroad workers and the store continued to be operated by the man known as Chew Kee. Chew Kee provided a social center along with groceries and supplies for the remaining Chinese population. The store was left to Chew Kee's "adopted" son, Jimmy Chow, in 1913, who lived there until his death in 1965. With its herb drawers, ceramic crocks, altar, gambling hall receipts, old photos, office, living quarters, and numerous associated artifacts, the store remains largely intact as the only remnant of the once thriving Chinese community in Fiddletown. The small store is a remarkable example of history frozen in time, "a fly in amber," since Jimmy threw nothing away during the time that he lived here.

● Daffodil Hill

1830 Ramshorn Grade. From Sutter Creek take Church Street. From Pine Grove (Highway 88), take Volcano/Pine Grove Road. (209) 223-0350/ 296-7048. Daily, mid-Mar.–mid-Apr., 9–5, weather permitting. Free. **All ages.** *www.historicdaffodilhill.com*

Although the hill is open only when the daffodils are in bloom around Easter, this is worth planning for. The McLaughlins, who have owned the farm since 1887, have planted about 300,000 daffodils in many varieties and colors, and, between the flowers and the 11 peacocks walking around, have created an enchanted hillside. Kids also enjoy the donkey, horse, pigmy goats, sheep, rabbits, and chickens.

● El Dorado County Historical Museum

104 Placerville Drive, El Dorado County Fairgrounds, Placerville 95667. (530) 621-5865. Wed.–Sat., 10–4; Sun., 12–4. Donation. **Ages 7 & up.** *W. www.eldoradocounty.org*

"Smokers and chewers will please spit on each other and not on the stove or the floor." This sign is one of many in this big old barn of a museum staffed by caring volunteers. There's an old cash register run by steel balls, lots of dolls, a model of gold mining, two well-stocked country stores, a surrey with a fringe on top, and lots more. Snowshoe Thompson, one of California's pioneering heroes, used to walk all over the Gold Country delivering mail and packages, even in winter. He stored a pair of his extra-long seven-foot skis and a cache of food every five miles along his 80-mile route, so he'd always have a way to keep going "in case." This museum is the proud owner of one set.

Right outside the door, wagons, engines, and a Shay engine No. 4 grab the kids' attention. There are also three locomotives and about 20 pieces of narrow-gauge rolling stock—cabooses and passenger cars.

In town, check out the 1852 **Fountain-Tallman Soda Factory Museum** (524 Main Street. 530-626-0773. Fri., Sat., and Sun., 12–4. Donation). The factory made bottled soda water, not ice cream sodas. Pieces of history of the area are presented in one of the original buildings of the town. You'll find another pair of Snowshoe Thompson's skis here.

● Hangtown's Gold Bug Mine Park

One mile north of Highway 50 on Bedford Avenue in Placerville, 2635 Gold Bug Lane, 95667. (530) 642-5207/642-5238. Gold Bug Mine, Stamp Mill and Gift Shop, and panning facilities open daily, 10–4, mid-Apr.– Nov. 1. Mine open 12–4 on weekends, Nov.1–mid-Apr. To Mine and Stamp Mill: adults, $3; ages 5–16, $1. Handheld cassettes for self-guided tours, $1. Guided tours by appt. Picnic areas. **Ages 8 & up.** *W. www.goldbugpark.org*

A ghost of an old gold miner narrates the entertaining, educational audio tour of Gold Bug, the only municipally owned, open-to-the-public gold mine in the world. It was worked as recently as 1947. The longer shaft (a 362-foot-long tunnel) of the mine ends at an exposed gold-bearing quartz vein. The occasional drip of water rings in the cool, eerie silence of the tunnel. There are educational displays in the Stamp Mill, the Hattie Museum, and the gift shop.

Placerville was originally called Old Hangtown after the Hanging Tree in the center of town. In one week, two Englishmen found $17,000 worth of gold on the main street of town. It is said that the legendary "Hangtown Fry" originated here when a miner walked into a restaurant and demanded a meal that used the three most expensive ingredients at once: eggs, bacon, and oysters.

● Gold Discovery State Historic Park and Visitors Center

Highway 49 (Mail: P.O. Box 265), Coloma 95613. (530) 622-3470. Museum: daily, 10–4:30, except holidays. $2 per vehicle. Park: 8–sunset. **Ages 7 & up.** *Partially W. www.parks.ca.gov*

"This day some kind of mettle found in the tailrace . . . looks like goald." A millworker noted this in his diary in January 1848. The gold found changed the face of California—and America.

Sutter's Mill has risen again on the American River. Across the highway, a modern museum is dedicated to the discovery of gold and the lives of the gold miners. Maps, tools, mementos, and pictures are displayed against informational panels and dioramas. On the grounds, follow a self-guiding trail to see the mill; a Chinese store; a mine; a monument to James Marshall, the discoverer; a miner's cabin furnished with corn, beans, a scale, a bible, and the miner in bed; a Mormon's cabin; an *arrastre* (ore crusher); and a town that's almost disappeared. If you feel lucky, take your own gold pan and boots.

● Placer County Historical Museum

101 Maple Street, County Court House, Auburn 95603. (530) 889-6500/ 889-6507. Tues.–Sun., 10–4. Free. Group tours by appt. **Ages 6 & up.** *W. www.placer.ca.gov/museum*

This state-of-the art museum displays an overview of the history of Placer County. Highlights include a Native American habitat complete with a sound presentation, a holographic image of an early miner, and a 10-minute video on the history of the transcontinental highway. A restored sheriff's office, circa 1915, focuses on the early days of the courthouse. The Pate Native American collection of more than 400 items includes artifacts from California, the Southwest, the Northwest Coast, Alaska, and the Eastern Tribes. The donor wished to show future children the lifestyle and culture of the Native American peoples.

● Gold Country Museum

1273 High Street, Gold Country Fairgrounds, Auburn 95603. (530) 887-0690; tours: (530) 889-6500. Tues.–Fri., 10–3:30; weekends, 11–4. Donation. Bags of gold and sand for panning are $1.25. **Ages 7 & up.** *www.placer.ca.gov/museum*

Old mining equipment and pioneer mementos recall the early days of Placer County. Kids will like the 45-foot-long walk-through model mine, the working stamp mill model, the miners cabin, the hands-on gold panning stream, and the replica of an early tent saloon complete with faro table. The exhibits change regularly but center on the personality of the forty-niner.

● Bernhard Museum Complex

291 Auburn-Folsom Road, Auburn 95603. (530) 889-6891; tours: (530) 889-6500. Tues.–Fri., 10:30–3; weekends, 12–4. Adults, $1; seniors and ages 6–16, 50¢. Groups by appt. **Ages 8 & up.** *www.placer.ca.gov/museum*

Benjamin Bernhard's restored home, built in 1851 as the Traveler's Rest Hotel, is one of the oldest wooden structures in Placer County. Bernhards have lived here from 1868 to 1957. The house is furnished in the style of the late Victorian era. The winery houses the Placer Arts League Gallery on the top floor; the wine storage building features exhibits on early wine growing. The carriage barn houses a variety of rolling stock.

● Whitewater Rafting Beyond Limits Adventures, Inc.

(Mail: P.O. Box 215, Riverbank 95367). (800) 234-RAFT/(209) 869-6060. Call for brochure or reservations. E-mail: www.rivertrip.com. Also **Whitewater Voyages,** *5225 San Pablo Dam Road, El Sobrante 94803. (800) 488-RAFT.* **Ages 10 & up.** *www.whitewatervoyages.com*

California's Gold Country is rich in history and gold. Much of that gold comes from rivers that range from mild to wild. Raft down the American River, where the Gold Rush began in 1848. The North Fork and Goodwin Canyon sections of the Stanislaus River, the Yuba River outside Lake Tahoe, the Merced River outside Yosemite Valley, and the rugged Tuolumne River beckon for adventure. Kayaking is also available on the Stanislaus.

● Griffith Quarry Park and Museum

Taylor and Rock Springs Roads, Penryn 95663. (530) 663-1837. Weekends, 12–4. Free. Group tours: (530) 889-6500. **Ages 8 & up.** *www.placer.ca.gov/museum*

The quarry in Griffith Park displays material on the granite works, the Griffith family, artifacts from historic Penryn, and Welsh clothing and furnishings. The park offers three miles of nature trails, picnic places, and views of the old quarry sites.

● Forest Hill Divide Museum

24601 Leroy Botts Park, Foresthill 95631. (530) 367-3988. Sat. and Sun., 12–4, May–Oct. Free. Groups: (530) 889-6500. **Ages 8 & up.** *www/placer.ca.gov/museum*

The history of the Foresthill and Iowa Hill divides is shown in exhibits featuring material on geology, prehistory, the Gold Rush, transportation, early business, recreation, and early firefighting. There's a scale model of the local logging mill and the original 1852 jailhouse, blacksmith shop, and livery stable. Special rotating exhibits keep kids coming back for more.

● Golden Drift Museum

32820 Main Street, Dutch Flat 95714. (530) 389-2126. Memorial Day– Labor Day; Wed. and weekends, 12–4. Free. Groups: (530) 889-6500. **Ages 8 & up.** *www.placer.ca.gov/museum*

Exhibits explain methods of mining, especially hydraulic mining, and show how railroading, especially the Central Pacific, has affected the local communities, the "Golden Triangle" of Dutch Flat, Gold Run, Alta, and Towle. Punched tinware from the 1800s, photographs of the early Dutch Flat area, and a Chinese joss house altar attract visitors.

● North Star Mine Powerhouse Museum

Lower Mill Street, at Empire, Grass Valley 95945 (Mail: P.O. Box 1300, Nevada City 95959). (530) 273-4255. Daily, May–Oct., 10–5. Donation. Picnic areas. **Ages 8 & up.** *W. www.gvncchamber.org*

Built by A. D. Foote in 1895, this is the first completely water-powered, compressed-air transmission plant of its kind. The compressed air, generated by 10-ton, 30-foot Pelton waterwheels, furnished power for the mine. The museum houses photos, ore specimens, safes, dioramas and models of the mines, an assaying laboratory, and a working Cornish pump. The star of the show is the 30-foot Pelton wheel itself.

● Grass Valley Museum

410 South Church, at Chapel Street (Mail: P.O. Box 203), Grass Valley 95945. (530) 273-5509. Tues.–Fri., 12:30–3:30, and by appt. Donation. **Ages 8 & up.** *W. www.gvncchamber.org*

The orphanage of the Holy Angels from 1865 to 1932 is now a quiet museum that displays antique clothing, an 1880s doctor's room, schoolrooms, and lace collection. The chapel is peaceful. There are lovely oil paintings in the Victorian-era parlor. The rose garden in front is splendid.

Grass Valley is a nicely preserved Gold Rush town. To relive a bit of history, have a Cornish pasty at one of the bakeries in town. The miners called these meat-and-potato pies "letters from home." While browsing, you may want to see the homes of Lola Montez and Lotta Crabtree on Mill Street. Lola was a Bavarian singer, dancer, and king's favorite who fled to America in 1853 when her king fell from power. Lotta Crabtree was Lola's protégé and soon became famous, rich, and beloved by the American public. Lola's home is open to the public (daily in summer, 12–4. Free).

● Empire Mine State Historic Park

10791 East Empire Street, Grass Valley 95945. (539) 273-8522. Daily except Thanksgiving, Christmas, and New Year's Day, Sept.–May 1, 10–5. May 1–Sept. 1, 9–6, daily. Adults, $1; under 17, free. Group tours. **Ages 7 & up.** *Partially W. www.empiremine.org*

Keeping alive the story of hard-rock gold mining and its significance in California's history, the Empire is the oldest, largest, and richest gold mine in the area. Some of the 20 stopping points along the mine's self-guided tour are in ruins, and the sites are being reconstructed. The William Bourn family "cottage" is furnished and also open for tours. Movies, tours, and Living History Days will help excite your imagination, so you'll think of the hundreds of Cornish miners who dug the 367 miles of tunnels, almost 11,000 feet deep (on an incline), and the mules that pulled the ore trains through the tunnels. Enterprising souls will want to know that there's still gold there.

● Museum of Ancient and Modern Art

Wildwood Business Center, 11392 Pleasant Valley Road, 1 mile off Highway 20 West (Mail: P.O. Box 975, Penn Valley 95946). (530) 432-3080. Daily, 12–5; classes for preschoolers and children, Sat., 10–12. Tours by appt. Free. **Ages 5 & up.** *W. www.MAMA.org*

Kids love mummies, and they won't be disappointed in the one displayed here. The Museum of Ancient and Modern Art is a multifaceted museum tucked away in the Sierra foothills. Its prestigious art book collections contain etchings, engravings, and woodcuts printed as early as 1529 and illustrate the history of printing. The collection of African masks and statues represents more than 20 different tribes from eight different countries. The large collection from 18th Dynasty Egypt is most intriguing to youngsters. Other notable artifacts, such as statues, pottery, masks, and objects of daily life, are from ancient Sumer, Ur, Assyria, Mesopotamia, Carthage, Alexandria, the Ottoman Empire, Persia, Phoenicia, and Byzantium. The ancient jewelry collection, which spans thousands of years of goldsmithing techniques, dates from Neolithic to historical times. There's also a beautiful diorama with real encased dinosaur bones as well as other dinosaur artifacts. Changing art exhibits can focus on anything from the work of local artists or beautiful butterflies and beastly bugs to an 11th-century illuminated manuscript. Be sure to ask for directions to Penn Valley's covered bridges, a treat for all.

● Bridgeport Covered Bridge

Interstate 80 east to Highway 49, Highway 49 to State 20, 10 miles to Pleasant Valley Road, turn right and drive 9 miles to Bridgeport. For spring through fall schedules of bridge tours, gold-panning expeditions, and trail maps, call (530) 432-2546. Free. **Ages 7 & up.** *www.ncgold.com*

California has 12 covered bridges and this, spanning the Yuba River, is the longest single-span covered bridge in the world today. Built in 1862, the 256-foot-long bridge allows no motor traffic, so it's a hidden oasis for walks, playing on the beach, picnicking, or walking along forest trails. The original builder, sawmill owner David Wood, collected tolls of $1 for a one-horse buggy and up to $6 for an eight-mule team.

● **Firehouse Museum**
Firehouse No. 1 Nevada County Historical Society, 214 Main Street at Commercial, Nevada City 95959. (530) 265-5468. Daily, 11–4 in summer; Thurs.–Sun., 11:30–4 in winter. Donation. **Ages 7 & up.** *www.hwy-49.com*

Located in one of this quaint town's most photographed buildings (its first permanent firehouse, built in 1861), the museum features Maidu Indian artifacts, relics of the Donner party, a unique Chinese exhibit that includes the original Joss (Temple of Gods/Altar) brought over from China by the local Chinese community around the time of the completion of the Central Pacific Railroad, and a Mid-Ch'ing Dynasty altar to Quan Yin, goddess of compassion and mercy. The museum is filled with a number of Gold Rush pioneer memories including toys, a Victorian dollhouse, and showshoes for horses. A favorite: the photography on the wall upstairs of a miner with an image of himself as a 12-year-old that appeared mysteriously as the picture was developed.

Nevada City, the best preserved of the gold-mining towns, is a thriving community with the feel of turn-of-the-century Gold Country. Walking along its gas-lit small streets is a pleasure. The Miners Foundry Cultural Center, California Historic Landmark #1012, with massive stone walls, iron doors, a fireplace and antiques, is a Historic Museum and Nevada City's premier event facility. (530) 265-5040. www.minersfoundry.nevcity.org

The **Nevada City Historical Society**'s latest completed project is the Nevada County Narrow Gauge Railroad Museum (NCNGRR), which features a steam locomotive that is driven inside the train museum. Universal Studios has "given back" this part of history to the town, so be sure to look for the list of the more than 100 movies that the train has appeared in. The NGNGRR comprised some 24 miles of track and the train met the CPRR, later the Southern Pacific RR, in Colfax, where passengers transferred to or from the East.

● **Malakoff Diggins State Historic Park**
23579 North Bloomfield Road, Nevada City 95959. North on Highway 49, 11 miles from Nevada City. Turn right on Tyler-Foote Road, travel 17 miles on the paved road and turn right on Derbec Road at the entrance sign. (530) 265-2740. Visitors center: 10–4 winter weekends; daily in summer. Museum: daily, 10–5 in summer; winter weekends, 10–4. Tours of the

*historic town at 1 P.M. on open days and by appt. Campsites, $7 in winter;
$10 in summer. Cabins, $15 in winter; $20 in summer. Day use: $2 per car.
Picnicking.* **Ages 7 & up.** *W. www.park.ca.gov*

Many millions of dollars worth of gold poured from these huge "hydraulic
diggins." A small sign tells visitors that there's still enough gold left here and
nearby to mine $12 million annually for the next 50 years. This park is a silent
monument to the hydraulic miners. The museum displays a model of the
monitor used in gold mines and shows how hydraulic mining worked. Photos
of the two-mile Bloomfield tunnel, the 12-foot-long miners' skis, a portable
undertaker's table, mementos of the Chinese miners, and an old-time bar and
poker room are some of the highlights. Visitors can also see a drugstore, a
general store, and a livery filled with wagons. Films round out the experience.

● Kentucky Mine Museum and Sierra County Historical Park and Museum

*Highway 49 (Mail: P.O. Box 260, Sierra City 96125). North of Sierra City
.5 mile. (530) 862-1310. Memorial Day–Sept. 30, Wed.–Sun., 10–5. Also
weekends in Oct. Guided stamp-mill tour, $5; junior rate for tours. Museum:
adults, $1; ages 7–17, 50¢.* **Ages 7 & up.** *W. www.sierracounty.org*

Among the northern mines, the Kentucky Mine is one of the earliest of
the hard-rock type mines, dating from 1854. The reconstructed stamp mill,
based on sections built in the 1860s and 1880s, was completed in 1933. It
is the only stamp mill in the area that is still operable, with the original
machinery intact. The informative guided tour begins at the opening of the
mine and follows the gold milling process from beginning to end. The Pelton
waterwheels still work, too! The museum constantly changes its displays on
Sierra County's past, which include mining equipment, logging machinery,
skis, clothing and household articles, local minerals, wildflowers, and other
natural history items. There are also exhibits on the early Chinese and the
Maidu Indians, and a schoolroom. Picnic facilities are available.

● Underground Gold Miners Museum

*356 Main Street (Mail: P.O. Box 907), Allegheny 95910. (530) 287-
3223. Weekends, Memorial Day to Labor Day, 11–4. Call in winter for
winter tours and times.* **Ages 10 & up.** *www.ugmm.org*

The Allegheny Supply Company building, originally a livery stable and,
recently, the town's general store, is being restored as a museum. The
museum gives tours to raise funds for its restoration and to serve the
community. This is what backwoods mining life was really like. One tour
($25) covers the mine site, shop and mill buildings, dry room, and videos. The
Underground Tour ($75) gets you down in a working underground gold
mine, rubbing elbows with real gold miners who are proud to have links to
the past.

● Forest City

Forest City. Up Ridge Road from Highway 49 in Yuba City, 15 miles. One mile on paved road on the left. Write: Forest City Historical Association, Allegheny 95910. (530) 287-3413/287-3207. Weekends, 12–4, Memorial Day–Labor Day, and by appt. Free. **Ages 9 & up.** *www.sierracounty.org*

The tiny town of Forest City not only has a museum, it is a museum, since most of the buildings date from the 1800s. The museum itself is located in the 1883 Dance Hall. Artifacts from the barbershop, saloon, and billiard hall that occupied the first floor are on display, as well as other items of 19th-century mining town life, including a forge, a Pelton wheel, and the gold scales used by the Forest City Meat Market.

● Downieville Museum

Main Street, on Highway 49 at mile marker SIE-17 (Mail: P.O. Box 484), Downieville 95936. (530) 289-3423. Daily, May–Oct., 10–5. **Ages 11 & up.** *www.sierracounty.org*

The Downieville Museum building dates to 1832 and was originally a store and gambling hall for the Chinese who settled in the community. Its construction of mortarless schist rock saved it from the many catastrophic fires that periodically razed the town. For half a century, until the 1930s, it was a grocery store run by the Meroux family. The local Native Daughters of the Golden West have completely renovated it to depict life in the area from Gold Rush days to the present in hands-on exhibits. Mining implements, Indian artifacts, household articles, and lodge regalia are exhibited, along with a one-sixth-scale model stamp mill and an ore-grinding *arrastre.*

● Loyalton Museum

Highway 49, mile marker SIE-61 on Sierra County Route A24 north to edge of town. Loyalton Community Hall, just past Loyalton Elementary School. (530) 993-6754. Thurs.–Mon., 11–3. Free. **Ages 10 & up.** *W. www.sierracounty.org*

The Loyalton Catholic Church is a small museum that displays 19th-century clothing and housewares, wooden skis, and a collection of glass from the 1930s. Handmade farm implements from the late 1800s and a "donkey," or logging steam engine, represent the agriculture and timber industries. There are also Washoe baskets, arrowheads, and photographs.

● Plumas-Eureka State Park Museum

310 Johnsville Road, off county road A-14, Blairsden 96103. (530) 836-2380. Museum: daily, 8–4 in summer; weekends in winter when staff is available. Adults, $1. **Ages 7 & up.** *W. www.parks.ca.gov*

The site of hard-rock gold mining, there are approximately 67 miles of mining shafts inside Eureka Peak. Bird-watchers see Caliope hummingbirds as well as pileated woodpeckers in early summer. Museum displays include hard-rock mining equipment, an assay office, models of a stamp mill and an *arrastre*, natural-history exhibits, and pioneer life remembrances. The outbuildings are fun, too.

● Plumas County Museum

500 Jackson, behind the Courthouse, Quincy 95971. (530) 283-6320. Mon.–Sat., 8–5, all year; May–Sept.; Sun. 10–4. Adults $1; ages 12–17, 50¢. Groups by appt. **Ages 7 & up.** *W. www.countyofplumas.com/museum*

This family-friendly "living museum" depicts local history with artifacts and displays about the lumbering, mining, and agricultural work that brought settlers to Plumas County. A large Maidu Indian basket collection centers the many exhibits. The three-story, 1878 Variel Victorian Home adjacent to the museum is restored and available for tour. Third-grader Kasey wrote, "I liked the Variel house too. It was amazing how Ran's ancestor's wedding dress was there. I thought it was cool how they used newspaper to insulate their house, and had a waffle iron. . . . I liked the tepee . . . because it actually felt like you were an Indian when you were in there. The mountain lion actually looked real. Thank you so much."

● Donner Memorial State Park

12593 Donner Pass Road, Donner Lake, Truckee 96161. (530) 582-7892. Daily, 10–4. Adults, $1; free for those 16 and under. $2 per vehicle for day use. **Ages 8 & up.** *W. www.parks.ca.gov*

During the disastrous winter of 1846, a party of 81 people stranded in this area tried to make it through the mountains to California. Only 49 people survived, and some of the survivors allegedly resorted to cannibalism. The settling of the Sierra Nevada and the tragic story of the Donner party are told with relics, dioramas, pictures, and models that are combined with natural history and Emigrant Trail history in The Emigrant Trail Museum. The pedestal of the memorial to the Donner party is 22 feet high—as high as the early snowfall that trapped them. Chinese railroad workers, the "Big Four" railroad tycoons, miners, and mountain men are also remembered here, as well as Native Americans. Picnic areas, campsites, and guided hikes are available. My favorite memento: the replica of Patty Reed's doll.

● Sierra Nevada Children's Museum/KidZone

11711 Donner Pass Road, Truckee 96161 (Mail: P.O. Box 2563, Truckee 96160). (530) 587-KIDS. Wed.–Sat., 10–5. Parties and groups by reservation. $3. Play Structure: $1 for those 2 and over. **Ages 2–13.** *W. www.ncgold.com*

The SNCM is located in the KidZone, a state of the art dome that also houses an indoor play structure, an infant/crawler area filled with soft mats and age-appropriate toys, and the Truckee Family Resource Center. The museum is the only hands-on discovery museum in the Lake Tahoe area. It invites children to "learn by doing," fostering creativity, independence, and self-esteem. Interactive exhibits such as the Junior Theatre, a mini-grocery store, and Emigrant Trail exhibit complete with a real covered wagon, a water play area, a computer lab, and a creative arts center are offered. The museum hosts science camps, art and music workshops, and fun.

● **Lake Tahoe**
Lake Tahoe Visitors Authority, 1156 Ski Run Boulevard, South Lake Tahoe 96150. (530) 544-5050/(800) AT-TAHOE. North Tahoe Visitors and Convention Bureau (Mail: P.O. Box 5578, Tahoe City 96125). (530) 583-3494. Road conditions: (800) 427-7623. Information: (530) 544-5050. Lake Tahoe magazine lists camping, dining, sporting, lodging information, and other services. **All ages.** *www.mytahoevacation.com*

Lake Tahoe is justifiably world famous for its crystal-clear water and beautiful setting. It was gouged from the crown of the Sierra during the Ice Age and named, in the language of the Washoe tribe, "Big Water." Visitors can ski, water-ski, boat, bike, ride, swim (only in August unless you're a polar bear), surf, sun, golf, windsail, hike, and enjoy the forest wilderness and the invigorating clarity of the air and sunshine.

For an exhilarating overall picture, ride the **Scenic Aerial Tram** (800-2-HEAVEN/775-586-7000), a spectacular 2.5-mile-long ride to the top of Heavenly. From there you can hike trails nearly 3,000 feet high and take the Nifty 50 Trolley from the South Shore (530-541-6328) or take the city bus to the base of the gondola.

Naturalist programs are given on summer weekends in the D. L. Bliss and Emerald Bay State Parks and at **Camp Richardson.** The U.S. Forest Service **Taylor Creek Stream Profile Chamber** near Camp Richardson is part of the **El Dorado National Forest Visitors Center** (daily, 10–5). You can take one of the self-guided nature walks through a mountain meadow and marsh and even down into the chamber for a fish-eye view of a mountain stream. Recorded messages help identify the fish and plants in front of you.

Vikingsholm Castle, a 38-room Nordic fortress (Emerald Bay State Park, Mail: P.O. Box 266, Tahoma 96142. 530-525-7277/541-3030. Daily, 10–4, mid-June–Labor Day) on Emerald Bay's southwest shore is open to the public. The **Ehrman Mansion** (Sugar Pine Point, Highway 89, Tahoma 96142. Summer tours, 11–4. Fee), is an outstanding example of turn-of-the-century Lake Tahoe architecture.

The Castle, **George Whittell's Thunderbird Lodge,** opened to the public in 2002. This three-story ranch chateau was built in 1939 with no expense spared and features masonry, iron, and woodwork by top European craftsmen. It offers a spectacular panorama of the lake. Tours can be booked at the visitors center at Incline Village (Adults, $22; children, $12, 1-800-GO-TAHOE. By reservation).

The **Gatekeeper's Log Cabin Museum** (130 West Lake Boulevard, Tahoe City 96145. 530-583-1762. Daily, spring to fall) displays Washoe and Paiute artifacts, local minerals and fossils, and other Tahoe memorabilia. On the lake, you can sightsee from the **Tahoe Queen**'s glass-bottom boat 800-238-2463. June–Oct., 11 A.M., 1:30 and 3:55 P.M.; noon daily in winter. Adults, $13; ages 11 and under, $6) or take the *MS Dixie* (775-588-3508/882-0786), a Mississippi paddlewheeler that shows you another view of Emerald Bay. The *Dixie* also does a breakfast cruise to Glenbrook. Other boats cruise the blue waters as well. In summer, you can also take a balloon ride with **Lake Tahoe Balloons** (800-872-9294; 530-544-1221).

The **Lake Tahoe Historical Society Log Cabin Museum** (3058 U.S. 50/Lake Tahoe Boulevard [Mail: P.O. Box 404, South Lake Tahoe 96150]. 530-541-5458. Daily, 10–4 in summer) features artifacts from Tahoe's early days, including Washoe Indian basketry, photos, pioneer implements and a model of the historic SS *Tahoe* and the area's oldest building. The visitors center in Truckee also offers information on dining, camping, sights, accommodations, skiing, transit, horseback riding, sleigh and hay rides, snowmobile rental, skating, wildlife scenic tours, four-wheel adventures, water sports, parasailing, and events. Pioneer belongings, railroad items, and historic photos decorate the renovated 1896 Southern Pacific Depot (530-587-2757).

The **Western America Ski Sports Museum** (Boreal Ski Area, Castle Peak exit on Interstate 80, [Mail: P.O. Box 729, Soda Springs 95728]. 530-426-3313. Late spring to fall, Sat.–Sun., 10–4. Free) features ski exhibits from 1860 to the present, vintage ski movies, and artifacts of Snowshoe Thompson.

Venture to the Nevada side of the lake for a visit to the **Ponderosa Ranch** at Incline Village (100 Ponderosa Ranch Road, Incline Village, off Highway 28 on the North Shore, NV 89451. 775-831-0691. Daily, 9:30–5, late April–October, weather permitting) to see the Cartwright Ranch House, Hoss's Mystery Mine and Shootin' Gallery, an entire Frontier Town, an antique car and carriage museum, a petting zoo in the Ponderosa barnyard, and other attractions. There are breakfast haywagon rides through the tall timber.

The Fresno Area and Madera County

Some people think that Fresno exists only as a stopping-off place from San Francisco to Los Angeles, but it's a big, booming city. The trip to Fresno is four hours by car from San Francisco (only an hour by plane), but there are so many motels you can usually be assured of a room when you arrive. Surrounded by orchards and rich farmland, pretty lakes, and an impressive irrigation system, Fresno is also the gateway to Sierra National Forest and Sequoia, Kings Canyon, and Yosemite National Parks. Hiking, skiing, spelunking, and wandering through groves of the largest living things on earth, the giant Sequoia redwoods, are all available within 40 minutes' drive. Closer to Fresno, seven lakes offer sailing, fishing, houseboating, waterskiing, and windsurfing.

● R. C. Baker Memorial Museum

297 West Elm, Coalinga 93210. (559) 935-1914. Mon.–Fri., 10–12 and 1–5; Sat., 11–5; Sun., 1–5. Donation. **Ages 7 & up.**
www.caohwy.com/r/rcbakmmu.htm

"I enjoyed going to your museum in Coalinga. I liked the photos of the earthquake, I loved those boxing cards that were $100 a card. I liked the old cameras, and that 1928 one dollar bill. I thought the car there was neat. I bet that would cost a lot of money. I liked all the different kinds of barbed wire. Speaking of barbed, I thought the barber or dentist chair was neat. And the big fossil was awesome. The uniforms and the guns were radical. The counting machines were weird, but I liked them too. One of the things that I liked the most was the telephone booth. I enjoyed the different rooms with dolls. But the thing I liked most about your museum was everything. Your museum was the best museum I have ever went to. Keep up the good work." This is the recommendation of Brandon, a visitor from Akers Elementary School.

The remodeled **R. C. Baker Museum,** named in honor of a Coalinga pioneer, oilman, and inventor, shows both the natural and man-made history of Coalinga. Visitors to Coalinga will enjoy a drive nine miles north on Highways 33 and 198 past the Grasshopper oil pumps—oil-field characters painted in many colors to look like clowns, birds, and animals.

● San Luis Reservoir

Romero Overlook, Highway 152, 15 miles west of Los Banos. Dept. of Water Research. 31770 Ganzaga Road, Gustine 95322. (209) 827-5353. Daily, 9–5. Closed major holidays. Free. **Ages 10 & up.** *www.DWR.water.CA.gov*

In the Romero Overlook on the reservoir, pictures, graphic wall displays, movies, and slide shows tell the story of the State Water Project and the Federal Central Valley Project, and how they work together at the San Luis

Complex. This is the history of California's water development from 1769 to 1962. Telescopes at the center offer a spectacular view of the area. The State Water Resources guides who staff the visitors center love to explain things.

● Tulare County Museum
27000 South Mooney Boulevard, Mooney Grove Park, Visalia 93277. (559) 733-6616. Fall and spring, Thurs.–Mon., 10–4. Winter weekends, 10–4. Summer, weekdays except Tues., 10–4; weekends, 12–6. Tours by reservation. $5 per car; $20 per bus. **Ages 6 & up.** *W. www.tularecounty.org*

End of the Trail, the bronze sculpture by James Earl Fraser portraying a tired Indian on a pony—once the most copied piece of art in the world—is the star attraction at this lively museum spread throughout 11 buildings in a park. That sculpture was first exhibited in San Francisco in 1915 at the Panama-Pacific Exposition. A one-room schoolhouse, newspaper and dental office, Yokuts Indian collection, and rooms from turn-of-the-century homes re-create the past. Furniture, clothes, cooking utensils, toys, baskets, World War I uniforms, antique cars, weapons, and early farm machinery are also on exhibit.

The 143-acre park offers picnic arbors and oak trees, boating, skateboard tracks, and more.

● Tulare Historical Museum
444 West Tulare Avenue (Mail: P.O. Box 248), Tulare 93275. (559) 686-2074. Thurs.–Sat., 10–4; Sun., 12:30–4. Adults, $5; seniors, $4; students, $2; under 5, free. **Ages 8 & up.** *W. www.tularehistoricalmuseum.org*

"Take a trip back in time" is the theme of this historic museum. You're greeted at the door by a life-size horse and doctor's buggy, then you step back to a Yokuts village around Tulare Lake. Walk through the coming of the railroad, the lives of some of the early settlers, the three great fires that swept Tulare during its first 14 years, and the incorporation of the city. Mini-replicas of rooms in an early Tulare home and local businesses bring to life a time gone by. Sports fans will like the statue of Olympian Bob Mathias.

● Boyden Cavern
Kings Canyon National Park, Highway 180, 77 miles east of Fresno. (209) 736-2708/(866) 762-2837 (Mail: P.O. Box 7), Vallecito 95251. June–Sept., daily, 10–5; May and Oct., daily, 11–4. Adults, $9; children, 6–12, $4.50; seniors, $8. Gift shop. Picnic area. **Ages 6 & up.** *www.caverntours.com*

A 45-minute tour takes you into a wondrous world deep beneath the 2,000-foot-high marble walls of the famous Kings Gates. Massive stalagmites, delicate stalactites, sparkling flowstones, rimstone dams, and splendid arrays of crystalline formations defy description. Boyden Cavern is in the deepest canyon in the United States. Evening flashlight tours by reservation, in summer.

● Clovis Big Creek Historical Society Museum

401 Pollasky Avenue, Clovis 93257. (559) 297-8033. Tues.–Sun., 11–2; in summer: Fri., 5–9, and by appt. **Ages 6 & up.**
www.fresno.com/cvonlinc/museums.html

This museum, in an old bank, is crammed with something for everyone. The bank is famous for being the first one in which nails were used in a robbery. The robbers threw nails out of their car (in the 1920s) to give every car in pursuit flat tires. Kids still get a thrill out of walking inside the bank vault. Joaquin Murietta's shotgun, baseball great Ty Cobb's letters, the boots Festus wore on the TV show *Gunsmoke,* Indian artifacts, a Holocaust exhibit, a military exhibit, and more crowd the building. There are Clovis High School pictures from 1918 to 1964. Youngsters are particularly fascinated by the flume that swept lumber to Shaver Lake.

● Wild Water Adventures

11413 East Shaw Avenue, Clovis 93611-8859. Exit Highway 99 at Shaw Avenue in Fresno; park is 7 miles east of Clovis Avenue. (559) 299-WILD. All-day admission, $21.99; 3-years-old to 48 inches tall, $15.99; seniors, $9.99. After 4 P.M., $13.95 and $9.95. Free parking. Special barbecue days. Weekends, 10–7; Tues.–Fri., 11–6. Closed Sept.–Memorial Day. **All ages.** W.
www.wildwater1.com

This 50-acre park has picnic spots with a great view of the Sierra mountains, a fishing lake, a toddler's wading pool, and a 15,000-square-foot children's water area. There's a pool with waves and a wet bumper cars area, body-surfing areas, speed slides, and a scary Black Hole.

● Porterville Historical Museum

257 North D Street, Porterville 93257. (559) 784-2053. Thurs., Fri., and Sat., 10–4, and by appt. Free. **Ages 5 & up.** W.
www.caohwy.com/p/porhismv.htm

The main room of the museum, a former Southern Pacific Railroad station waiting room, houses an interesting collection of Yokuts Indian baskets and other artifacts along with a collection of mounted birds and animals. Cattle industry memorabilia, including branding irons, barbed wire, and saddles and tack, are in the Wilcox Room. A graciously furnished turn-of-the-century bedroom, a lovely collection of glassware and china, and vignettes of a drugstore, dentist's office, and lawyer's office are in the arcade and baggage room areas of the museum. Outdoor exhibits include antique farm equipment, fire engines, a mill wagon, an oil wagon, a baggage wagon, a broom-making machine, and a fully restored blacksmith shop.

● Zalud House

393 North Hockett, Porterville 93257. (559) 782-7548. Wed.–Sat., 10–4; Sun., 2–4. Adults, $2; children, 50¢. Groups by appt. **Ages 8 & up.** *www.chamber.porterville.com*

One of the state's unsung treasures is this remarkably preserved and lovingly cared-for Victorian home. Pearle Zalud was born in 1884 and lived there until her death in 1970. Her world tour at age 29 was the first of many. The home bears the beautiful fruits of her worldwide souvenir hunting. The house is exactly as she left it—which is exactly as her father liked it in 1912, when her mother died. The art and furnishings, hats, dolls, collars and laces, framed antique valentines, and the family photos all create a house that is a home.

Since there was so much left in the closets, the curator changes the exhibits in the rooms with the seasons. The beautiful flower gardens outside are available for private parties and weddings. Kids love the story of Pearle's brother Edward, a cowboy who was killed while riding, and her brother-in-law William, who was shot to death by a woman in the Porterville Pioneer Hotel in 1917. The chair with the bullet hole is upstairs.

Third-grader Carrie wrote, "Thanks for taking us through the Zalud House. It was fun. Some people say that it is haunted but I don't think it is because it is beautiful. And I wish that I lived there."

● Colonel Allensworth State Historic Park

Allensworth. On Highway 43, 18 miles north of Wasco; on Highway 99, 9 miles west of Earlimart. (661) 849-3433. Visitors center open daily, 10–4, except Thanksgiving, Christmas, and New Year's Day. Parking fee, $2, $10 per bus. Camping available. Buildings, 10–4, by appt. To schedule a tour, write: P.O. Box 148, Allensworth-Earlimart 93219. **Ages 5 & up.** *www.parks.ca.gov*

The only California town to be founded, financed, and governed by and for African Americans is now perpetuated for the public's use and enjoyment. It is dedicated to the spirit of Colonel Allen Allensworth, who escaped slavery and served with the Union Army during the Civil War. When he retired in 1906, he held the rank of lieutenant colonel and was the highest ranking African-American officer in the U.S. military. A visitors center with exhibits and films, picnic area, two museums, the colonel's residence, and the original schoolhouse are open to the public upon request, as is the 15-unit campground. The Mary Dickinson Memorial Library is open now, along with the Morris Smith House.

● Pioneer Village Museum

Art Gonzales Parkway, adjoining Highway 99 (Mail: 1814 Tucker), Selma 93662. Undergoing renovation. Call (559) 896-8918 for hours and info.

Victorian homes and cherished buildings are being restored in this museum-in-progress. Visitors will be able to walk through a 1904 Queen Anne, an old barn, the Ungar Opera House, Selma's 1887 Southern Pacific Depot, and a 1901 Little Red School house—and more.

● Fort Roosevelt Science Center

870 West Davis (Mail: P.O. Box 164), Armona 93202. (550) 582-8970. By appt. only. Adults, $2; children, $1.25. Picnic areas, overnights, and birthday parties. **All ages.** *www.museumsusa.org*

Local businesses and families have worked with the California Department of Fish and Game to set up this natural-history museum and rehabilitation center. The museum itself is in the 1893 Hanford Railroad Freight Depot. There's an old two-story log cabin, covered wagons, a windmill, and a waterwheel by the pond. There's an adopt-an-animal program, and on-site educators really get the youngsters involved with the world around them, especially with the museum's collection of mammals and birds.

● Kearney Mansion and Kearney Park

7160 West Kearney Boulevard, Fresno 93706. In Kearney Park, 7 miles west of downtown Fresno. (559) 441-0862. Fri.–Sun., 1–4. Tours at 1, 2, and 3, Fri., Sat., and Sun. Adults, $4; seniors, $3; students and children, $2. Groups by appt. Gift shop. **Ages 8 & up.** *www.valleyhistory.org*

Built between 1900 and 1903, the home of M. Theo Kearney, pioneer Fresno land developer and raisin baron, is administered by the Fresno Historical Society, which has preserved many of the original furnishings, including European wallpapers, art-nouveau light fixtures, and replicas of original carpets and wallpapers. The adjoining servants quarters house the ranch kitchen and museum store. The 225-acre park surrounding the mansion features picnic and playground facilities.

● Discovery Center

1944 North Winery Avenue, Fresno 93703. Take Highway 9 to McKinley, then east to North Winery Avenue. (559) 251-5531. Tues.–Sat., 10–4. Donation. Group by appt. Summer science camp and astronomy program. Picnic areas and playgrounds. Gift shop. **All ages.** *W. www.TheDiscoveryCenter.net*

This hands-on science center helps children try things out for themselves. There's a bubble machine, a tree that lights up by sound, pipe phones, an electricity learning lab, a Gemini space capsule, and hands-on table stations. The Indian room has a Yokut hut and shows the many things that Indians have introduced to civilization. Dioramas of the animal and vegetable life of the valley and streams are also fun to look at. Outside, there's a little zoo of local animals, a desert tortoise colony, and a pond for exploring. Children have a great time here.

● Fresno Arts Museum
2233 North First Street, in Radio Park, between Clinton and McKinley Avenues, Fresno 93703. (559) 441-4221. Tues.–Fri., 10–5; weekends, 12–5. Adults, $2; seniors and students, $1. Tues., free. Tours by reservation. Gift shop. **Ages 8 & up.** *W. www.fresnoartmuseum.com*

This forum for the arts of the 19th and 20th centuries, with revolving exhibits, classes, planned tours, and lectures, offers artists-in-residence and permanent collections of Mexican art and French postimpressionist graphics.

● Meux Home Museum
1007 R Street at Tulare (Mail: P.O. Box 70), Fresno 93707. (559) 233-8007. Fri.–Sun., 12–3:30. Adults, $4; ages 13–17, $3; ages 5–12, $2. Groups by appt.: 209-431-1926. Storytelling afternoons. Gift shop. **Ages 5 & up.** *Partially W. www.meux.mus.ca.us*

The docents in this sweet blue-and-white Queen Anne enjoy talking about Victorian family life and explaining how things worked back then. Special events such as the Teddy Bears' picnic make this a class favorite. Indeed, Fresno schoolchildren were some of the many contributors to the refurbishment of this elegant family home. A plaque thanks them for the sponsorship of the breezeway in the kitchen area. Visitors enjoy Dr. Thomas R. Meux's Confederate uniform and surgical tools as well as his portrait in a Rhett Butler mustache, and the clothing, jewelry, wedding gowns, and photographs.

● Library Museum of Germans from Russia
3233 North West Avenue, Fresno 93705. (559) 229-8287. Mon.–Fri., 12–4; Sat., 9:30–12. Groups by appt. Free. **Ages 10 & up.** *W. www.ahsgr.org*

The Central California Chapter of the American Historical Society of Germans from Russia offers genealogy workshops, a large assortment of maps, and discussions about the folklore of their forefathers. The collection of art, literature, and folklore is housed in an old city firehouse. Exhibits include photographs and items brought from the Soviet Union as well as artifacts of early Fresno immigrants.

The nearby **African-American Historical and Cultural Museum of the San Joaquin Valley** (1857 Fulton Street, Fresno. 209-268-7102) offers changing exhibits celebrating African-American heritage, from art and crafts from the Congo to an exhibit focused on the Buffalo Soldiers.

● Fresno Metropolitan Museum of Art, History and Science

1555 Van Ness Avenue, Fresno 93721. (559) 441-1444. Tues.–Sun., 11–5; Thurs. until 8. Adults, $7; seniors and students, $4; 3–12, $3. Free evenings, first Thurs. of the month. Tours by appt. **Ages 5 & up.** *W. www.fresnomet.org*

Explore art, history, and science in the San Joaquin Valley's largest museum. From giant dinosaurs to original drawings by Michelangelo, major touring exhibitions change regularly. The Met's permanent collections feature a collection of rare Chinese snuff bottles, the Oscar and Maria Salzer Collection of trompe l'oeil paintings, and the largest collection of puzzles in the world. The Met is also home to the Reeves Exploration Center in the Rotary Playland Science Gallery, which includes more than 50 interactive exhibits for children. A permanent exhibition devoted to Fresno's most famous native son, William Saroyan, includes artifacts from his life and times and examines upbringing in Fresno. He wrote, "If you want to behold a truly religious man in action, go to Fresno and watch a farmer watering his trees, vines, and plants."

● Chaffee Zoo and Rotary Storyland and Playland

890 West Belmont Avenue, Roeding Park, Fresno 93728. Freeway 99 between Olive and Belmont. (559) 498-2671. Zoo: ages 5–11, $4; ages 12–61, $7; over 62, $3. Daily, Nov.–Feb., 10–4; Mar.–Oct, 9–5. Groups: 264-2235. **All ages.** *W. Rotary Storyland: ages 3–12, $2.75; ages 12–61, $3.75; over 62, $2.25. Spring and fall weekends and holidays, 10–5. Closed Dec. and Jan. May 1–Labor Day, 10–5.* **Ages 2–11.** *Playland: 486-2124. Prices and hours vary depending on season; usually, 10–5 when school's out. Boating costs also vary.* **Ages 2–13.** *www.Chaffeezoo.org*

The Fresno Zoo is one of the most progressive in the country. In the South American tropical rain forest exhibit, visitors walk through a lush habitat of free-flying birds and small primates. One favorite is the golden lion tamarin, a tiny, fluffy, fierce-looking monkey. The computerized state-of-the-art reptile house has been extremely successful in breeding almost-extinct animals. The elephants thrive in the waterfall and deep pool in their section. Winding paths and lush foliage add to the pleasure of a stroll through the zoo, as does the "Ask Me!" cart program. Kids especially like meeting hawks and owls face to face when the docent takes them out of their cages for discussions with visitors. Enjoy birds from Australia in the Australian aviary.

In Storyland, talking storybook keys ($1.50) persuade the blue caterpillar to tell eight classic fairy tales. Then when children have heard the stories, they can go on to visit the heroes of the tales. They can play in King Arthur's castle, Red Riding Hood's Grandmother's cottage, or Mr. Toad's cart, or they can talk to Simple Simon's pie man, the knaves of Alice's court, or Little Miss Muffet and Winnie the Pooh.

Young children will find Playland irresistible. There's a roller coaster, a Ferris wheel, a kiddie car ride, a scenic miniature train ride, and a merry-go-round. Paddleboats, motorboats, and rowboats to rent by the hour on Lake Washington attract the seaworthy, and there are concessions and picnic areas.

Fort Millerton, also in the park (weekends, May 1–Sept. 30, 1–4. Donation), houses a small exhibit of pioneer life, with antique toys, lumber tools, and the medical kit of Fresno's first doctor.

● San Joaquin Fish Hatchery

Friant 93626. Off Highway 41, 13 miles northeast of Fresno. (559) 822-2374. Daily, 8–4:30; in summer, 7:30–4. Free. **All ages.** *www.dfg.ca.gov*

There are more fish in this one spot than you'll ever see again: more than two million trout in sizes that range from pinhead to fingerlings ready to catch are raised in these trout-hatching ponds. Four times a day the fish are fed high-protein dry pellets. When they're a year old and 10 inches long, they're taken in tanks by plane and truck to the heavily fished lakes and streams of California. But while they're here, it's really fun to walk along the 48 ponds and watch the fish leap over and slide down the little dams between them. A photo exhibit explains about trout habits and the trout-seeding program. California's Fish Hatchery and Planting Program runs 22 hatcheries, most open to the public. Call your local Fish and Game Department office for information on the one nearest you.

● Friant Dam and Millerton Lake State Recreational Area CHP

Millerton Lake (Mail: P.O. Box 267, Friant 93626). Off Highway 41, north of Fresno. (559) 822-2332. Daily, daylight hours. Park entry, $6 per car. Camping: 882-4363. **Ages 8 & up.** *www.parks.ca.gov*

Fed by Sierra snows, the waters of Millerton Lake are released into the Friant-Kern and Madera irrigation canals to feed the rich croplands of Fresno and Madera Counties. The dam is 319 feet high and 3,488 feet long, with a reservoir capacity of 520,000 acre feet. You can walk halfway across the dam while guides tell you the history of the project.

● Madera County Museum

210 West Yosemite (Mail: P.O. Box 478), Madera 93637. Off Highway 99, 17 miles north of Fresno. (559) 673-0291. Sat. and Sun., 1–4, and by appt. Free. **Ages 6 & up.** *www.maderahistory.org*

This meticulous museum tells the story of Madera County and its people. Third-grader Patrick wrote, "Thank you for letting us come. I saw a lot of interesting rooms. I saw a lot of great ones. The best ones are mining, store, parlor, saloon, war and peace, Native Americans, and downtown."

Three floors of displays in this 1900 granite courthouse emphasize the county's mining, logging, and agricultural history. There's a miner's cabin, a country store, a blacksmith shop, and an amazing section of flume from the Madera Sugar Pine Lumber Company. The "downtown" room shows what the city looked like in 1900 and even has a stagecoach in which people rode to Yosemite Park.

● Sierra Mono Museum

(Mail: P.O. Box 275, North Folk 93643) At the intersection of Roads 225 and 228, off Highway 41 from Fresno toward Bass Lake. (559) 877-2115. Tues.–Sat., 9–3:30, and by appt. Adults, $3; seniors, $2; students, $1. Gift shop. **Ages 3 & up.** *W. www.yosemite-sierra.org*

The only Indian museum in California owned and operated by an Indian tribe without any outside help, the Sierra Mono Museum is a triumph of care, hard work, and attention to detail. The dioramas of wildlife in nature and vignettes portraying Indian foods and culture are well labeled and beautifully designed. Did you know that rattlesnakes are born alive, not hatched from eggs? You can see some unborn baby rattlesnakes if you look carefully. The museum offers classes and demonstrations on basket making, beadwork, acorn gathering, and other arts and crafts.

● Fresno Flats Historic Park

School Road, Oakhurst. School Road is Road 427, off Highway 41. (559) 683-6570/683-7766. Tues.–Fri., 10–3; weekend tours, 11–3. Tours: adults, $3; children over 6, $2. Costumed docents host groups. (For appt., write to SHSA, P.O. Box 451, Oakhurst 93644.) Free. Picnic Area. **Ages 6 & up.** *www.fresnoflatsmuseum.org*

Designed to capture the flavor of family life in Central California's foothills and mountains a century ago, Fresno Flats is preserving buildings along with memories. The old Fresno Flats school is now a museum with interesting artifacts and revolving exhibits, but the Laramore-Lyman 1878 house and the 1869 Taylor log house are living museums. A jail, blacksmith shop, old barn, wagon-stage collection, and flume are also on the grounds. One side of the Taylor log house is a re-creation of an early-day forest ranger's office, complete with maps, old tools, and a display on how the house was constructed.

One young visitor wrote, "I especially enjoyed the jail. I learned how they put their houses together and how they used horses and wagons to get around. Fresno Flats is an important part of Oakhurst's history. It's great to see how much our community has changed by visiting Fresno Flats."

If you're driving through Oakhurst, you must stop in the center of town, on Highway 41 and Road 426, and visit the **Talking Bear.** He'll give you and the kids a brief history of the now extinct California grizzly and ask for respect of the forest and its wildlife.

● Children's Museum of the Sierra

49269 Golden Oak Drive (Mail: P.O. 1200), Oakhurst 93644. (559) 658-5656. Tues.–Sat., 10–4 in winter, until 5 in summer. Adults and children over 2, $2; under 2, free. **Ages 2 & up.** *W. www.childrensmuseumofthesierra.org*

This kid-friendly museum is a wonderland of touchable, interactive exhibits, from stuffed animals to pet to an emergency station where you can call 911 for the fire engine or ambulance. There are butterflies and fossils to check under the microscope, doctor's X-rays to examine, and a "dig site" to uncover deer bones and then put the skeleton back together. The shadow room, ship room, crafts room, karaoke station, and stage—with costume collection—are all great to play in.

● Mariposa County History Center

(Mail: P.O. Box 606, Mariposa 95338) At 12th and Jessie Streets, off Highway 49. (209) 966-2924. Daily, Apr.–Oct., 10–4:30, until 4 in March; weekends, 10–4 in Feb., Nov., and Dec. Donation. **Ages 4 & up.** *www.mariposacounty.org*

In what proud Mariposans call "the finest small museum to be seen anywhere, " you'll see a typical miner's one-room cabin with all his worldly possessions; the more comfortable home of the West's most famous explorer, John C. Fremont, and his wife, Jessie; a street of shops reminiscent of the 1850s; a one-room schoolhouse; a five-stamp mill used for crushing gold-bearing quartz; the Gazette Building, a newspaper office from 1860 to 1930; and art and artifacts showing how gold was formed and extracted. Of special interest are the "Dear Charlie" letters posted throughout: letters written by Horace Snow in 1852 through 1854 to Charlie, his boyhood friend in Cambridge, Massachusetts. They give a miner's-eye view of life in the mines more than a century ago. The Indian Village with bark houses, sweathouse, mining exhibits, and old wagons and buggies on the grounds are also worth seeing.

The **Mariposa County Courthouse** (10th and Bullion Streets. 209-966-2005. In winter, Mon.–Fri., 9–5; Apr.–Oct., 10–4, on weekends; and by appt. Free) is the oldest courthouse still in use in California, and is also part of the History Center. The clock in its tower has been marking time since 1866.

● California's State Mining and Mineral Exhibit.

(Mail: P.O. Box 1192, Mariposa 95338.) Mariposa County Fairgrounds, near Highway 140. (209) 742-7625. May 1–Sept. 30, Wed.–Mon., 10–6;

Oct. 1–Apr. 30, Wed.–Sun., 10–4. $1; under 14, free. Group rates: (209)742-7625. Gift shop. **Ages 5 & up.** *www.parks.CA.gov*

The 20,000-piece collection flourishes on a hillside where forty-niners once mined the gold-rich ore. There are Mother Lode gold specimens, including the fabulous 13-pound Fricot Nugget. Visitors can also see a turn-of-the-century assay office, model stamp mill, and historic mining equipment. Dramatic crystals and minerals from around the world are on display, as well as rare benitoite, the California state gem. You can walk through a 200-foot mine tunnel and see underground mining tools from the early 1900s. A miniature stamp mill and simulated mine tunnel will intrigue.

● Yosemite Mountain Sugar Pine Railroad

56001 Yosemite Highway 41, Fish Camp 93623. (559) 683-7273. Adults, $9–12.50; children, $4.50–6.25. Gift and book shop. Call or write for complete schedule. Groups and parties are welcome. The logger steam train is wheelchair accessible. **All ages.** *www.ymsprr.com*

Just four miles from Yosemite National Park's south entrance, this narrow-gauge steam railroad operates on a restored section of old logging rails for a four-mile narrated trip through magnificent forest scenery. Jenny A railcars operate daily, March through October; logger steam trains run less frequently. Special runs are also available. Moonlight specials can include a melodrama or a barbecue dinner and music around the campfire. An 1856 log cabin is the site of the Thornberry Museum with artifacts and photos of the logging era. Food service is available at the station.

● Yosemite National Park

Enter through Fish Camp on Highway 41, at El Portal on Highway 140, or on Highway 120 (this road to Tioga Pass is closed during the winter, which can last until May). (Mail: Park Admin. Headquarters, P.O. Box 577, 95389.) (209) 372-0200. Visitors center: (209) 372-0200. Center open daily: in summer, 8–6; in spring, fall, and winter, 9–5; museums open daily. Cars, $20 for 7 days. **All ages.** *www.NPS.gov/YOSE*

If you and your family had only one sight to see in California, your best choice would be Yosemite National Park. Yosemite is one of the world's wonders, a world within itself. Elevations range from less than 2,000 feet to over 13,000, and in these 11,000 feet, five different plant belts exist. Each sustains a part of the park's wildlife population of 220 bird and 75 mammal species. In this natural splendor, you can hike, swim, camp, fish, ski, ride horseback or mule, bicycle, or simply wander.

Your first stop should be the visitors center in Yosemite Valley, where you can learn about the park from the center's pamphlets, exhibits, audio-visual programs, lectures, and guided walks. The *Yosemite Guide* and *Yosemite Today,* free, at entrance stations, give the latest schedules.

Where you go in Yosemite will, of course, depend on your time, interests, and the season. You can choose from mountains, giant sequoia groves, towering waterfalls like Bridal Veil, and sites with breathtaking vistas of Sentinel Rock and El Capitan.

There are also museums in Yosemite for rainy days or a change of pace. The **Indian Cultural Center** (daily, 9–4), near the visitors center, is of interest. Be sure to go through the self-guiding reconstruction of the **Ahwaneechee Indian Village,** which is open at all times. During the summer, there are cultural demonstrations in the Indian Village. At the **Pioneer Yosemite History Center** at Wawona, you can wander through a collection of horse-drawn vehicles, an old jail, a miner's hut, a working wagon shop, and a covered bridge. In the summer, you can talk to costumed historian-interpreters who portray the original occupants of the cabins, representing the different stages in the development of Yosemite National Park.

The **Yosemite Travel Museum** in the administration area near the Arch Rock entrance, now under renovation, tells the story of early-day railroad and auto transportation in the region. It has a caboose, a locomotive, and a couple of cars on the grounds. The **Geology Museum** at the visitors center in Yosemite Valley shows how the mountains, waterfalls, and gorges were formed. The natural history of the area is also explored at the **Happy Isles Nature Center,** which is youth oriented, with summer Junior Ranger programs, dioramas, and interactive displays.

Yosemite By Air is one way to see it all. Tours leave from Fresno Air Terminal. Call or write, but be sure to reserve in advance, (800) 622-8687/ (209) 251-7501. 4885 East Shields Avenue, Suite 201, Fresno 93727. Yosemite Air Tours, Courtney Aviation: (209) 532-2345. (Mail: P.O. Box 1196, Columbia 95310) www.flyyosemite.com

For trail rides and pack trips, contact the **Rock Creek Pack Station,** Box 248, Bishop, CA 93515. Winter: (760) 872-8331; summer: (760) 935-4493. www.RockCreekPackStation.com. And to see the area by water, contact (Ahwahnee Whitewater. P.O. Box 1161, Columbia 95310). (800) 359-9790/(209) 533-1401. www.ahwahnee.com

Yosemite is busy in summer, so aim for other times, if possible. For information about the park, write to Superintendent, Yosemite National Park, CA 95389, or telephone (209) 372-0200. Camp reservations may be made through Destinet, (800) 436-7275. Hotel reservations are a must. Call (209) 252-4848 or contact Yosemite Concession services, Yosemite National Park, CA 95389. For road and weather information, call (209) 372-0200. For recorded general information, call (209) 372-0265; live, (209) 372-0265 (weekdays, 9–12, 1–5). Yosemite Valley/Big Trees Tour will give you an overall picture of the park (209-658-TOUR). For a brochure on access for disabled visitors, including special programs, parking, free shuttle bus service, guides, rest rooms, and more, call (209) 372-0200 or write to Yosemite National Park, P.O. Box 577, Yosemite National Park, CA 95389. All facilities and services are listed in the free quarterly Yosemite Guide, (209) 372-0200.

Just outside the park, the **Wassama Roundhouse** (daily, 11–4. Adults, 75¢. Tours by appt. Write: The Wassama Roundhouse Assoc., P.O. Box 328, Ahwahnee, CA 93601, or call 209-683-3631) is a rare authentic ceremonial Indian roundhouse open to the public. Its oak-shaded grounds include picnic areas, old Native American grinding stones, and other Native American artifacts. By the way, Ahwahnee is the Miwok Awani name for "deep grass valley."

● Bodie State Historic Park

Bodie is 13 miles east of Highway 395; take Highway 270, 7 miles south of Bridgeport. The road is paved for 10 miles, rough dirt the final 3 miles. (Mail: Friends of Bodie, P.O. Box 515, Bridgeport 93517) Museum open May–Sept. 30, at least, usually 9–6. Park open daily, year-round, weather permitting. Roads do close in winter. Call for current conditions and park hours: (760) 647-6445. There are no facilities. Admission, $1 per person over 17 per car. Smoking in parking lot only. **Ages 6 & up.** *www.parks.ca.gov*

Nestled high in sagebrush country, Bodie, the largest ghost town in the West, has escaped the commercialism often found in ghost towns. The 170 original buildings that still stand are maintained in a state of arrested decay— neither restored nor allowed to decay further. You walk through the townsite, passing the 1882 Methodist church, the old jail, a frame schoolhouse, a small home that once belonged to President Herbert Hoover's brother, the morgue with caskets still on view, and the brick vault of the bank. The Boone Store at Main and Green Streets looks as if Harvey Boone, a direct descendent of Daniel, has just locked the door and walked away—the shelves are still full of merchandise and the window displays are still in place. Information comes from a self-guiding tour pamphlet ($1), sold, in summer, at the entrance station. The only commerce here, for Bodie memorabilia, is in the park's museum and visitors center, housed in the Miner's Union Hall built in 1877. Just wander through this quiet, ramshackle town and imagine all the high adventures that occurred here, more than a century ago. As Mark Twain wrote, "The smoke of battle almost never clears away completely in Bodie."

■ North Central California: Butte, Lassen, Modoc, Siskiyou, and Trinity Counties

When I first caught sight of it . . . all my blood turned to wine," wrote naturalist John Muir on his first trip to Mount Shasta, in 1874. The north-central to northeastern area of California is the most rugged, remote section of the state, offering many unique and extraordinary sights. Here you'll find the nation's sixth-highest waterfall, Feather Falls, and the world's smallest mountain range, the Sutter Buttes. The world's largest gold nugget was found here, on the Middle Fork of the Feather River, by General John Bidwell. It weighed more than 54 pounds!

Lassen Volcanic National Park, Lava Beds National Monument, and Modoc National Forest are snowed-in in winter and blazingly hot in summer. Distances between towns are long, so be sure to arrange overnight camping or lodging before you set out. Take picnics, sweaters, and wetnaps. Nature lovers will enjoy the Whiskeytown-Lake Shasta-Trinity area and McArthur Burney Falls Memorial State Park and all the wonderful open spaces whose inaccessibility leaves them unspoiled. These Fun Places are laid out for the reader throughout the book from San Francisco outward. In this chapter, you'll be going north from Sacramento to the Oregon border, down again and east to Susanville, and up to the most northeastern point in California.

● Community Memorial Museum

1333 Butte House Road, Yuba City 95993. From Sacramento take Highway 99 north, turn left in Yuba City at the Highway 99/20 intersection, then turn right at Civic Center Boulevard and right onto Butte House Road. (530) 822-7141. Tues.–Fri., 9–5; Sat. and Sun., 12–4. Free. **Ages 6 & up.** *W. www.suttercounty.org*

This small community museum uses local artifacts, from Maidu Indian baskets and grinding stones, to antique pianos and dishes, to celebrate and explain the life and times of Sutter County. John Sutter's settling at Hock Farm is exemplified by his six-foot rampart gun, air rifle, and Bowie knife. And the 1915 Yuba ball tractor manufactured in Marysville stars in the new agricultural wing, which shows how the county became the "Peach Bowl of the World." The section on the nearby Sutter Buttes, with a table relief map and geological information on the "world's smallest mountain range," is of great interest to area visitors. Changing exhibits reflect the diverse interests of Sutter County today. Eight-year-old Tasha's "favorite thing was Lola Montez's dressing table." Brittany P. wrote, "Thanks for showing us the player piano and the iron without a cord to heat it on the stove and for telling us a story of the girl that had a pet grizzly bear."

FRESH PRODUCE

$1.00

FRESH
LETTUCE!

● Mary Aaron Memorial Museum

704 D Street, at 7th Street, Marysville 95901. (530) 743-1004. Call for times and prices, since the museum is being remodeled. Gift shop is open Sat., 10–5. **Ages 8 & up.** *www.museumsusa.org*

Warren P. Miller built his crowned gray and white Gothic family home for $5,000 in 1857. Today, it is a museum with period furniture and clothing and an interesting display of dolls, documents, and photos. Our favorite: the 1860s wedding cake that was discovered perfectly intact and petrified in a wooden Wells Fargo storage box.

On the levee of the river, the Bok Kai Temple (on D Street; 530-742-ARTS; by appointment), an 1879 Chinese temple for the River God of good fortune, houses many cultural artifacts.

● Museum of the Forgotten Warriors

5865 A Road off North Beale Road, Marysville 95901. (530) 742-3090. Open the first Sat. of the month, Veterans and Memorial Days, 10–4, and Thurs., 7 p.m. –10 p.m. Groups by reservation. Free. **Ages 9 & up.** *W. www.museumsusa.org*

Dedicated to veterans of the Vietnam War, this museum houses 18,000 artifacts, photographs, and personal histories collected from veterans across the United States. There are uniforms and patches, including the black garb of the Viet Cong, nurse uniforms, and a mannequin of a Navy Seal, complete with camouflage and paint. Other exhibits highlight World War II, the Korean War, and the Persian Gulf War. The owner, Dann Spear, started collecting when he was 10 years old, in 1964, and is especially proud of his 400 GI Joes and their huge GI Joe Firetower. You know you've found it when you see the light observation helicopters, two Marine Corps tanks, two cannons, and an equipment trailer.

● Sacramento Valley Museum

1491 E Street, Highway 20 at Interstate 5 (Mail: P.O. Box 1437), Williams 95987. (530) 473-2978. May–Nov., Thurs.–Sat., 10–4; and by appt. $2, 4–17, $1. Picnic area. **Ages 6 & up.** *Partially W. www.caohwy.com/s/sactovmu.htm*

This 21-room museum captures the past with a fully stocked general store, a blacksmith shop and saddlery, an apothecary shop, a barbershop, and restored early-California rooms filled with memories. The double cradle from the 1700s is special. The fashion doll collection is a history of civilization from ancient Greece to the 1930s. In the document room, there's an 1800 newspaper reporting George Washington's death.

Lacey wrote, "I like the big bell, the buggy, and the old quilts." Her friend Liliana said, "I like the dresses the best and I liked the store the best. I liked the hats the best of all. I found out that women couldn't ride boy saddles so that was what I didn't know. Thank you."

● Oroville Chinese Temple Complex

1500 Broderick at Elma Street, Oroville 95965. (530) 538-2496. Thurs.– Mon., 12–4; Tues. and Wed., 1–4. Closed Dec. 1–Feb. 1. Ages 12 and over, $2. In groups, by appt., $1.50. **Ages 10 & up.** *www.cityoforoville.org*

This complex of Buddhist, Taoist, and Confucian temples houses one of the finest collections of Chinese artifacts, art, and folk art in the United States. At the door of one building stands a two-ton, cast-iron urn given to the temple by Emperor Quong She. Carved teakwood altars, old tapestries, gods and goddesses, dragons, rare lanterns, and shrines decorate the buildings.

The Moon Temple, used for Buddhist worship, is entered through a circular doorway, which symbolizes the circle of life. The arts and lives of the thousands of Chinese who migrated to the gold fields are reflected in this peaceful spot. One young visitor wrote, "I enjoyed when the dragon was playing with the Moon. And the room where I saw the big guardians at the door and the big swords."

● Judge C. F. Lott Historic Home in Sank Park

1607 Montgomery Street, Oroville 95965. (530) 538-2497. Fri., Sun., and Mon., 11:30–3:30. Over 12, $2. In groups by appt., $1.50. **Ages 6 & up.** *www.cityoforoville.org*

"I like the courting chair because I think it was neat that the father got to know the daughter's fiancé. I also liked the kitchen and the bride's room and the guest room." A fourth-grader from the Camptonville Elementary School wrote this in her thank-you note. This sweet Victorian has a lot of love in it—from the plaque in the front trellis that says, "In commemoration of a kiss and a promise given between these columns," to the semiprecious stones from the local riverbed spelling out "Love" in the front parlor. Visitors of all ages will walk through authentically furnished rooms and learn what it was like to live in the late 19th and early 20th centuries. The nature center in the park is also of interest.

● Butte County Pioneer Memorial Museum

2332 Montgomery Street (Mail: P.O. Box 1743), Oroville 95965. (530) 534-0198. Fri.–Sun., 12–4, and by appt. Closed Dec. 15–Feb. 1. Donation. **Ages 6 & up.** *www.cityoforoville.org*

This grand collection of pioneer memorabilia is housed in a replica of a miner's cabin and has been expanded to include rooms furnished in Victorian style. Visitors will see, among other things, early typewriters, a doll collection, kitchenware, an old fire engine, and pictures of the Oroville floods.

The **Butte County Historical Society** has opened the **Ehmann Home** (1480 Lincoln Street, Oroville 95965. (530) 533-5316. Sat., 11–3; Sun., 12–4, and by appt. Donation. W). This furnished Colonial Revival home features displays from the society's collection of historical artifacts and a gift store specializing in Ehmann-brand olives.

● Feather River Fish Hatchery and Oroville Dam

5 Table Mountain Boulevard, Oroville 95965. (530) 538-2222. Hatchery, daily, 8–6. Dam overlook (530-2219): daily, except major holidays, 9–6. Tours, (530) 534-2306. Free. **All ages.** *www.cityoforoville.org*

A large window in one of the world's largest chinook salmon and steelhead trout hatcheries enables visitors to see the salmon climb the fish ladder to spawn, usually in September through November. Tours of the nursery reveal the artificial spawning process in action. More than 15,000 adult salmon and 2,000 steelhead make their homes here and you can see 20 million eggs and 9.6 million fingerlings. Ten miles up the road, you can get a good view of the 770-foot dam across the Feather River.

● Sacramento National Wildlife Refuge

752 County Road 99 W, 7 miles south of Willows on the east side of Interstate 5, Willows 95988. (530) 934-2801. Daily, Oct.–Mar., 7:30–4. $3 per day per vehicle. **All ages.** *www.sacramentovalleyrefuges.fws.gov*

The visitors center of this wildlife refuge has a diorama featuring three dozen bird species and a helpful staff that will send you on a two-mile trail where you'll see ponds and marshes, vernal pools, blue herons, great egrets, and other migratory wild birds.

● Portola Railroad Museum/Feather River Rail Society

700 Western Pacific Way (Mail: P.O. Box 608), Portola 96122. (530) 832-4131. Daily, 10–5. **Ages 7 & up.** *$5 donation requested. E-mail: mywprr@compuserve.com*

There are 85 cars and 36 diesel locomotives as well as railroad artifacts and equipment in this stellar collection, where children of all ages can get hands-on experience in an authentic railroad facility. The model train exhibit is also of interest. Rides, summer weekends, 11–4, are available at $5 per person. To operate a diesel locomotive, call (530) 832-4532 for reservations.

The **Jim Beckworth Museum** (Rocky Point Road, Portola 96122. 530-832-4888), the refurbished hotel and trading post, circa 1852, of a Plumas County pioneer, is open by appointment.

● Yuba Feather Historical Museum

19096 New York Flat and Forbestown Roads, Forbestown 95941. (530) 675-1025/675-0194. Weekends and holidays, Memorial Day through

Labor Day, 10–4; Sat., Sun., and holidays, 12–4, and by appt. Free. **Ages 6 & up.** *www.YFHMuseum.org*

Visitors can step back in time at this historical museum and park. Museum exhibits highlight the region's history with logging and blacksmith artifacts, photographs, and, in the Junior Museum, exhibits by local school-children. Step up to a miner's cabin, a saloon, a doctor's office, a chapel, a mining display, a harness shop, an old fashioned general store, or a Wells Fargo Office and pretend. The one-room schoolhouse has a teacher in authentic period garb and a bell to call children to class.

● Gold Nugget Museum

502 Pearson Road, at Mallan Lane, Paradise 95969. (530) 872-8722. Wed.–Sun., 12–4, Free. **Ages 8 & up.** *www.goldnuggetmuseum.com*

This local history museum is named for the Willard Nugget, a 54-pound gold nugget discovered in nearby Magalia Canyon in 1859. Kids will enjoy the doll collection, mining tools, a gun collection, antique furniture, and the exhibit about Yellowstone Kelley, the famous Indian guide.

● Bidwell Mansion

525 The Esplanade, Chico 95926. (530) 895-6144. Wed.–Sun., 12–5. 45-minute tours on the hour. Special kids programs in the morning. Adults, $1. **Ages 8 & up.** *www.parks.ca.gov*

Rancho del Arroyo Chico, covering 26,000 acres, was purchased in 1849 by agriculturalist and politician John Bidwell. His large Victorian home soon became the social and cultural center of the upper Sacramento Valley. Bidwell's is a California success story. He arrived in California in 1841, worked as a clerk for John Sutter, rose to the rank of general in the Mexican War, and then on July 4, 1848, struck it rich at Bidwell Bar. He set himself up at Chico and built a model farm. He raised corn, oats, barley, peaches, pears, apples, figs, quince, almonds, walnuts, wheat, olives, and casaba melons. He was elected state senator and congressman and even ran for president. Visitors may walk through the graciously furnished rooms.

Children like the cabinet of stuffed birds in the general's office and the Victorian hair wreaths in the parlor, as well as the numerous 19th-century gadgets and Maidu crafts programs.

Bidwell Park, the fourth-largest municipal park in the nation, is also part of the Bidwell estate. There are picnic and barbecue areas and playgrounds.

The **Chico Creek Nature Center** in Bidwell Park enlightens thousands of school-aged children and the public with nature-based educational programs, a living-animal museum, and year-round exhibits (1968 East 8th Street, Chico 95928. 530-891-4671. Tues.–Sun., 11–4. Donation. www.chico.com/naturecenter).

The **Stansbury Home** nearby (530-895-3848/343-0442. Weekends, 1–4, and by appt. Adults, $2; students, $1; under 8 free, 305 West 5th Street, at Salem, 95952. **Ages 7 & up**) is an 1883 Italianate Victorian filled with period furnishings. The house is remarkable because only Stansburys have lived in it and it has never been remodeled or modernized. The children's room, filled with toys and games, is popular. Guests often remark on the "quiet" of the house.

● Chico Museum

141 Salem Street, Chico 95926. (530) 891-4336. Wed.–Sun., 12–4. Donation. **Ages 8 & up.** *W. www.chicomuseum.com*

Household items, clothing, and photographs show what Chico was like in yesteryear in this sweet museum. Youngsters will be fascinated by the 19th-century musical instruments and the altars, ceremonial pieces, and other memorabilia from Chico's Taoist temple. In another section, history and art exhibits rotate with children's interactive science exhibits. One room offers a Chico Timeline from 1830 to 2000.

● South Shasta Lines

G. A. Humann Ranch, 8620 Holmes Road, Gerber 96036. Holmes Road is 2 miles south of Gerber. (530) 385-1389. Sundays in Apr. and May, 12–4, and by appt. Adults, $4; under 12, $3. **Ages 5 & up.**

G. A. Humann, engineer and conductor, started creating this quarter-inch-scale model railroad based on the Southern Pacific, Gerber to Dunsmuir, in 1950, in his spare time. There are 16 steam-type locomotives and 100 freight and passenger cars on 900 feet of track. There are 1,500 miniature trees, 1,000 people, and hundreds of animals on this detailed miniature system. The bells ring in the church steeple. The sawmill works. The smell of hot oil and smoke will bring back memories of real steam engines. In addition, a real steam locomotive takes visitors for a mile-long ride. A steam and gas antique farm machinery museum is also on hand, next to the country store.

● Corning Museum

1110 Solano Street (Mail: P.O. Box 1385), Corning 96021. (530) 824-7033. Tues.–Fri. 1–4. **Ages 7 & up.** *www.caohwy.com/c/corningm.htm*

The Corning Museum preserves and exhibits artifacts that represent the cultural heritage of Corning and Tehama County. Many displays at the museum include articles of period clothing, tools, pictures, and other items dating back to the early days of the town.

● Tehama County Museum

275 3rd Street, at C, Tehama, 96090. (530) 384-2420/384-2594. Fri.– Sun, 1–4, and by appt. Free. **Ages 8 & up.** *www.tco.net/tehama/museum*

Artifacts, photos, and records of the history of the whole county, including Ishi and his friends and ancestors. The largest artifact is the building itself, which was built in 1859 and is the oldest building in Tehama County with continuous service to the people of the county. Turn-of-the-century pianos, pioneer pistols and muzzle-loaders, dolls, and books mingle with memories of earlier ranchers and lumbermen.

● William B. Ide Adobe State Historic Park

21659 Adobe Road, Red Bluff 96080. Off Interstate 5, north of town 1 mile. (530) 529-8599. Park open 8 to sunset for picnics and fishing. Adobe open whenever the ranger is on hand, and by appt. Craft and living history demonstrations summer weekends. Parking fee, $2. **Ages 6 & up.** *W. www.ideadobe.tehama.k12.CA.US*

"He hereby invites all good and patriotic citizens in California to assist him—to establish and perpetuate a liberal, a just and honorable government, which shall secure to all civil, religious and personal liberty." So wrote William B. Ide to introduce the Bear Flag Republic to California. As first president of the Bear Flag Republic, he brought California into the Union. But when the republic failed, Ide went to the gold fields.

This adobe, which served as a ferry station between Sacramento and Shasta's northern gold mines, is one of the state's earliest and best-preserved examples of an American pioneer homestead. It has been restored and refurnished to its full 1852 glory by volunteers. The house is small and unassuming, with family photos, cradle and high chair, a furnished kitchen, and an unusual sleeping platform under the eaves. A smokehouse and a carriage house are also open to the public. The simple timber-framed period workshop has been crafted by volunteers using tools and methods used in 1852. The visitors center/exhibit trailer display panels help explain the exhibits. The garden and chickens will be the kids' favorites.

● Kelly-Griggs House Museum

311 Washington Street, Red Bluff 96080. (530) 527-1129. Thurs.–Sun., 1–4. Donation. **Ages 8 & up.** *www.redbluff.net*

Visitors walk into the past in this early 1880s classical Victorian house, which is furnished and "peopled" with costumed mannequins depicting life in the Victorian era. Our favorite item is the minutely detailed Victorian dollhouse in the master bedroom. It was built by Bob Grootveld, who also hand-carves and paints carousel horses. The fence around the house is made from bars of the old jail. Ben, a third-grader, wrote, "I like the Indian room and dress room, the pictures of Mt. Lassen and the steamboat. I wonder how it was like back then with all those great clothes and neat hidden places in the dressers. Getting to see all that was nice!"

● Red Bluff Round-Up Museum

650 Antelope Boulevard, Red Bluff 96080. (530) 528-1477. Thurs.–Sat., 1–5. Donation. **Ages 8 & up.** *www.redbluffroundup.com*

This relatively new museum houses an extensive collection of photographs and memorabilia relating to the Red Bluff round-up since its beginning in 1921.

Red Bluff Fire Station No. 2 Museum (835 Cedar Street. 530-527-1226, by appt. Free. **All ages**) is nearby. Red Bluff's Fire Department's first motorized pumper is one of the treasures on view in this interesting display of early firefighting equipment, tools, and photographs.

● Tehama County Aviation Museum

Luther Road, Red Bluff Municipal Airport, Red Bluff. (530) 527-6226. Sat. and Sun., 1–4. Free. **Ages 8 & up.** *www.californiahistory.com*

The Tehama County Aviation Museum aims to provide information about the aviation history of Tehama County. Displays include photographs of classic airplanes, information about the Red Bluff Naval Air Station, distinguished local pilots, and the first U.S. Navy aircraft carrier and its connection to Red Bluff.

● Salmon Viewing Plaza

Lake Red Bluff Recreation Area, North Central Valley Fish and Wildlife Office, 10950 Tyler Road, Red Bluff 96080. Exit Interstate 5 at Antelope Boulevard and follow Antelope Boulevard west to first stoplight, which is Sale Lane. Continue on Sale Lane 2 miles to the plaza. (530) 527-3043. Daily, 6 A.M.– 8 P.M., May–Sept. 15. Free. **Ages 7 & up.** *www.caohwy.com/s/salviepl.htm*

Visitors may see, on TV monitors, king salmon on their way past fish ladders to upstream spawning grounds at the Salmon Viewing Plaza near the Diversion Dam in the Red Bluff Recreation Area. They can also see fish trapping from an elevated walkway. The site is self-guided with several interpretive displays. The best time to visit is September and October.

The **Sacramento River Discovery Center** nearby (1000 Sale Lane, 96080. 530-527-1196. Tues.–Sun., 11–4. Donation. **Ages 5 & up**) is an interpretive center offering educational programs and interactive displays and tours assisted by the Forest Service and Bureau of Reclamation.

The U.S. Fish and Wildlife Service also operates the **Coleman National Fish Hatchery** 20 miles away, next to the Battle Creek Wildlife Area on the boundary between Shasta and Tehama Counties. From Interstate 5 take the Balls Ferry Road exit in Cottonwood and go east on Balls Ferry Road (2411 Coleman Fish Hatcher Road. Route 1, Box 2105, Anderson 96007. 530-365-8622. Oct. 1–Dec. 1, 8–4. Free). Here chinook salmon eggs are spawned daily in October, less frequently in November, December, and January.

● Yreka Western Railroad

300 East Miner Street (Mail: P.O. Box 660), Yreka 96097, just east of Interstate 5 via the Central Yreka exit. (530) 842-4146. Three-hour-long summer excursions depart at 11 A.M., Wed.–Sun.; on weekends only in Sept. and Oct. Adults, $12.50; seniors, $10.75; children 3–12, $6. Reservations suggested. Gift shop, daily, 9–4 in summer. Mon–Fri. 10–3 in winter. **Ages 5 & up.** *www.snowcrest.net/yrekawesternrr*

Established by the local citizenry in 1889 to link Yreka with the Southern Pacific tracks, the local short-line railroad has been in continuous operation, hauling freight, ever since. The excursion train now takes new pioneers brave enough to be carried by Ol' No. 19, a boot-shined black 1915 Baldwin 2-8-2 steam locomotive, pulling two Harriman 1920s coaches, a wooden caboose, and a flat car for open-air viewing, through the Shasta Valley into Montague, with a one-and-a-half-hour stop. There's a quaint 1887 Southern Pacific depot/museum. Bandits have been known to attack the train to snatch bags of "gold" away from the kids—and replace them with candy.

● Turtle Bay Exploration Park

800 Auditorium Drive, Redding 96001. (800) TURTLEBAY/ (530) 243-8550. Daily, 9–6 in summer; Tues.–Sun., 9–5 in winter. Adults, $11; children, $6; under 3, free. **Ages 4 & up.** *W. www.turtlebay.org*

Turtle Bay Exploration Park is a gee-whiz experience for everyone, with hands-on exhibits that captivate and educate. Still in its final stages, this $84 million complex encompasses the McConnell Arboretum, with trails through 220 acres of Oak Savannah and river wetlands, five gardens and animal habitats, an art gallery, a glass-walled riverside café, and a 20-story towering Sundial footbridge.

The new 34,000-square-foot glass-walled museum includes art, history, and science, from exhibits on the early Wintu Native Americans to pioneers, to underwater fish viewing from the river aquarium. Birds of prey live in the Natural Science Museum, and interpretive talks are offered regularly. The Mill House specializes in the history of the Shasta Cascade lumber industry. Everything is hands-on, and kids are encouraged to feel and smell and make things work. Paul Bunyan's oversized Forest Camp, with log slides and eagles' nest lookout towers, is a great place to work off extra energy.

● Waterworks Park

151 North Boulder Drive, Redding 96003. (530) 246-9550. Memorial Day to Labor Day; call for times and prices. Season passes, group rates, and team and barbecue nights. Gift and food shop. **All ages.** *W. www.waterworkspark.com*

Beat the heat and cure those summertime blues with the wildest, wettest time of your life. Three giant, twisting, turning, serpentine water slides, an awesome "Flash Flood, " a 400-foot wild white-water inner-tube river ride, a children's aquatic playground with fountains, pool, and slides, and beach volleyball, picnic grounds, and games add up to a great vacation day.

● **Fort Crook Museum**

(Mail: P.O. Box 397, Fall River Mills 96028) (530) 336-5110. North-east of Redding 75 miles on Highway 299 East. Tues.–Sun., 12–4. Closed Nov. 1–May 1. Donation. **Ages 6 & up.** *www.geocities.com/ftcrook*

There are seven little buildings, including an 1884 one-room school-house, a jail, two working blacksmith shops, and a settlers home in this historical museum, reflecting the history of the area. Old farm machinery, buggies, an old fire hose, baskets, a dugout canoe, and dolls all attract youngsters.

● **Shasta State Historic Park and Court House Museum**

(Mail: P.O. Box 2430, Old Shasta 96087) Highway 299, west of Redding. (530) 243-8194. Wed.–Sun., 10–5. Adults, $1; children, free. Picnic areas near the stagecoach and pioneer barn. **Ages 7 & up.** *www.parks.CA.Gov*

Once the center of the rich northern gold mines, Shasta is a quiet almost-ghost town now restored. The old county courthouse contains a remarkable collection of California art along with displays of photographs and relics of the Indians, Chinese, gold miners, and pioneers who once lived here. Modoc handicrafts, Chinese wooden pillows and money, an 1879 *Godey's Ladies Book,* and the pistol John Brown used in his raid at Harpers Ferry are among the highlights. The courtroom is furnished as it was when in use, and the jail is still equipped with chains, leg irons, and a gallows. The Litsch General Store looks just as it did in the 1880s, with barrels of meat and wine, old hats, and picks and shovels for sale. The Blumb Bakery, kitchen for the town in the 1800s, boasts a giant Peel Oven. Within the park are the ruins of what was once the longest row of brick business buildings north of San Francisco, the town's Catholic cemetery, the Union Pioneer cemetery, and other sites that are fun and safe to explore along a Ruins Trail.

● **J. J. (Jake) Memorial Museum and Trinity County Historical Park**

508 Main Street, Highway 299 West (Mail: P.O. Box 333), Weaverville 96093-0333. (530) 623-5211. Daily, May–Oct., 10–5; Apr., Nov., and Dec., 12–4. Donation. **Ages 10 & up.** *W. www.tcock12.org/~museum*

Clear displays trace Trinity County's history from the days of the Indians through the gold-mining years. Ray Jackson's collection of antique firearms, Chinese tong-war weapons, and a reconstructed miner's cabin, 1904 steam-powered stamp mill, and blacksmith shop help to recall this bygone era. One popular item is the boots worn by a woman who tried to poison the entire town of Weaverville during the Tong War of 1854. A copper Ming Dynasty teapot and a Redding/Weaverville stagecoach are also of note.

● Weaverville Chinese Joss House

Main Street (Mail: P.O. Box 1217), Weaverville 96093. Highway 299 West. (530) 623-5284. Wed.–Sun., 10–4, except holidays. Adults, $1; under 17, free. **Ages 9 & up.** *www.trinitycounty.com/joss.htm*

The Temple of the Forest Beneath the Clouds is open for worship now, as it has been since 1874. A small museum offers Chinese art, mining tools, weapons used in the tong wars, and photos of Chinese laborers building the railroads. A Lion Dance headdress, an abacus, opium pipes, and a huge gong are also shown. Inside the temple, you see the paper money that is burned for the gods and the drum and bell that wake the gods so they'll hear your prayers. In the rear of the temple, the attendant's quarters are furnished as they were a hundred years ago, with bunk beds and wooden pillows. Colorful altars, temple saints, celebration drums and flags, and the mirror-covered king's umbrella that guarded him against evil spirits create a vivid picture of what to many is another world.

● Shasta Dam

Highway 15 off Interstate 5, 10 miles north of Redding (Mail: 16349 Shasta Dam Boulevard, Shasta Lake 96019). (530) 275-1554/275-4463. Daily, 8–4. Visitors can drive or walk on the dam at any time. Information center, 8–4:30, weekdays; Sat. and Sun., 8:30–5. Guided walks and videos on request. Free. **Ages 8 & up.** *www.mp.usbr.gov*

It's said that once you see Shasta Dam you'll never forget it. Completed in 1945, Shasta is the second-largest concrete structure ever built in the United States (Grand Coulee dam is the largest). Its spillway is three times the height of Niagara Falls. The Bureau of Reclamation offers one-hour tours of the dam and power plant, including an elevator ride up to the top to view both the construction and the lake side of the dam. There are picnic areas near the visitors center.

Snow-capped Mount Shasta (which the athletic can climb) looms in the distance, accentuating the differences between natural and man-made wonders. Jet-boat tours, camping, houseboating, and every kind of water sport are popular in this Shasta-Whiskeytown-Trinity National Recreation Area.

● Lake Shasta Caverns

(Mail: P.O. Box 801, O'Brien 96070) Off Interstate 5 on Shasta Caverns Road. Twenty minutes north of Redding. (800) 795-CAVE/(530) 238-2341. Tours every half hour in summer, 9–4; hourly, 9–3 in Apr., May and Sept.; at 10, 12, and 2, Oct.–Mar. Closed Thanksgiving and Christmas. Reservations suggested. Adults, $14; ages 4–12, $7. Group rates. Gift shop. **Ages 7 & up.** *www.lakeshastacaverns.com*

Discovered in 1878 by J. A. Richardson (you can still see his inscription), the Lake Shasta Caverns are a natural wonder. Stalactite and stalagmite formations range from eight inches to, in the Cathedral Room, 60-foot columns of stalactite draperies that are studded with crystals.

Multicolored formations unfold before you during your tour, as you hear geological facts and Wintu Indian legends from a knowledgeable guide. The two-hour tour consists of a boat ride and bus ride, as well as the one-hour guided tour of the caverns.

● Sisson Museum

1 North Old Stage Road at Hatchery Lane, Mount Shasta 96087. (530) 926-5508. Mon.–Sat., 10–4; Sun., 1–4. Closed Jan.–Mar. Free. **Ages 7 & up.** *W. www.parks.ca.gov*

Early life in a mountain town is portrayed in this little museum in the Old Fish Hatchery Building. The history of Mount Shasta City and the hatchery is on display, with wildflower displays, antique photographs, Native American baskets, a 1920s "dining room," a 1915 Ford fire truck, and an exhibit of the geology of Mount Shasta. A large mural portrays the wildlife of the Sacramento River.

● Heritage Junction of McCloud

320 Main Street, Box 607, McCloud 96057. (530) 964-2604. Mon.–Sat., 11–3; Sun., 1–3. Donation. **Ages 8 & up.** *www.mccloudchamber.com*

McCloud has been put on the National Register of Historic Places as an early logging center. This museum celebrates the logging industry with memorabilia of the people and their tools, such as saws of all kinds, measuring sticks, mill office equipment, and clothing and accessories from the mid-1800s to the early 1900s. The big equipment is on the grounds: firefighting equipment, the Corliss engine from a 1903 McCloud Steam Log Mill.

● McCloud Railway Company

Reservations: (800) 733-2141/(530) 964-2141. Three-hour dinner train: $70 for adults; $35 for those under 12. Sat., mid-May–Sept., 5:30 P.M. One-hour excursions in open-air rail cars depart every Sat. at 4. Adults, $8; children under 12, $5. **Ages 6 & up.** *www.shastasunset.com*

Dine in 1916 splendor in two beautifully restored dining cars. The four-course dinner is served on tables covered with white linen tablecloths, fine china, and sterling silver. Lace curtains frame the outstanding views as the train winds its way through the forest.

● Siskiyou County Museum

910 South Main Street, Yreka 96097. (530) 842-3836. Tues.–Fri., 9–5; Sat. 9–4. Closed Nov.–Apr. Adults, $1. Children 2–12, 75¢. **Ages 7 & up.** *www.co.siskiyou.ca.us/museum*

In this reproduction of the Callahan Ranch Hotel, one of the first stage stops in Siskiyou County in the 1850s, visitors learn the story of Siskiyou County from the first Native American inhabitants up to the 20th century. Exhibits detail local Indian cultures, early trappers, military history, gold mining, and Chinese and pioneer settlements. A schoolhouse, black-smith shop, church, 1856 pioneer log cabin, 1876 miner's cabin, skid shack, and an operational replica of a Denny Bar General Merchandise store (the first chain store in California) are situated in the 2½ acre outdoor museum.

In the center of town, the foyer of the **Siskiyou County Courthouse** (311 4th Street. Weekdays, 9–4. Free) shows off raw, natural gold nuggets taken from Siskiyou County placer mines during the Gold Rush in one of the largest displays of gold south of Alaska.

● Fort Jones Museum

11913 Main Street, Fort Jones 96032. (530) 468-5568. Summer hours: Mon–Fri., 10–4; Sat., 11–3. By appt. in winter. Donation. **Ages 7 & up.** *www.siskiyouhistory.org/fjm*

The museum contains an excellent collection of Indian and pioneer artifacts including a rare ceremonial white deer skin and many Indian baskets. The walls of the building are of native stone and include mortars, millstone pestles, and arrastra wheels. On the north side of the museum is the famous ceremonial "rain rock." Hands-on favorite item: the two-headed calf.

● Weed Lumber Museum

303 Gilman (Mail: P.O. Box 447), Weed 96094. (530) 938-5050. Daily, 10–5, May 30–Sept. 30, and by appt. Free. **Ages 8 & up.** *www.snowcrest.net/whm*

Memories of the logging industry in its early days attract visitors. Inside are photographs and personal mementos of Weed, including an old movie projector. Outside you'll find logging equipment, including a D-8 Cat, a snag pusher, and rail cars for hauling lumber. Third-graders love the jail cells and stagecoach.

● Lava Beds National Monument

1 Indian Well Headquarters, Tulelake 96134. Off Highway 139. (530) 667-2282. Fee: $5 per vehicle. Camping: $10 in summer (800-326-6944 for information on lodging and dining). Monument visitors center: in summer, 8–6; in winter, 8–5. Tours and maps for independent exploring. Closed Christmas. **Ages 8 & up.** *Visitors center, rest rooms, and one campsite are wheelchair accessible. www.nps.gov/labe*

"Thank you for letting us go to the Lava Beds. I really enjoyed it. The reason skull ice cave was my favorite cave is because of the ice at the end. My second favorite was Hopkins Chocolate. That's because it's long and narrow." So wrote Michelle about her visit.

Natural and Native American history vie for visitors' attention in this monumental landscape of lava formations. The area abounds with natural wonders, including cinder cones that reach up to 500 feet. Most of the sights at this 70-square-mile monument are underground. More than 435 lava tube caves can be explored with care. Some caves hold Native American rock images that date back centuries. Captain Jack's Stronghold, formed of natural lava fortifications, is a grim reminder of later history: In the winter of 1872–73, a young Modoc leader, Captain Jack, led a band of Modoc warriors in a war against the U.S. Army in an unsuccessful attempt to retain their homeland. A short visit to the monument's visitors center will help you understand the geology, natural history, and past events of the area.

● Indian Valley Museum

(Mail: P.O. Box 165, Taylorsville 95983) (530) 284-6511. Fri., Sat., and Sun., 1–4, and by appt. Donation. **Ages 8 & up.** *www.indianvalley.net*

The Mount Jura Gem and Mineral Society sponsors this private museum, so the room of rock and mineral displays and carvings is one they're most proud of. Another building houses old blacksmith tools and a forge and early logging implements as well as a 1932 fire truck. Children enjoy using the butter churn and the sewing machine in the two kitchens, one from the early 1800s, the other from the 1930s. And they like ringing the school bell and grinding acorns on the grinding rocks.

● Lassen County Historical Museum

75 North Weatherlow Street (Mail: P.O. Box 321), Susanville 96130. (530) 257-3292. May 1–Oct. 31, Mon.–Fri., 10–4; Sat., 11–3, Free. **Ages 8 & up.** *W. www.shastacascade.org/lassen*

Lassen County memorabilia, farming and lumbering machinery, artifacts of the Native Americans, and remembrances of the first settlers fill this interesting museum. Many wagon trains stopped here at Roop's Fort, which is undergoing restoration. Susanville is named after the daughter of Isaac Roop, one of the founders of the Provisional Territory of Nevada and

Nataqua. Peter Lassen, one of the Danish pioneers of the area, was shot in Black Rock Desert, a murder that remains unsolved to this day. Historic murals are painted all over town, including one of Susan and her father on Lassen Street.

The **Susanville Historic Train Depot** (601 Richmond Road, 96130. 530-257-3252) is totally restored to its original condition.

● Chester Museum

210 First Avenue (Mail: P.O. Box 977), Chester 96020. (530) 258-2742. Mon., Tues., Wed., 10–1 and 1:30–5:30; Thurs., 12–5 and 6–8; Sat., 10–2. Free. **Ages 7 & up.** *www.shastacascade.org/plumas/plumas.htm*

This photo museum of the Chester/Lake Almanor area celebrates the early Maidu culture and early dairy and cattle ranchers. It's housed in a log cabin structure designed to resemble the 1929 log cabin building to which it is connected. During special programs, kids are encouraged to use grinding stones and touch pottery and baskets. The video of a Maidu basket maker is very popular. A compact, century-old steam locomotive known as "dinky," found in the bottom of nearby Butte Valley Reservoir is on the site.

● Lassen Volcanic National Park

38050 Highway 36E, Mineral 96063. (530) 595-4444. Road closed in winter. Call for road, park, trail, camping, accommodations, education, and interpretation information. **Ages 8 & up.** *Limited wheelchair access. www.nps.gov/lavo. E-mail: lavo_information@nps.gov*

Among the attractions in this rugged area are boiling springs and pools, mud pots, sparkling lakes, and four types of volcanoes. Cinder cone erupted more than 300 years ago. An Indian lore program at Manzanita Lake Visitor Information Center presents the story and customs of the Native Americans who once lived here. Other programs are scheduled irregularly. Read the National Park Services newsletter *Peak Experience* for up-to-date programs and information.

The **Loomis Museum at Manzanita Lake,** open 9–5 weekends from Memorial Day to mid-June, and daily, 9–5, June 11–Sept. 23, offers exhibits, orientation videos, permits, publications, and Jr. Ranger Journals. Information may also be obtained at Park Headquarters in Mineral, the Southwest Information Center, and Lassen Crossroads Information, at the junction of Highways 44 and 89. During the pioneer programs, naturalists use a covered wagon and other artifacts to show how people lived when they were on the Nobles Immigrant Trail. Subway Cave, north of Manzanita Lake on Highway 44, just outside the park, is also worth a trip.

One note of warning: The grounds and thermal areas are treacherous, so keep hold of your children at all times. Lassen Peak erupted for seven years beginning in 1915 but is now considered dormant. Remember, the geothermal areas are named Devil's Kitchen, Sulphur Works, and Bumpass Hell for good reason. With the smell of sulphur in the air and fenced boardwalks over land that changes from cracked mud to hissing steam as you walk, you'll think you're on another planet.

● Big Valley Museum

(Mail: P.O. Box 355, Bieber 96009) (530) 294-5368. Tues., Wed., Thurs., 11–4 in summer. Free. **Ages 8 & up.** *www.shastacascade.org/lassen/lassen.htm*

The Big Valley Museum features displays and collections relating to the settlement and development of northeastern California. Exhibits of pioneer life and Native American artifacts are shown on a rotating basis.

● Alturas Modoc County Historical Museum

600 South Main Street (Mail: P.O. Box 1689), Alturas 96101. (530) 233-6328. Tues.–Sat., May 1–Oct. 31, 10–4. Donation. **Ages 6 & up.** *W. www.caohwy.com/y/ymodcomu.htm*

To learn more about Captain Jack, who earned his fame in the Modoc Indian Wars in the Lava Beds, and see pictures of him, go to this pleasant museum in the far corner of the state. There are beads, baskets, arrowheads, and other artifacts of the Pit River, Paiute, and Modoc tribes, along with pioneer memorabilia. The collections of mounted animals and birds and antique guns are popular with visitors. Becky wrote, "I liked the old dolls. They were beautiful. Thank you." Tom said, "Way cool dude. I like the old guns." Rebecca, "I like the swords because they are nice to look at." And Jose, "I like the knives. They are cool." Janie wrote, "I'm bringing my friends tomorrow!"

Special Annual Events

THE FOLLOWING ANNUAL EVENTS in Northern California are arranged in order of the estimated time of the month the event will take place, from the first weekend to the last. Some celebrations, such as Fourth of July and Halloween, inspire events in most major towns. So, if something sounds intriguing but is listed in a city that's far away, call around to see if you can find something similar but much closer to you.

For exact dates and prices, please call the local chamber of commerce. The California Trade and Commerce Agency (801 K Street, Suite 1700, Sacramento 95814-3520. gocalif.ca.gov) offers a free calendar of 1,000 special events and insider tips. *VIA,* the magazine of the California State Automobile Association of America, also lists events in California in each monthly issue.

January
Teddy Bear Exhibit, Lakeport
San Francisco Sports and Boat Show, Cow Palace
San Mateo Auto Show, Fairgrounds
Winter's Eve at Chaw-Se State Historic Park, Jackson
Golden Gate Kennel Club All Breed Dog Show, San Francisco
Four-Dog Sled Races, Prosser Lake and Donner Lake
Whalefest, Monterey
Gold Rush Discovery Day Festival, Coloma (Jan. 24)
Whale watching begins, Point Reyes National Seashore
Fiddlers Contest and Crab Cioppino Feed, Cloverdale
Crab, Wine and Art Festival, Eureka
Sealabration, Año Nuevo State Reserve, Big Sur

February
Sutter Creek Doll, Toy, and Miniature Show
Chinese New Year's Celebration, San Francisco, Fresno, and other towns.
National Roadster Show, Oakland Coliseum

Crab Festival, Crescent City
Crab Feast, Bodega Bay
Redwood Region Logging Conference, Eureka
Chinese Bomb Day, Bok Kai Festival, Marysville
Cloverdale Citrus Fair
Monarch Migration Festival, Santa Cruz
Black History Month, Col. Allensworth State Historic Park
Napa Valley Mustard Festival
Clam Beach Run, Trinidad
Carnival and Spring Fair, Lakeport
California Special Olympics Water Games, Sonora
Winterfest, Chester
Almond Blossom Festival, Ripon

March

St. Patrick's Day parades and celebrations take place almost everywhere.
Irish Days, Murphy
Celtic Music and Arts Festival, San Francisco and Sonora
Daffodil Hill Blooms, Volcano
Snowfest, Lake Tahoe and Great Ski Race
Hot Dog Skiing Festival, Alpine Meadows, Tahoe
Annual Winter Round-Up, Red Bluff
Camellia Show, Santa Rosa, Fresno, Sacramento, and Modesto
Crab Feed, Ukiah
Draggin' Wagons Dance Festival, Sonora
Sierra Dog Sled Races, Sierra City, Truckee, and Ebbetts Pass
Candlefishing at Night, Klamath River
Junior Grand National Livestock Expo, Cow Palace, San Francisco
Jackass Mail Run, Porterville
Whale Festival, Mendocino and Fort Bragg
Storytelling Festival, Yosemite
Back Country Horsemen Annual Rendezvous, Anderson
Women's History Day, Sacramento

April

Ducky Derby, Santa Cruz
Teddy Bear Convention, Nevada City
Log Race, Petaluma River
Fisherman's Festival, Bodega Bay
Annual Trinidad Crab Feed
Gem and Mineral Show, Cow Palace, San Francisco

Yacht Parade, Redwood City
Sheepshearing, Petaluma Adobe
South Shasta Lines Railroad runs, Gerber
Annual Trail Days, Bothe-Napa Valley State Historic Park
Clovis Rodeo and Big Hat Days Festival
Cherry Blossom Festival, Lodi and San Francisco
Earth Day celebrations in San Francisco and many other towns
Easter Egg Hunt, Casa de Fruita, Hollister, Lakeport, and Monterey
Great Duck Race, Sutter Creek
Dunsmuir River Festival
Carmel Kite Festival
Gold Nugget Days, Paradise
Children's Lawn Festival, Redding
Tuolumne County Cowboy and Cowgirl Days, Sonora
Scottish Games and Gatherings, Roseville
Red Bluff Romp and Rodeo Round-up
Tea and Musicale, Vintage Cars Display, Anderson Marsh State Historic
    Park
Pebble Beach Concours d'Elegance
Stockton Asparagus Festival
Coalinga Water Festival
Nikkei Matsuri Festival, San Jose
Apple Blossom Festival, Sebastopol
Fresno Folk Festival
Angels Camp Celtic Faire
Kool April Nights, Redding
Fisherman's Festival, Bodega Bay
Rhododendron Festival, Eureka
Red Bluff Roundup
Boonville Buck-a-Roo Days
Scottish Games, Woodland
Motherlode Dixieland Jazz Festival, Sonora
Auburn Wild West Stampede
Butter and Eggs Day Parade, Petaluma
Trinity River Rodeo

May
Laguna Seca Races, Monterey
Cinco de Mayo Festivals, San Francisco, San Jose, others
Japanese Mochi Pounding Ceremony, San Francisco
Youth Arts Festival, San Francisco

Opening Day Yacht Parade, San Francisco
Ione Homecoming Picnic, Parade, and Carnival
Avenue of the Giants Marathon, Garberville
Bay to Breakers Race, San Francisco
Luther Burbank Rose Parade and Festival, Santa Rosa
Living History Days, Petalume Adobe State Historic Park
Native American Cultural Day, Anderson Marsh State Historic Park
Mt. Folk Festival, Potter Valley
West Coast National Antique Fly-In, Watsonville Airport
Bok Kai Festival and Parade, Marysville
Lake Berryessa Art and Wine Festival
Red Suspenders Day, Gridley
Sacramento State Fair
Grand Prix of Sonoma
Salinas Valley Fair, King City
Lillie Langtry Day, Middletown (May 11)
Sacramento Jazz Jubilee
Silver Dollar Fair, Chico
Shasta Art Fair and Fiddle Jamboree
Native American Pow Wow, Hollister
Dixieland Monterey Jazz Festival
Castroville Artichoke Festival
Migratory Bird Festival, Alturas
Big Foot Gemboree, Weaverville
Antique Fly In and Air Show, Watsonville
Calaveras County Fair and Frog Jumping Jubilee, Angels Camp
West Coast Relays, Fresno
Roaring Camp Mining Company Gold Prospecting Days
Chamarita Festival and Parade, Half Moon Bay, Sausalito, and Pescadero
   (Pentecost Sunday)
Feather Fiesta Days, Oroville
Old Settler's Day, Campbell
Fireman's Muster, Columbia
Lamb Derby Days, Willow
Miniature Horse Show, Amador County Fairgrounds
Russian River Wine Festival, Healdsburg
Stump Town Days and Rodeo, Guerneville
Coarsegold Rodeo, Madera County
Fiddletown Gold Country Hoedown
Prospector's Daze, Willow Creek
Carnival, San Francisco
Oakdale Chocolate Festival

June

Black Bart Celebration, Redwood Valley and Cloverdale
Sonoma/Marin Fair, Petaluma
Upper Grant Avenue Street Fair, San Francisco
Lewistown Fiddler Fair
Fly-In and Moonlight Flight, Porterville
Alameda County Fair, Pleasanton
Merienda, Monterey's birthday party
Scottish Highland Games, Modesto
California Cowboy Show, Carmel Valley
Gualala Whale Festival
Valhalla Renaissance Festival, South Lake Tahoe
San Antonio Mission Fiesta, Jolon
Springfest, San Mateo Fairgrounds
Grand Prix of Monterey
Campbell Scottish Games
Shasta District Fair, Anderson
Modoc Co. "Super Bull" Event, Surprise Valley
Old Auburn Flea Market
Italian Picnic and Parade, Sutter Creek
Klamath Salmon Barbecue
Street Painting Festival, San Rafael
California Railroad Festival, Sacramento
Eagle Lake Bicycle Challenge, Susanville
Shasta Bridge Jamboree, Redding
Malakoff Homecoming, Nevada City
Solano County Fair, Vallejo
Novato County Fair
Pony Express Days, McKinleyville
Garberville Rodeo and Western Celebration
Father's Day Kite Festival, San Francisco
Bear Flag Day and Ox Roast, Sonoma
Pioneer Wagon Train, Yosemite
Tuolumne Jubilee, Tuolumne City
Kit Carson Days, Jackson
Butterfly Days, Mariposa
Cornish Miner's Picnic, Grass Valley
Fiddler's Jamboree, Railroad Flat
Bonanza Days, Gilroy
Redwood Acres Fair, Eureka
Western Daze, Fairfield
Western Weekend, Novato

Vaquero Days, Hollister
Scandinavian Midsummer Festival, Ferndale
Rice Festival, Gridley
San Juan Bautista Peddler's Fair
Midsummer Music Festival, Stern Grove, San Francisco
Highway 50 Wagon Train, Placerville
Secession Day, Rough and Ready (June 27)
San Francisco's Birthday Celebration
Russian River Rodeo and Sumptown Days, Guerneville
Truckee-Tahoe Air Show
Trinidad Fish Festival
Middletown Days, Middletown
Living History Days, Johnsville
California High School Rodeo Finals, Red Bluff
Oakland Festival at the Lake

July
San Francisco Waterfront Festival
Old Time Fourth of July Celebration, Columbia
Old-Fashioned Fourth, Mt. Shasta, Modesto, Arcata, Redding, Clovis,
    Martinez, Truckee, Nevada City, Mt. Shasta, Crescent City
San Jose America Festival
Napa County Fair, Calistoga
Willits Frontier Days
Hoopa Fourth of July Celebration, Hoopa
Salmon B-B-Q, Noyo
Sonoma County Fair, Santa Rosa
C.B. Radio Convention, Eureka
Bach Festival, Carmel
Freedom Festival, Redding
California Rodeo, Salinas
Obon Festival, San Jose, Monterey, and Fresno
Clearlake Worm Races
Paul Bunyan Mountain Festival, Westwood
Gold Dig Days, Greenville
Indian Gathering, Ahwahnee
Annual Antique and Arts and Crafts Show, Oakdale
Asian Festival, Oakland Museum
Christmas in July Jazz Band Festival, Sutter Hill
Pony Express Celebration, Pollack Pines
Arcata Salmon Festival
Trinity County Fair, Hayfork

McCloud Lumberjack Festival
Mendota Sugar Festival
Garberville Rodeo
Folsom Rodeo
San Mateo County Fair
Woodminster Music Series, Oakland (through September)
San Francisco Fair and Exposition
Hangtown Festival, Placerville
Sacramento Water Festival
Dune Daze, Samoa, Eureka
Fortuna Rodeo
Water Carnival, Monte Rio
Jeepers Jamboree, Georgetown to Lake Tahoe
Fiesta Rodeo de San Juan Bautista
Holy Ghost Celebration, Benicia
Gilroy Garlic Festival
Lassen County Fair, Susanville
Placerville County Fair, Roseville
Captain Weber Days, Stockton
Scotts Valley Days
Gold Rush Jubilee, Callahan, Siskiyou County
Feast of Lanterns, Pacific Grove
Orick Rodeo
Roaring Camp '49er Day (July 22)
Gasket Raft Races
Turtle Races, Cloverdale
Nightboat Parade, Lakeport and Clearlake Highlands
Marin County Fair, San Rafael
Amador County Fair

August
Old Adobe Days, Petaluma Adobe State Historic Park
Monterey County Fair
Humboldt County Fair, Ferndale
Dipsea Race, Mill Valley
Nihonmachi Street Fair, Japantown, San Francisco
California State Horseman's American Horse Show, Sonoma
"Annie and Mary Day," Blue Lake
Santa Clara County Fair, San Jose
Butte County Fair, Gridley
Indian Fair Days, Sierra Mono Museum, North Fork
El Dorado County Fair, Placerville

San Mateo County Fair
Stanislaus County Fair, Turlock
Japanese Culture Bazaar, Sacramento
California State Fair, Sacramento
Oakland Chinatown Streetfest
Nevada County Fair, Grass Valley
Plumas-Sierra County Fair, Quincy
Portola RR Days
Monterey County Fair
Steinbeck Festival, Salinas
Modoc County Last Frontier Fair, Surprise Valley
Olive Festival, Corning
Zucchini Festival, Hayward
Petaluma River Festival
Wildwood Days and Peddlers' Fair, Rio Dell
Siskiyou County Fair and Paul Bunyan Jubilee
Calamari Festival, Santa Cruz
Jamestown Pioneer Days
El Dorado Days at Mt. Ranch, San Andreas
Mother Lode Fair and Loggers' Contest, Sonora
Susanville Rodeo
Pony Express Day, McKinleyville (August 22)
Children's Fairytale Birthday Week, Oakland
Air Round-Up, Red Bluff
Willow Creek Bigfoot Days
Adobe Day, Ide Adobe, Red Bluff
Del Norte County Fair, Crescent City
Gravenstein Apple Fair, Sebastopol
Lake County Fair, Lakeport
Renaissance Pleasure Faire, Novato
Sonoma County Fair, Santa Rosa
Paul Bunyan Days, Fort Bragg
Nevada County Fair, Grass Valley

September
Renaissance Pleasure Faire, Novato
Sausalito Art Festival
Alturas Balloon Festival
Tribal Stamp, Hayfork
California Int'l Air Show, Salinas
Santa Cruz County Fair
Big Foot Jimboree, Happy Camp

Begonia Festival and Sand Castle Contest, Capitola
Monterey Jazz Festival
Mendocino County Fair and Apple Show, Boonville
A la Carte, a la Park, Golden Gate Park, San Francisco
San Francisco Art Festival
Redwood Empire Logging Festival, McKinleyville
Constitution Days, Nevada City
Vintage Festival, Hall of Flowers, Golden Gate Park, San Francisco
Festival of Viewing of the Moon, Japantown, San Francisco
Scottish Games, Santa Rosa
Shasta County InterMountain Fair, McArthur
Gold Country Fair, Auburn
Valley of the Moon Vintage Festival, Sonoma
Pleasanton Pasta Festival
Columbia Admission Day
Blue Grass Festival, Amador County Fairgrounds
Pageant of Fire Mountain, Guerneville
Vintage Car Fair, Fremont
Moon Festival with Chinese Dragon, Chinatown, San Francisco
Opera in the Park, Golden Gate Park, San Francisco
National Indian Observance Day, Crescent City
American Indian Pow Wow, Volcano
Paul Bunyan Days, Fort Bragg
Black Bart Day, San Andreas (Sept. 14)
Atwater Fall Festival
Cedar Grove Pow Wow, Chico
Miwok Indian Acorn Festival, Tuolumne City
California Prune Festival, Yuba City
Concord Jazz Festival
Indian "Big Time" Days, Amador County
Santa Cruz County Fair, Watsonville
Vintage Festival, Sonoma
LEAP Sand Castle Contest for Architects, Aquatic Park, San Francisco
San Francisco Blues Festival, Justin Herman Plaza and Fort Mason, San
    Francisco
KQED Ice Cream Social, San Francisco
Blessing of the Fishing Fleet, Fisherman's Wharf, San Francisco
Northcountry Fair, Arcata
Carmel Mission Fiesta
Fiesta del Pueblo, San Jose
Porterville Pow Wow
Redwood Invitational Regatta, Big Lagoon, Humboldt County

Harvest Festivals in Mt. Shasta, Columbia, Felton, and Tuolumne
September Fest, Downieville
Salmon Festival, Oroville
Turlock Poultry and Dairy Festival
Tehama District Fair, Red Bluff
Lodi Grape Festival
Fiesta Patrias, Woodland
Castroville Artichoke Festival
Walnut Festival, Walnut Creek
Worldfest, Live Oak Park, Berkeley
Sourdough Days, Sutter Hill
Weaverville Bigfoot Daze
Bridge to Bridge Run, Bay Bridge to Golden Gate Bridge, San Francisco

October

Oktoberfest, San Jose, San Mateo Fairgrounds, and other towns
Laguna Seca Grand Prix, Monterey
Fortuna Arts Festival
Sonoma Country Harvest Festival, Santa Rosa
U.S. National Gold Panning Championship, Coloma
Fresno Fair
National Livestock Expo, Cow Palace, San Francisco
Marin Grape Festival, San Rafael
Pumpkin Festival, Half Moon Bay, Manteca
Spanishtown Art and Pumpkin Festival
Columbia Fiddle and Banjo Contest
West Coast Monster Truck Nationals, Red Bluff
Butterfly Parade, Pacific Grove
Johnny Appleseed Days, Paradise
Autumn Moon Festival, San Francisco
Western Opera Fiddle Championships, Red Bluff
Candle Lighter Ghost House, Fremont
Pro-Am Surfing International, Santa Cruz
Old Mill Days, Bale Grist Mill State Historic Park
Redding Children's Art Festival
Fall Festival, Clearlake Oaks
Selma Parade and Band Festival
Johnny Appleseed Day, Paradise
Lumberjack Day, West Point
Harvest Festival, Pacific Grove
Great Sandcastle Building Contest, Carmel
Great Snail Race, Folsom

Oktoberfest, Tahoe City
Old-Timers' Day, King City
Columbus Day Festival, San Francisco
Reedley Festival
Chinese Double Ten Celebration, San Francisco
San Francisco International Film Festival
Discovery Day, Bodega Bay
Harvest Hoedown, Healdsburg
Victorian Village Octoberfest, Ferndale

November

Miniatures Fair, Nevada City
North California Boat and Sports Show, Oakland
Christmas Balloon Parade, San Jose (day after Thanksgiving)
Thanksgiving Art Fair, Mendocino
Santa's Steamboat Arrival and Antique Wagon Procession, Petaluma
Teddy Bear Exhibit opens, Lakeport

December

Christmas fairs, lightings, house tours, and celebrations in almost every
    town.
Grandma's Christmas Open House, Anderson Marsh State Historic Park
Dixieland Christmas, Jamestown
Pioneer Christmas, Bale Grist Mill State Historic Park
Christmas at the Mission, Sonoma Mission State Historic Park
Christmas Art and Music Festival, Eureka
Great Dickens Faire, San Francisco
Nutcracker Suite, San Francisco Ballet and Oakland Ballet
Native American Christmas Fair, Sacramento
Los Posada Nativity Procession, Columbia State Historic Park
Currier and Ives Christmas Open House, Sutter Creek
Festival of the Trees, Monterey and San Rafael
Pioneer Christmas, Roaring Camp, Felton
Oakland Temple Christmas Pageant, Oakland
Children's International Craft and Food Fair, Santa Cruz
Lighting of the Tree of Lebanon, Santa Rosa
Native Christmas Tree Ceremony, Sequoia National Park
Christmas Tree Lane, Fresno
Christmas Boat Parade, Eureka
Pioneer Christmas Party, Ide Adobe, Red Bluff
Rice-Pounding Ceremony, Japantown, San Francisco
Miner's Christmas, Columbia

Amador Calico Christmas
Christmas in the Adobes, Monterey
Lighted Boat Parade, Petaluma
San Juan Bautista de Posada Fiesta
Adobe Luminaria Fiesta, Petaluma
Victorian Christmas, Nevada City
Festival of Lights, Volcano, Yountville and Auburn
New Year's Eve Fireman's Ball, Cloverdale
Claim Jumper's New Year's Eve Square Dance, Plymouth
New Year's Eve Pro Rodeo and Celebration, Red Bluff

Index by Age Group

Alphabetical Index

An Appreciation

I'd like to close with a note of special thanks to people who have written with suggestions for this new edition of *Fun Places to Go With Children in Northern California*. The book could not have lasted as long as it has (thirty years!) without friends and fans who keep me aware of the new things that are happening in this wonderful state of ours.

I'll be sending books to the following people: Yvonne Hoppe of Plesasanton, Scheely Conneely of San Mateo, Lisa Hettler-Smith of San Jose, Monica Castillo-Barraza of Foster City, Karyn Ruth Cheng of Antelope, Deanna Fale, and others who have asked that their names not be published.

Happy trails!

Elizabeth Pomada

Notes . . .